JUN 1 1 2010

Great Negotiations

Great Negotiations

Agreements that Changed the Modern World

Fredrik Stanton

WESTHOLME
Yardley

Frontispiece: Ralph Bunche at the United Nations Security Council session in Paris, October 19, 1948. (*United Nations*)

Westholme Publishing, LLC
904 Edgewood Road
Yardley, Pennsylvania 19067
Visit our Web site at www.westholmepublishing.com

First Printing February 2010
10 9 8 7 6 5 4 3 2 1

ISBN: 978-1-59416-099-8

Printed in United States of America

For my parents

Contents

INTRODUCTION

WORDS, as much as weapons, shape history. Whether to avert, assist, or secure the resolution of a conflict, in the modern age diplomacy has had great triumphs and bitter failures, from the Cuban Missile Crisis in 1962, which narrowly spared humanity from nuclear Armageddon, to the Treaty of Versailles after World War I, which created problems that still confront us today.

In negotiations, great opportunity lies alongside the potential for disaster, and the rules are often written as the action takes place. Every successful negotiation is a triumph of reason over force, and a confirmation that conflict is not an inevitable outcome of a clash of interests. These unique moments provide individuals, armed only with cunning, determination, and personal charisma, an opportunity to leave an immediate and lasting mark on the fates of nations. German military theorist Carl von Clausewitz described warfare as "politics by other means," and in the same vein negotiations can be perceived as war by other means. Looking at the powerful role great negotiations have played in the course of history and how they still affect our lives helps us understand policy alternatives available today and informs our choices for the future.

When it works, it seems like magic—the ability to reconcile opposing elements, or to create a situation that leaves both sides better off than before. Major negotiations, which Winston

Churchill called "conversations of silk and steel," are made of contradictions: confrontation and collaboration, conflict and seduction. The stakes are high, the margin for error is small, and the clock is ticking. With lives and nations' fates in the balance, participants must use perseverance, creativity, bluff, and the ability to capitalize on the unexpected to overcome obstacles to agreement, which may include their adversary, the strategic environment, and even the demands of their own side.

Not surprisingly, in addition to inspiring stories of nobility and sacrifice, one finds colorful figures and a full array of treachery, blackmail, betrayal, and assassination. The characters' weaknesses, as well as their strengths, make each negotiation a fascinating insight into cardinal moments in history.

Despite their challenges, the negotiators accomplished amazing victories. The Louisiana Purchase turned a potential war into an opportunity for one of history's greatest acquisitions. In securing the Treaty of Portsmouth, Theodore Roosevelt helped save a quarter-million lives and prevented a world war. Kennedy and Khrushchev successfully navigated a crisis that insiders had given a 50 percent chance of leading to nuclear holocaust.

Europe, Asia, and the Middle East have been fundamentally changed by decisions made at the negotiating table. America has as well. Its birth, growth, and emergence as a world power were driven to a large extent by negotiating successes, and for all its military might, the United States has gained more from negotiations than from all of its wars combined.

Essential to the colonies' success in the American Revolution was the support they received from France as a direct result of Benjamin Franklin's negotiations in Paris. France's coming to America's aid turned the tide against the British and paved the way for the colonists' victory over what was then the greatest empire on earth.

Twenty-five years later, the young American republic pulled off what has been described as the best real estate deal in history. By manipulating the strategic tension between France and England, American envoys James Monroe and Robert Livingston were able to convince Napoleon to sell all eight hundred thousand square miles of the Louisiana Territory to the United States for fifteen million dollars. The Louisiana Purchase sent the nation down a new, entirely unexpected path, and turned the collection of former colonies into a continental power. The transaction nearly doubled the size of the United States, making it one of the largest nations in the world.

In 1814, Napoleon's adventures (partly financed by his sale of the Louisiana Territory to the United States) led to France's defeat by the great powers and his exile to Elba. The Congress of Vienna was intended to be a dictation of terms, but by driving a wedge between the victorious powers and exploiting their differences, Talleyrand, the French foreign minister, was able to gain a seat at the table and ensure that despite its military defeat France's interests were protected as Europe was redrawn. The resulting agreement restructured Europe, restored the power of monarchy, and established a framework that provided a durable peace in Europe for almost a century.

In the summer of 1905, Theodore Roosevelt invited Japanese and Russian representatives to Portsmouth, New Hampshire, in an attempt to broker a peace between them and end the Russo-Japanese War. Although Russia had suffered serious setbacks and the war was costing both parties dearly, neither side was exhausted, and influential elements in each country pressed to continue fighting. After tortuous negotiations, an agreement was reached only after the Russian negotiator disobeyed direct instructions to break off the talks and presented terms he was not authorized to give. The resulting peace irretrievably altered the balance of power in the Far East and raised America's status as an emerging great power on the world diplomatic stage.

In January 1919, diplomats met at Versailles to negotiate an end to World War I, which had bled Europe dry with over forty million casualties. The war's cost in life and treasure had raised the stakes for all sides, and the results were both sweeping and tragically flawed. The outcome reordered Europe and the Middle East, eliminated the German, Austro-Hungarian, and Ottoman Empires, and planted the seeds of conflict on two continents.

Sometimes a first, tentative step toward peace becomes a lasting accomplishment in its own right, as in the Egyptian-Israeli armistice accords. In late 1948, Ralph Bunche took over as United Nations mediator in Palestine. The previous mediator, Bunche's colleague and friend, had just been assassinated. The parties were at war, and none of their representatives would look at, speak to, or shake hands with each other. Through meticulous diplomacy over a period of several months, Bunche was able to bring all sides to agreement, securing an armistice that ended the crisis. For his efforts, Bunche became the first black American and the youngest-ever recipient of the Nobel Peace Prize.

Sometimes it is enough to avoid catastrophe, as in the Cuban Missile Crisis, when Kennedy and Khrushchev navigated a way through the crisis and averted a nuclear war that could have destroyed mankind. In the depths of the Cold War, with the balance of power teetering between the two superpowers, American intelligence discovered a clandestine attempt by the Soviet Union to place nuclear missiles in Cuba. If successful, the United States would have been placed in immediate jeopardy, and it was prepared to go to war to prevent it. Over the course of thirteen days, President Kennedy and his advisers found an accommodation with Premier Khrushchev that averted the threat and avoided a global nuclear war.

In 1986, at the high-water mark of the Cold War, President Reagan met with Soviet leader Gorbachev in a summit in Iceland. That two-day meeting led to the first arms-control agreement to reduce nuclear weapons and marked the turning point in the conflict between the superpowers.

By averting wars or restructuring continents, each of these negotiations has had a profound and enduring impact on history. While they addressed different situations and problems, all of the figures faced the common challenge of bringing home a deal on the best terms against competing forces. As a result, one finds strategic patterns, as well as the recurring elements of persistence and the ability to capitalize on the unexpected. These examples provide timely evidence of how people have used reason and persuasion to avoid violence and prevail over adversity and can do so again. Negotiating, always at the heart of diplomacy, remains one of the indispensable tools of statecraft. The better we understand what has worked in the past and which mistakes to avoid, the less often states may find the need to resort to violence to settle differences.

Benjamin Franklin appears before the French court at Versailles on March 20, 1778, in a German print from 1784. (*Library of Congress*)

Chapter 1

Franklin at the
French Court

1778

W HEN the United States declared independence in July 1776, the Continental Army suffered from a shortage of weapons and gunpowder, and the Continental Congress struggled to feed, clothe, and supply thousands of troops in the face of a British trade ban and naval blockade. General George Washington's forces had less than five rounds of ammunition per soldier. "This was kept secret even from our people," Benjamin Franklin confided in a letter to a friend. "The world wondered that we so seldom fired a cannon. We could not afford it."[1]

Congress naturally turned to France, England's traditional adversary for hundreds of years, which had already covertly provided money and supplies, as a possible ally against Britain. Supporting the American Revolution offered France an opportunity to settle old scores, punish its historic enemy, and, by depriving England of a principal source of its wealth and power, restore the balance of power in Europe in France's favor. America's vast reserves of timber, furs, and raw materials fueled the British economy, and former British prime minister Lord

Chatham called the American colonies "the fountain of our wealth, the nerve of our strength, the nursery and basis of our naval power."[2]

In late September 1776, Congress appointed a commission of three prominent Americans, Arthur Lee, Silas Deane, and Franklin, to travel to Paris to persuade the French monarchy to join America in the conflict against Britain. Franklin, a former member of the Continental Congress and one of the authors of the Declaration of Independence, already enjoyed fame as a printer, author, inventor, and scientist, and his successful experiments on the nature of lightning had made him an international celebrity. French philosopher Voltaire called him "a man of genius, a first name in science, a successor to Newton and Galileo."[3] Deane, a Connecticut merchant who had also served in the Continental Congress, and Lee, a doctor and lawyer from a prominent Virginia family, were already in Europe. Franklin left Philadelphia on October 27, 1776, with his two grandsons, six-year-old Benjamin Franklin Bache and seventeen-year-old Temple Franklin, who would be his personal secretary. They traveled aboard the *Reprisal*, a sixteen-gun sloop carrying a cargo of thirty-five barrels of indigo. Despite several close calls with British cruisers during the passage, the *Reprisal* slipped through the British fleet and captured two British merchant ships off the French coast. Franklin's rough, thirty-day trip across the frigid North Atlantic "almost demolished me,"[4] he wrote. Franklin called the *Reprisal* "a miserable vessel, improper for those northern seas,"[5] and the poor food aboard left him too feeble on his arrival to stand. "Our voyage," Franklin wrote John Hancock, president of the Congress, "though not long was rough, and I feel myself weakened by it, but I now recover strength daily, and in a few days shall be able to undertake the journey to Paris."[6]

Franklin reached the French capital on December 21 where he joined Deane, and Lee arrived the following day. After a rest in Paris he settled into a villa on an eighteen-acre estate in the village of Passy, half a mile outside of Paris. Franklin and the Americans held a weak hand. General Washington's force of five thousand men was outnumbered six to one, and Franklin reached Paris the same day as news of Washington's defeats in New York and New Jersey. On the continent, few expected the rebellion would be able to last the year. While supportive of the colonists, France was deeply in debt, and King Louis XVI and his

Silas Deane drawn from life by Pierre Du Simitière in Philadelphia, c. 1781. (*Library of Congress*)

ministers had no interest in provoking a war with England. Furthermore, as a monarchy, France was reluctant to openly support colonists in rebellion against their king. "The spirit of revolt, wherever it appears, is always a dangerous example," French Foreign Minister Charles Gravier, the Comte de Vergennes, wrote. "Moral maladies, just as physical maladies, can prove contagious. Because of this consideration, we should prevent the spirit of independence . . . from spreading over that hemisphere."[7]

The American commissioners requested a meeting with Vergennes two weeks after their arrival. Although he refused them an official audience, he received them as private citizens, while assuring the British ambassador to France, Viscount Stormont, that there was no cause for alarm. "A minister's residence," Vergennes told Stormont, "is like a church. Anyone can enter, although there is no guarantee he will be absolved."[8] The Americans presented a proposal for a commercial treaty offering preferential trade with North America. Vergennes received them respectfully but told them that as things stood, France would remain neutral, although he sympathized with the rebels and would support them unofficially so far as he could, including greater help with covert supplies.

The modesty of their request puzzled Vergennes, and he wondered whether the American commissioners "might be hiding something in their pockets."[9] "I don't know whether Mr. Franklin told me everything," Vergennes confided to France's ambassador in Madrid, the Comte de Montmorin, "but what he told me is not very interesting with regard to the situation of his country. The ostensible object of his mission, the only one which he has revealed to me, is a treaty of commerce which he desires to conclude with us; he even left me an outline. . . . Its modesty causes surprise, because they do not demand anything which they do not already enjoy, at least from our side. If it is modesty or fear to be a burden to those powers on whose interest they hope to be able to rely, then these sentiments are very laudable; but could it not be possible that this reserve is the result of a more political consideration?"[10] He suspected that Franklin intended to create an open rupture between Spain and France on the one hand and England on the other, over the profitable trade with the American colonies that England had jealously guarded as its own monopoly. Vergennes wrote that he had no interest in war with England, and Franklin reported to Congress, "The cry of this nation is for us, but the court, it is thought, views an approaching war with reluctance."[11]

The American commissioners followed up with a second memorandum a week later that took a more direct approach, asking for eight fully manned ships of the line, thirty thousand muskets and bayonets, a large quantity of gunpowder and brass artillery pieces, and a formal alliance against England. In exchange they offered protection for French and Spanish colonies in the West Indies and access to America's large and growing commerce. The Americans warned that "if the Commerce of America is much longer obstructed, the Party who dislikes the War will be so strengthened as to compel the rest to an accommodation with Britain." The commissioners concluded: "North America now offers to France and Spain her amity and commerce. She is also ready to guarantee in the firmest manner to those nations all their present possessions in the West Indies, as well as those they shall acquire from the enemy in a war that may be consequential of such assistance as she requests. The interest of the three nations is the same. The opportunity of cementing them, and of securing all the advantages of that commerce, which in time will be

French Foreign Minister Charles Gravier, the Comte de Vergennes. (*Library of Congress*)

immense, now presents itself. If neglected, it may never again return. We cannot help suggesting that a considerable delay may be attended with fatal consequences."[12]

Vergennes replied that if France granted their request it would "compromise her openly" and serve as a "legitimate motive of war."[13] France would provide covert aid, but nothing that could provoke Britain or jeopardize France's neutrality. He would not rule out the possibility of another war between France and England, but France, he maintained, "must await, not force, events."[14] Vergennes wrote Montmorin that he had no interest in an American alliance, but the Americans could prove useful should war erupt between Britain and France, so he would leave the door open for future negotiation. Vergennes softened his rejection with two million livres in covert support, although the gift was so secret that not even Congress could know that the aid came from the French treasury.

Arthur Lee traveled to Spain in February to petition the Spanish court for assistance and an alliance. Spain promised some token aid, but, as Spanish Foreign Minister Jerónimo

Grimaldi confided to Vergennes, only "a little so as to nourish their hopes."[15] "The example of a rebellion" Grimaldi wrote the Spanish ambassador in Paris, "is too dangerous for his Majesty to wish to support it openly."[16] Congress also sent envoys to Tuscany, Vienna, and Berlin, but the prevailing belief that the revolution would soon fail caused them to turn the American representatives away.

While waiting to hear from the French government, the commissioners received a letter from Robert Morris, writing on behalf of Congress, saying that unless help arrived soon the future of the revolution looked bleak. British General Henry Clinton had taken Rhode Island. The Continental Army suffered military defeats on Long Island and in the Hudson River valley, and the British, who occupied New York, had chased Washington's ragged, barefoot soldiers through New Jersey and driven them across the Delaware River into Pennsylvania. The revolution was on the verge of collapse for lack of muskets and gunpowder. Inflation was out of control, and with the American currency nearly worthless, Congress found it increasingly difficult to find funds to keep the army in the field. The British fleet blockaded American ports, and England was making preparations for a final campaign to finish off Washington's army.

Robert Morris described the situation as so desperate that only France entering the conflict could prevent catastrophe. "I must add to this gloomy picture," he wrote, "one circumstance, more distressing than all the rest, because it threatens instant and total ruin to the American cause, unless some radical cure is applied and speedily; I mean the depreciation of continental currency. The enormous pay of our army, the immense expenses at which they are supplied provisions, clothing and other necessities, and, in short, the extravagance that has prevailed on most departments of the public service, have called forth prodigious emissions of paper money, both continental and colonial."

He concluded: "If the Court of France open their eyes to their own interest, and think the commerce of North America will compensate them for the expense and evil of a war with Britain, they may readily create a diversion, and afford us succors that will change the fate of affairs; but they must do it soon; our situation is critical, and does not admit of delay."[17]

Arthur Lee. (*Library of Congress*)

The commissioners also received a letter from Arthur Lee's brother Richard Henry Lee, a member of Congress from Virginia, separately relaying Congress's warning that independence would be in jeopardy if they could not arrange an alliance with France and Spain and obtain money for arms, supplies, and ships, and emphasizing "how all important it is to the security of American independence that France should enter the war as soon as possible."[18]

Franklin submitted a second offer of a military alliance to Vergennes on February 1. With no answer from the French ministry, the commissioners decided to exceed their instructions and extend France an assurance that the United States would not make a separate peace with England, in exchange for a similar commitment from France, should a commercial treaty with America lead to war between France and England. "[I]n the present peril of the liberties of our Country," they insisted, "it is our duty to hazard everything in their support and defense. Therefore, Resolved unanimously: That if it should be necessary, for the attainment of any thing, in our best judgment, material to the defense and support of the public cause; that we should pledge our persons or hazard the censure of Congress by exceeding our instructions—we will, for such purpose, most cheerfully risk our personal liberty or life."[19]

On March 14, new instructions arrived. In desperation, Congress authorized the commissioners to sweeten their proposal, confirming the course they already had independently taken, and allowed them to make any offers they felt necessary to obtain French assistance. "Upon mature deliberation of all circumstances," Congress wrote the commissioners, "Congress deems the speedy declaration of French and European assistance so indispensably necessary to secure the independence of these states, that they have authorized you to make such tenders to France and Spain as they hope will prevent any longer delay of an event that is judged so essential to the well-being of North America."[20] The Americans requested an additional loan of two million livres from France and presented Vergennes and the Spanish ministry with a proposal for a formal triple alliance with France and Spain for immediate war against Britain to last until the establishment of American independence, the Spanish conquest of Portugal, and French and American forces' ejection of British forces from North America and the Caribbean. The Americans included a new demand, that France not only join an alliance and provide aid, but also help with the conquest of Canada, a particular aim of Franklin's. Canada and Newfoundland would go to the colonists, and France would take possession of the British West Indies. To encourage Spain to join the alliance, America offered to declare war against Portugal and to "continue the said war for the total conquest of that kingdom to be added to the dominion of Spain."[21] The proposal ended by warning that unless France intervened directly America might be forced to sue England for peace.

Uninterested in new territory and apprehensive about American military prospects, the French politely but firmly rejected the proposal, as did Spain. France did not share their impatience, Vergennes told the American commissioners. "Even a precarious peace for now would be better than war,"[22] the French prime minster, Count Jean-Frederic Maurepas, wrote the

French naval minister. The Americans decided not to press the offer. "It is proper to observe," Deane recalled, "that Doctor Franklin was from the first averse to warm and urgent solicitations with the Court of France. His age and experience, as well as his philosophical temper, led him to prefer a patient perseverance, and to wait events, and to leave the Court of France to act from motives of interest only. He used often to say that America was a new and young state, and, like a virgin, ought to wait for the addresses of other powers, rather than to make even the first advances; and what confirmed him in these sentiments was, his having early in the contest made it a fixed and certain point with him that France would not in any circumstances or situation suffer America to return under the domination of Great Britain."[23]

In fact, the French were providing surreptitious aid to the colonists. To the Americans' great relief, in late April 1777, two French ships, the *Amphitrite* and the *Mercure*, evaded the British blockade and arrived in Boston with twenty thousand muskets, gunpowder, balls, and lead. To ferry supplies to the United States, other French ships sailed under forged bills of lading to the French West Indies, where the cargo was unloaded at night into small ships and smuggled into American ports. This French support was a welcome reprieve, but not enough to alter the balance against the British.

American military defeats continued with the fall of Fort Ticonderoga to General John Burgoyne's army in July, which left the headwaters of the Hudson in the hands of the British, threatened to sever communication between New England and the other colonies, and reinforced a belief in France that the American Revolution was doomed. "It is a problem," Vergennes wrote, after hearing of the loss of Ticonderoga, "whether they can preserve the liberty for which they have taken up arms; attacked in the rear by the English army of Canada, while General Howe assails them in front. Have they the force, the unity, the leadership, to resist this storm?"[24] Vergennes moved cautiously. "Everyone does what he has to do," he wrote, but if the American interests prompted them to "embrace anything that might benefit their cause, ours is not to allow ourselves farther than it is in our interest to go."[25] Rather than commit France to an uncertain proposition, Vergennes preferred to wait and sign a treaty with the United States after it gained independence.

On September 25, Franklin approached Vergennes for an additional fourteen million livres of aid. Congress needed eighty thousand blankets, forty thousand uniforms, one hundred thousand pairs of stockings, one million flints, and two hundred tons of lead.[26] Having almost exhausted their funds, the American envoys were themselves on the verge of bankruptcy, as they had received no payments from Congress and the French loans were spent. Their financial outlook was so grim that Franklin suggested they cancel contracts for weapons and uniforms and sell guns and supplies they had bought but not yet shipped. Lee read his colleagues part of a letter from his brother Richard Henry warning that "without an alliance with France and Spain, with a considerable loan to support their funds it would be difficult to maintain their independence."[27] The American commissioners agreed their best hope was for France to keep paying the interest on their debts, which would spare them from going to jail.

Less than two weeks later, shortly before noon on December 4, a messenger from Boston arrived with word that Philadelphia, the American capital, had fallen to the British, and the Continental Congress fled to Baltimore, where it continued to meet in an old tavern. But that was outweighed by other news of far greater strategic importance: General Burgoyne and his entire army had surrendered to American forces at Saratoga. Two thousand British soldiers were killed, and almost six thousand men taken prisoner, including four members of Parliament, six generals, three hundred officers, five thousand five hundred enlisted men, and thirty-seven pieces of artillery. The British pincer had been broken, its northern army had been wiped out, and American forces had triumphed in the field against the best the British had to offer.

The American victory at Saratoga had an immediate effect on the French calculations and drove home to Vergennes the need to make a decision regarding the colonies. "Recent military victories seem to offer a new perspective," Vergennes declared, since it removed French doubts about the "solidity"[28] of American resistance

Portrait of Benjamin Franklin engraved by Pierre Le Beau in France, c. 1780. (*Library of Congress*)

to Britain. The French worried that the American victory would strengthen those within the British government who favored reconciliation with America, and Vergennes felt France would have to act before a newly humbled Britain offered the colonies tempting peace terms. "What ought to lead France to join with America," he wrote Montmorin, "is the great enfeeblement of England to be effected by the subtraction of a third of her Empire."[29]   Within two days, Vergennes's deputy, Conrad Alexandre Gerard, called on the American representatives at Passy. As "there appeared no doubt now," he told them, "of the ability and resolution of the States to maintain their independency," he could assure them that American overtures would find a more willing ear, and invited the Americans to resubmit their proposal for an alliance, adding that "it could be done none too soon."[30]

Two days later, Franklin, Deane, and Lee gave Vergennes a renewed proposal for an alliance. In it they reminded him that it had been almost a year since they had approached the French court for help, and called on France for "immediate and public action to correct the ill impressions on the minds of our people, who, from the secrecy enjoined us, cannot be informed of the friendly and essential aids that have been so generously but privately offered us." Otherwise, the commissioners implied, the American public, unaware of the covert French support, might be tempted by British peace offers.[31]

On December 12, Vergennes and Gerard secretly met the Americans at a house a half mile outside of Versailles. The French foreign minister let them know he was willing to consider a treaty of alliance and trade, and recognition of American independence, before explaining: "If we enter into a treaty with you, we will be affirming your independency. Necessarily this will bring about war with England. We cannot do this without consulting Spain, without whose concurrence nothing can be done." According to the Bourbon Family Compact of 1761, part of the compromise that ended the War of the Spanish Succession, France and Spain committed to act in concert in matters of war and peace, so an alliance with the United States required Spain's consent. Vergennes ended by warning them: "Your independency must still be considered in the womb. We must not endeavor to hasten its birth prematurely."[32] He dispatched a courier to Madrid and told the Americans they would hear back in three weeks. "Take for your motto," Vergennes advised the Spanish ambassador in Paris, "and make them adopt it: *Aut nunc aut numquam*" (either now or never).[33] Otherwise, if they let slip "the most interesting conjecture that heaven could present us, the reproaches of the present generation and of the generations to come will accuse us forever of our culpable indifference."[34] "Let us not be mistaken," Vergennes wrote Montmorin, "the Power which first recognizes the independence of the Americans will be the first to gather all the fruits of this war."[35]

King George III's government, shaken by Saratoga and concerned by Franklin's presence in Paris, decided to forestall any

alliance between France and the
Americans with an offer of reconciliation between the colonies and
Britain. It sent an envoy, Britain's
chief spy in Europe, Paul Wentworth,
to meet Deane (Franklin refused to
meet Wentworth, and the British
believed Deane was the most
approachable of the commissioners) at
Deane's apartment on the rue Royale
on December 15 and 16. Over dinner,
the British emissary outlined a proposal for reconciliation in which the
colonies would be self-governing in
all matters except trade and foreign

A portrait of Lord North
from the London Magazine,
October 1779. (*Library of
Congress*)

affairs. Deane refused Wentworth's offer, telling him independence was the only road to peace. While Vergennes and the
American representatives waited to hear from Spain, Lord
North, the British prime minister, announced that he intended to
submit a proposal for amnesty and reconciliation with the
American colonies when Parliament reconvened January 20.
With British overtures appearing imminent, the Americans
pressed Vergennes on whether the colonies would be able to rely
on France and Spain for help. "England's aim being no longer
doubtful," Vergennes wrote, "it seems that neither should our
decision be so; for the question we have to decide is to know
whether it is more expedient for us to have war against England
and America together, than with America for us against
England."[36]

Vergennes felt pressed to preempt the British peace overtures.
"If the English," he worried, "learned wisdom from their misfor-
tunes and made terms of peace, what could France do to prevent a reconciliation?"[37] Vergennes feared that the North government, reeling from the loss at Saratoga, was close to making

a generous peace offer that would include independence in all but name that the exhausted colonies, fighting alone and deprived of the prospect of outside help, would find difficult to refuse if France continued to deny them open support. French fears took the upper hand, and Vergennes decided he had to do something. "There remains hardly any time for a decision," he wrote. "The moment is decisive." If France did not act, Vergennes worried, "the British Ministry . . . may cut us out, and leave us nothing but useless regret at having wantonly lost the most fortunate opportunity which Providence ever offered the House of Bourbon." Vergennes did not want to lose what he called "the only opportunity which may perhaps happen for many centuries for putting England in its true place." [38] He instructed Gerard to "make glitter before his [Deane's] eyes, . . . everything necessary to keep the legation in the lap of France."[39] On December 17, Gerard visited the commissioners at Franklin's house at Passy and told them that after long and careful deliberation, Louis XVI had resolved to recognize their independence and would grant a treaty as soon as confirmation arrived from Madrid.

The confirmation never came. On December 31, Vergennes's courier returned with word that Spain rejected an alliance. Spain's interests differed from France's, and the Spanish stood to gain less than the French from a successful American uprising, and had more to lose. The settlement of a dispute between Spain and Portugal had removed a source of friction with England, and Spain's less industrialized economy and smaller merchant fleet were not well-positioned to benefit from the opening of American trade. While France saw reducing British power as the key to reestablishing itself as the dominant nation in Europe, Spanish ambitions were directed to its overseas colonies, which were easy targets for the British navy and vulnerable to rebellion should the American example succeed. Spain had little appetite for committing itself to a war whose main purpose was to humble France's rival. "One does not make war," Spain's new foreign minister, Count Floridablanca, explained, "except to preserve one's own possessions or to acquire those of others."[40] The Spanish preferred to provide just enough aid to draw out the conflict. "Certainly it is for our advantage," he wrote, "that the revolt of these people should continue; we must wish that they and the English should exhaust each other."[41]

That winter the revolution hung by a thread. The Continental Army, camped at Valley Forge, had twenty-five barrels of flour for eleven thousand men, and many starved. "An army of skeletons appeared before our eyes naked, starved, sick and discouraged,"[42] Gouverneur Morris, a member of the Continental Congress, reported after a visit. Almost three thousand died, some frozen to death, others of illness or hunger. "The unfortunate soldiers," wrote the Marquis de Lafayette, who had traveled to the United States to fight with the Continental Army, "were in want of everything; they had neither coats nor hats, nor shirts, nor shoes. Their feet and their legs froze until they were black, and it was often necessary to amputate them."[43] George Washington wrote: "Naked and starving as they are, we cannot enough admire the incomparable patience and fidelity of the soldiery, that they have not been ere this excited by their sufferings, to a general mutiny or dispersion. Strong symptoms, however, of discontent have appeared in particular instances; and nothing but the most active efforts everywhere can long avert so shocking a catastrophe."[44] In February 1778 he wrote: "Our present sufferings are not all. There is no foundation laid for any adequate relief hereafter. All the magazines provided in the States of New Jersey, Pennsylvania, Delaware and Maryland, and all the immediate additional supplies they seem capable of affording, will not be sufficient to support the army more than a month longer, if so long."[45]

With no word from Vergennes after the Spanish refusal, Franklin decided to force Vergennes's hand. After brushing off Wentworth for weeks, Franklin invited him to dinner. His meeting Wentworth, which he knew would be reported by the efficient French secret service, signaled that the Americans might be willing after all to entertain reconciliation with Britain, and left Vergennes under the impression that Franklin had begun negotiating terms. Lord North had sent Wentworth to Paris to approach the American commissioners to head off a deal with France, but Franklin used it as the means he needed to seal one. Franklin met Wentworth on January 6, and they spoke alone for two hours. Wentworth told Franklin if they set aside their personal grudges, a rejoined Britain and America would be "the greatest empire on earth," and asked what terms it would take for reconciliation. Franklin replied that he would accept independence or nothing. In that case, Britain was willing to fight for another ten years to prevent American independence, Wentworth told Franklin. "America," Franklin retorted, "is ready to fight fifty years to win it." Franklin would not budge. He wandered on, talking about the past, complaining about British atrocities in the colonies, keeping the conversation going for the benefit of Vergennes's spies outside without revealing or agreeing to anything. Deane joined them at the end of their talk, and the three sat down for dinner. Franklin's purpose, of course, was not to engage Wentworth in a meaningful discussion on the substance of his proposals, but to keep him occupied in conversation long enough to generate a convincing impression of entertaining his offer, for the benefit of Vergennes and the French cabinet.

Wentworth returned to London the next day empty-handed, and the British concluded that it must be because the Americans already had an agreement with France in their pocket, but Franklin now had a decisive tool to convince the French government to move quickly, which he sealed by failing to report to the French ministry (as he usually did religiously when receiving foreign visitors) his meeting with the British representative. Franklin's meeting with Wentworth, as intended, led Vergennes to believe that unless he acted quickly, the Americans might do the unthinkable and come to terms with Britain. "I am certain that they are negotiating briskly," Vergennes wrote. "I see proposals most eagerly listened to, and I am afraid."[46] "They play us off against one another," the British ambassador, Lord Stormont, cautioned Vergennes. "Franklin's natural subtlety gives him a great advantage in such a game. It is easy to see that on such a situation peace between England and the House of Bourbon hangs by the slightest of all threads."[47]

The day after Franklin met Wentworth, Vergennes, concerned by the meeting, convened the Royal Council of Ministers in French Prime Minister Maurepas's bedroom, where the prime minister lay stricken with gout, and convinced them that if France did not act, the once-in-a-lifetime opportunity would slip from their hands. The council voted unanimously in favor of an alliance despite Spain's opposition.

Gerard met the commissioners at Deane's apartment in Paris on the Rue Royale the following day. He asked them two questions: "What is necessary to be done to give such satisfaction to the American commissioners as to engage them not to listen to any propositions from England for a new connection with that country?" and, "What would work the same effect on the American people?" Franklin consulted privately with his colleagues, and when Gerard returned an hour later, Franklin gave their reply to the first question (they hadn't had a chance to get to the second.) "The immediate conclusion of a treaty of commerce and alliance," he said, "would close their ears to any proposal which should not have as its basis entire liberty and independence." Gerard informed the American commissioners that the king was finally prepared to conclude a treaty. Franklin, according to Gerard, "softened by this resolution, which he did not appear to expect, observed that this was what they proposed and solicited vainly for a year past." Gerard assured them he would produce a document within days that would include a commercial treaty and, more importantly, a treaty of military alliance, although to Franklin, Deane, and Lee's disappointment, French involvement in the war would not be automatic, as Gerard insisted that France retain its ability to decide when to enter the conflict.[48]

Three days later the American commissioners replied in writing to Gerard's second question, laying out in greater detail what was needed to prevent the United States from coming to terms with England: either France's immediate entry into the war, or enough financial support to sustain the revolution until the English were thrown out of North America and American independence was secure. The commissioners demanded "an immediate engagement" by France "to guarantee the present possessions of the Congress in America, with such others as they may acquire on the continent during the war, and either to enter into a war with England or furnish Congress with the money," until "all that the English now possess on the continent shall be conquered."[49] A gift from France of six or eight warships would ensure victory arrived more quickly. "Their first word," Vergennes wrote, "when I caused them to be sounded, and they have not yet altogether retracted it, was that only an immediate war could make them engage to come to no arrangement with the mother country without our consent."[50] For diplomatic reasons, it was important for France not to be the party initiating hostilities in a war with England. However, as signing an alliance with and providing open aid to the rebellious colonies would be an intolerable infringement on English sovereignty, a declaration of war by Britain would be the inevitable outcome.

Franklin, Deane, Lee, and Gerard signed the Franco-American treaties in the French Ministry of Foreign Affairs in

Paris on February 6, 1778. The treaty of alliance declared that the two countries "mutually engage not to lay down their arms, until the independence of the United States shall have been formally or tacitly assured by the Treaty or Treaties that shall terminate the War." The alliance, which would come into effect at the outbreak of hostilities between France and England, was "to maintain effectually the liberty, sovereignty, and independence, absolute and unlimited of

Conrad Alexandre Gerard. (*New York Public Library*)

the said United States, as well in matters of Government as of commerce."[51] France promised to continue the conflict until American independence was secured. Significantly, the treaties avoided entangling the United States in permanent alliances that might involve it in future European wars and left the United States free to grant equal political and commercial privileges to other nations. "No monopoly of our trade was granted," Franklin pointed out in a letter to Congress. "None are given to France but what we are at liberty to grant to any other nation."[52]

Within five months France and England were at war. Spain joined the fight against Britain a year later in return for a French promise to help it capture Gibraltar from the British. French help was indispensible in turning the tide of the war. Ninety percent of the gunpowder used by Washington's army came from France. The French shipped over thirty thousand muskets, four hundred tons of gunpowder, five thousand tents, and sixty pieces of field artillery. American soldiers wore French clothes, fired French weapons, and their wages were largely paid by France. The combined might of the French and Spanish navies broke the British navy's monopoly in the Atlantic and,

The French fleet under command of Comte d'Estaing off the coast of New England, August 17, 1778. (*Library of Congress*)

by threatening an invasion force off the English Channel (as well as fighting in the Mediterranean, Gibraltar, the Caribbean, and India), turned the war into a global conflict and forced a dispersion of British forces that fatally weakened the British war effort. At the decisive battle of Yorktown in 1781, which marked the defeat of the British and secured American independence, a French fleet, French troops, and French heavy cannon provided the margin of victory. The fleet, commanded by Admiral Francois-Joseph De Grasse, prevented British reinforcements from relieving General Charles Cornwallis's besieged force, while over eight thousand French soldiers under Count Rochambeau fought in the final engagement. Support for the American war cost the French treasury over a billion livres (equal to three times France's national budget), drove the country deeply into debt, and led to taxes that provoked the French Revolution in 1789. Louis XVI was beheaded in 1793.

A map of Louisiana from 1804. (*Library of Congress*)

Chapter 2

The Louisiana Purchase

1803

T HE United States' first major international crisis, and its most profitable, began twenty-two years after the British surrender at Yorktown, when France in 1803 secretly bought the Louisiana Territory from the Spanish monarchy in exchange for the kingdom of Tuscany. The Spanish had governed the Louisiana Territory, an uncolonized expanse of wilderness that extended from the Mississippi River to the Rocky Mountains, as an absentee landlord, but Napoleon Bonaparte planned to make it the centerpiece of a French empire in the New World. He assembled an occupation fleet to take possession of his new prize and ordered authorities in the strategic port of New Orleans to block American goods from passing down the Mississippi, bringing half the country's trade to an abrupt halt. "Since the question of Independence," Alexander Hamilton observed, "none has occurred more deeply interesting to the United States than the cession of Louisiana to France. This event threatens the early dismemberment of a large portion of our country; more immediately the safety of all the Southern States; and remotely the independence of the whole union."[1]

Residents of the states west of the Appalachian Mountains called for war and threatened secession if Washington would not act, and Senator James Ross of Pennsylvania took to the floor of the U.S. Senate to demand an immediate attack on New Orleans. "The people of the west are impatient to do themselves justice," he declared, "and if the French are allowed time to arrive, the Americans, in those parts of the Union, will refuse to pay taxes to a government too feeble to protect them. Never will there be so favorable an occasion to annex [a gateway] without which half our states could not exist."[2]

The resolution failed narrowly, but the political pressure forced President Thomas Jefferson to call out the militia and put the country on a war footing. "This little event," President Jefferson predicted, "of France's possessing herself of Louisiana . . . is the embryo of a tornado which will burst on the countries on both sides of the Atlantic and involve in its effects their highest destinies."[3]

The European situation, meanwhile, was in flux. Unusually cold weather kept the French flotilla bound for New Orleans ice-bound in Holland, creating a brief window for negotiation before French forces arrived. In the New World, a successful uprising in Santo Domingo, in which thirty thousand French troops, including Napoleon's brother-in-law, perished, curbed France's appetite for colonial adventures. The Peace of Amiens, a fragile, yearlong pause in the Napoleonic wars between England and France, was falling apart and it became obvious that France would soon once again be at war with England. Twenty British warships patrolled the Gulf of Mexico, and the British made no secret of their plans to seize New Orleans from the French at the first sign of hostilities. If the British gained control of New Orleans and the Mississippi, they could easily roll back what had just been so hard won in the Revolutionary War.

Jefferson knew France needed money for the approaching European war. Years of revolution, mismanagement, and conflict had left the French treasury desperate for cash, and even the French treasury minister admitted that the revolutionary government "had made the disorders of the French finances too well known for a foreign state to expect to treat in any other way than with ready money."[4] President Jefferson and Secretary of State James Madison hoped there might be a chance to turn this to their advantage.

Thomas Jefferson in an 1804 portrait. (*Library of Congress*)

Still, a peaceful solution seemed unlikely. "There is not the most remote possibility," Hamilton wrote, "that the ambitious and aggrandizing views of Bonaparte will commute the territory for money. Its acquisition is of immense importance to France, and has long been an object of her extreme solicitude. The attempt therefore to purchase, in the first instance, will certainly fail, and in the end, war must be resorted to, under all the accumulation of difficulties caused by a previous and strongly fortified possession of the country by our adversary."[5]

On January 10, 1803, Jefferson asked former Virginia Governor James Monroe for his help. "I have but a moment to inform you," Jefferson wrote his fellow Virginian, "that the fever into which the western mind is thrown by the affair at New Orleans . . . threatens to overbear our peace. In this situation we are obliged to call on you for a temporary sacrifice of yourself, to prevent this greatest of evils in the present prosperous tide of our affairs. I shall tomorrow nominate you to the Senate for an extraordinary mission to France, and the circumstances are such as to render it impossible to decline; because the whole public hope will be rested on you."[6]

The burly, six-foot-tall Monroe, one of Jefferson's closest friends, had previously served as the American ambassador in

Paris. A revolutionary patriot, he suffered the hardships of Valley Forge as a young lieutenant and was wounded in the shoulder at the Battle of Trenton, where General Washington promoted him for bravery under fire. After the victory at Yorktown, Monroe returned to school before apprenticing as a lawyer under Jefferson. His service as a delegate to the Continental Congress and as a U.S. senator from Virginia established his political credentials, and in 1794 President Washington chose him to be the American ambassador to France, a position he held for three years. His term as governor expired in December 1802, and he had been looking forward to making some money and returning to practicing law when he received President Jefferson's letter.

Monroe left for Paris on March 9 with a heavy heart. Once he arrived he would be completely isolated, as communication across the Atlantic was so poor it could take up to three months to send an urgent message and receive a reply, and there was no guarantee that Napoleon, who once famously said, "Peace is opposed to my interests," [7] would even agree to meet with him. The failure of several previous diplomatic attempts, as a result of France's refusal to acknowledge the Spanish treaty's existence, led the American ambassador in Paris to write despondently "with respect to a negotiation for Louisiana I think nothing will be effected here." [8] Before Monroe departed, President Jefferson warned him: "All eyes, all hopes are now fixed on you . . . for on the event of this mission depends the future destinies of this republic." [9]

Monroe would join the American ambassador to France, Robert Livingston. Fourteen years older than Monroe, Livingston was in certain respects an unlikely diplomat. He spoke barely a word of French and was almost completely deaf. He had, however, an agile mind and unshakable persistence. He had served with Jefferson on the committee of five that drafted the Declaration of Independence, had chaired the New York

Constitutional Convention, and as chancellor of New York in 1789 administered the oath of office to George Washington when he became the first president of the United States. Charles Maurice de Talleyrand–Perigord, the French foreign minister, had developed a dry respect for his abilities, calling him "the most importunate negotiator I have ever encountered." Tall and self-confident, Livingston's austere aristocratic exterior concealed an affable temperament and a keen intellect. His family was prominent politically (his brother was district attorney and mayor of

James Monroe. (*Library of Congress*)

New York), and rumors circulated of his ambitions to run for vice president in 1804. Monroe ranked high on the list of potential rivals, and Livingston resented and feared his new partner's arrival.[10]

Monroe reached Le Havre on April 8, exhausted and ill after a rough Atlantic crossing. As Monroe's carriage made its way toward Paris, Napoleon gathered his advisers at his palatial estate at St. Cloud. Napoleon's longstanding dreams of building a French empire in the New World faded as, with war inevitable in Europe, he worried about losing Louisiana to the British. He saw, as Jefferson and Madison hoped, that a sale to the United States could place Louisiana permanently beyond England's reach and raise money for the coming war. There was little time. He ordered his ministers to open negotiations with the Americans immediately, not just for New Orleans, which was what they asked, but the entire Louisiana Territory. However, he warned that the price must be high. Otherwise he preferred to make "a desperate attempt to keep these fine countries,"[11] as he accurately foresaw that "whatever nation held the Mississippi Valley would eventually be the most powerful on earth."[12]

Napoleon, concerned about possible interference by the British, wanted the matter handled discreetly. "The cabinet of London is informed of the measures adopted at Washington," he cautioned, "but it can have no suspicion of those which I am now taking. Observe the greatest secrecy, and recommend it to the American Ministers. You will acquaint me, day by day, hour by hour, of your progress."[13] Emphasizing that he knew what he offered was priceless, and his need for money, he continued: "If I should regulate my terms, according to the value of these vast regions to the United States, the indemnity would have no limits. I will be moderate, in consideration of the necessity in which I am making a sale. But keep this to yourself. I want fifty million francs, and for less than that sum I will not treat."[14]

Napoleon's key ministers were Talleyrand and Francois de Barbé—Marbois. Short, fat, and clubfooted, Talleyrand was also charming, treacherous, and effective. "He understands the world," Napoleon said. "He knows thoroughly the Courts of Europe; he has finesse to say the least of it; and he never shows what he is thinking."[15] A skillful negotiator, Talleyrand's favorite tactic was delay. "The lack of instructions and the necessity of consulting one's own government are always legitimate excuses in order to obtain delays in political affairs,"[16] he once wrote. He was also entirely without scruples and breathtakingly corrupt. His contemporaries thought of him as a reptilian character, and treated him with a mixture of fear and awe, but mostly fear. One described him as having "no fixed principles, he changes them as he does his linen,"[17] while Gouverneur Morris, a former American ambassador to France, found him "polished, cold, tricky, ambitious and bad."[18]

The oldest son of minor Parisian nobility, Talleyrand began his career in the clergy, and despite elastic morals and a fondness for atheism, he became a bishop at age thirty-four. He left

French foreign minister Charles Maurice de Talleyrand–Perigord, left, and Francois de Barbé–Marbois, right. (*Musée national du Château de Versailles*)

the priesthood soon after to join the French diplomatic corps, which better suited his talents. Although he had been an early supporter of the French Revolution, Talleyrand moved to England when it spiraled out of control. Expelled from England at the request of the French revolutionary government, he spent two years in exile in America, which he detested. "Refinement," he complained, "does not exist" in the United States.[19] When things calmed down, Talleyrand returned to France and became foreign minister in 1797.

Barbé-Marbois was Napoleon's finance minister. A keen admirer of the United States, he spoke perfect English, had traveled extensively in America, and knew Monroe and Livingston well. His wife was the daughter of the former governor of Pennsylvania, and Barbé-Marbois provided indispensable help during the American Revolution as the French consul general in Philadelphia. Barbé-Marbois was promoted to the Council of Ancients in the French Revolutionary Government before he fell out of favor for objecting to the misappropriation of funds and was sent on trumped-up charges to exile in a prison camp in French Guiana that became notorious as Devil's Island. Needing someone of integrity and experience to restore France's neglected finances, when Napoleon took power he released Barbé-Marbois and placed him in charge of the French treasury. Napoleon charged him with carrying out the negotiation for Louisiana under Talleyrand's guidance.

The French negotiators began with several disadvantages. Months of French prevarication and stonewalling had exhausted Ambassador Livingston's patience and filled him with mistrust. Barbé-Marbois described Livingston's firm belief "that the United States would never possess New Orleans by treaty, and that it ought to be taken by force. His intercourse with the French ministry confirmed him in this impression."[20] The French knew that American goals for the negotiation were much narrower than theirs, as New Orleans and navigation rights along the Mississippi were the only objects Monroe and Livingston had in mind. Napoleon warned his negotiators that neither Monroe nor Livingston was "prepared for a decision which goes infinitely beyond anything that they are about to ask of us."[21]

The morning after Napoleon's meeting at St. Cloud, Livingston received an urgent request to meet with Talleyrand at his residence on the Rue du Bac in Paris. Livingston went there in the early afternoon, and after light conversation, Talleyrand asked him almost as an afterthought whether the United States "wished to have the whole of Louisiana?" Livingston said no. Unaware of the events at St. Cloud, he assumed this proposal was one of what Barbé-Marbois described as "the many deceptions that had previously been practiced upon him"[22] by Talleyrand. "But if we gave New Orleans, the rest would be of little value," Talleyrand continued. "I should like to know what you would give for the whole."[23] Suspicious but slightly intrigued, Livingston volunteered the token amount of twenty million francs, or just under four million dollars. Talleyrand, bristling at the low price, urged Livingston to think it over, adding coyly that he did not speak from authority. "The idea merely struck me," he said.[24]

They met again the following morning. Livingston, puzzled by Talleyrand's probing the day before, pressed the French foreign minister on his mysterious proposition, but Livingston's eagerness made Talleyrand more aloof and evasive. Talleyrand reiterated implausibly that the idea was just an idle brainstorm of his, but again encouraged Livingston to make an offer. The American

Robert Livingston. (*Center of Military History*)

ambassador declined. Although intrigued, he told Talleyrand he needed to first consult with Monroe, who was about to arrive in Paris. At this, the Frenchman shrugged his shoulders and dropped the subject.

Monroe reached Paris that afternoon at one o'clock and spent the afternoon with Livingston at the American Embassy reviewing their instructions from Jefferson and Madison. News of the failure of Senator Ross's resolution depressed Livingston, who felt negotiation was pointless and Talleyrand's gesture was simply a way of toying with him. "I wish," he told Monroe, "that the resolution . . . had been adopted. Only force can give us New Orleans. We must employ force. Let us first get possession of the country and negotiate afterwards."[25]

After dinner, Barbé-Marbois stopped by while Monroe and Livingston enjoyed coffee with guests. Over cognac, the French finance minister let them know that he had something important to share with them in private. Monroe had not yet officially received his diplomatic credentials, so Livingston excused himself and hurried alone to Barbé-Marbois's office at the French treasury.

While Talleyrand's fumbled overture had heightened Livingston's confusion and desperation, Livingston and Barbé-Marbois had a strong working relationship, and in the candle-light the American ambassador tried to impress on his friend the gravity of the situation. Livingston pointed out that at any moment either the Americans could lose their patience or the British could declare war on France and seize Louisiana them-selves. He related his conversations with Talleyrand and shared his misgivings over "the extreme absurdity of his evasions."[26]

Barbé-Marbois listened closely before playing his hand. France, he told Livingston, was prepared to offer the entire Louisiana Territory along with New Orleans to the United States in exchange for one hundred million francs. The American ambassador flatly rejected the offer. Barbé-Marbois's demand amounted to five times the operating budget of the U.S. govern-ment, more money than existed in the United States. Undeterred, Barbé-Marbois conceded that the number was high and probed Livingston, asking what the United States might be willing to pay. Livingston gave no reply. Instead, he stalled, telling Barbé-Marbois that he lacked the authority to go any-where near Napoleon's number, and he needed to consider the matter and discuss it with Monroe.

Livingston tried to draw him out. Since Barbé-Marbois admitted the price was high, Livingston pressed him on what he considered fair. The French minister, in a clearly preplanned move, said he felt that the territory was actually worth eighty million francs. Sixty million could be in cash, and twenty mil-lion in the assumption of old debts the French government owed American merchants. Even at the reduced price, Livingston countered, he could never agree to something so far beyond their ability to pay. "Our fellow citizens," he explained to the French minister, "have an extreme aversion to public debts. How could we, without incurring their displeasure, burden them" with such an "enormous charge?"[27] He also reminded Barbé-

Marbois that the incumbent American administration was friendly to France, while the opposition was more inclined to support England. If Napoleon demanded too much, it could lose Jefferson the upcoming election and turn the White House over to those openly hostile to the French government. He laid this out, and asked Barbé-Marbois whether "the few millions acquired at this expense would not be too dearly bought?" Livingston reminded Barbé-Marbois of the danger of the territory falling into the hands of the British. He stressed the "ardor of the Americans to take it by force," and "the difficulty with which they were restrained by the prudence of the President."[28]

The French minister acknowledged Livingston's points but told him the demand was nonnegotiable. Instead, he cautioned the American in a thinly veiled threat that Napoleon could quickly change his mind and withdraw the offer. "You know the temper of a youthful conqueror," Barbé-Marbois said, "everything he does is rapid as lightning."[29] Barbé-Marbois reiterated the benefits to the United States: "Consider the extent of the country, the exclusive navigation of the River, and the importance of having no neighbor to dispute with you, no war to dread." With these in mind, he asked Livingston, "Try to see if you cannot come up to my mark."[30] Livingston stood his ground: "There was a point beyond which we could not go, and that fell far short of the sum he mentioned."[31] Livingston left Barbé-Marbois's office at midnight and returned to the American Embassy, where he quickly wrote a letter to Madison. "A negotiation is fairly opened," he reported. "The field opened to us is infinitely larger than our instructions contemplated."[32]

After Monroe presented his diplomatic credentials to Talleyrand, Monroe and Livingston spent the next day deciding on a strategy, as their instructions never anticipated anything on the scale of the offer before them. They recognized the value of the opportunity but knew that such an unprecedented acquisition would bring great and potentially unforeseeable consequences. Beyond the impact on the approaching election, there was no provision in the U.S. Constitution for the addition of territory. No one could tell how doubling the size of the United States would affect America's delicate political landscape, especially on sensitive issues such as slavery. The federal government carried heavy debts from the Revolutionary War, and too high a price would bankrupt the nation. Monroe argued that they should ask for guidance from Washington before proceeding, but both he and Livingston knew that the opportunity would not survive the wait. After deliberating, the American negotiators decided to go as high as fifty million francs for all of Louisiana, but to give themselves leeway, they agreed "only to mention forty in the first instance."[33]

The following day, April 15, they presented their offer to Barbé-Marbois, who responded that it was so low "that the whole business might be defeated,"[34] but agreed to bring it to Napoleon. Barbé-Marbois returned the next afternoon with news that Napoleon had received the offer "very coldly."[35] Napoleon's interest had faded, the French finance minister warned the Americans, and he feared the negotiation was in jeopardy.

Monroe and Livingston sweetened the offer to fifty million francs, which Livingston informed Barbé-Marbois was "the greatest length"[36] they could go. While this met Napoleon's initial demand, Barbé-Marbois believed the territory was worth more and decided not to settle for less than eighty. Over dinner on April 18, Barbé-Marbois told them that Napoleon asked for one hundred twenty million francs (slightly more than the estimated value of Tuscany, which he had traded for Louisiana) and would not consider anything below eighty million. The Americans insisted they could not go above fifty million, but a meeting the following day left Barbé-Marbois with an impression of more flexibility in the American position than they let on.[37] He reported to Talleyrand: "The negotiation is on a good track. . . . In the course of a rather long meeting . . . enough progress was made to make me hope a satisfactory result was possible for the two countries. I did not hear it expressed direct-ly, but I could infer it from various expressions which [Livingston] let escape involuntarily."[38]

Despite Barbé-Marbois's hopes, the parties remained far apart on price, with no indication either was willing to make further concessions and time running out. Each side believed that it had the upper hand and that delay would work in its favor. The Americans, convinced that things were moving in their direc-tion, relaxed their pace. "We resolved," Livingston explained, "to rest for a few days upon our oars."[39] It was a serious miscal-culation. Unknown to the American negotiators, powerful forces within the French government began to move against a sale. Talleyrand had just accepted a large bribe from the British to avert the war with England and thwart the sale of Louisiana needed to fund it, as had Napoleon's brothers, Joseph and Lucien. They began putting considerable pressure on Napoleon to reject the deal and abandon the negotiation.

Deadlocked on price, the negotiators turned to other aspects of the transaction, starting with the less contentious issues. Once the representatives agreed to negotiate for the entire terri-tory, they faced the curious problem that neither side knew how far the territory actually extended. Beyond New Orleans and scattered settlements along the Mississippi's banks, most of the Louisiana Territory consisted of unexplored wilderness. Without the benefit of charts or defined borders, the envoys struggled to define exactly what it was they negotiated for. From mid- to late April, Barbé-Marbois and Livingston met Monroe, who suffered a back injury so painful it prevented him from sitting up, in the salon of Monroe's hotel, where he could talk while lying on a sofa. They pored over maps and descriptions from journal entries written by the few fur traders and explorers who had traveled into the interior, but their efforts yielded nothing except vague and conflicting accounts that were useless for the purposes of a treaty.[40]

The French, who owned the region, had no idea where its boundaries lay. There was no time to find out from the Spanish authorities what they thought they had traded to France. Previous treaties offered no help, and a proper survey was out of the question. As Barbé-Marbois puzzled over an old map with the American negotiators in the middle of April, he marveled that "many of these countries are not better known at this day than when Columbus landed at the Bahamas; no one is acquainted with them."[41] Canada, governed by the British, stood to the north. Neither the French, who had ceded Canada to England forty years earlier, nor the Spanish had laid out where Canada ended and the Louisiana Territory began. Barbé-Marbois admitted the northern regions were so remote that the English themselves had never explored them. The Rocky Mountains to the west formed an unpenetrated natural barrier. The Mississippi traced the eastern border, at least as far south as Spanish-owned Florida. At that point, the lines became muddled—and a matter of some importance, because of American designs on Florida for its strategic ports and rivers.

With time running short and both sides under mounting pressure, the Americans decided at Barbé-Marbois's suggestion to take the Louisiana Territory as the French had received it from Spain: without clearly described contours, as a vast and largely undefined country. This invited future conflicts, but it was a price the Americans were willing to pay. Sensitive to the ramifications, Barbé-Marbois warned them that the ambiguities "may in time give rise to more difficulties, . . . but if they do not stop you, I, at least, desire that your government should know that you have been warned of them."[42] When Barbé-Marbois reported this, Napoleon, perhaps sensing opportunity for further mischief, replied that "if an obscurity did not exist, it would per-haps be good policy to put one there."[43]

The inhabitants posed a different challenge. For the second time in almost as many years, their fate was being decided without their knowledge or consent in secret deliberations thousands of miles away. Barbé-Marbois, Monroe, and Livingston, each of whom had played prominent roles in the American Revolution, were uncomfortable with the prospect of an action that went so directly against the United States' founding principles. But with their hands tied, Barbé-Marbois wrote, "This difficulty, which could not be solved, was at once set aside."[44] However, the French did their best to ensure fair treatment for Louisiana's residents. With the Americans' support, Barbé-Marbois inserted language guaranteeing them "the enjoyment of all of the rights, advantages, and immunities of the United States," and stipulating their incorporation into the Union as citizens of one or more future states "as soon as possible."[45]

The negotiators next took up the prickly subject of the French debts. Several years earlier, France and the United States had been entangled in a brief conflict called the Quasi War over maritime rights and alleged American smuggling to the anti-French rebels in Santo Domingo. France's capture of a large number of American merchant vessels left bad blood between the two countries, and while the conflict ended with France promising to make the ship owners whole, it never followed through. For months Livingston, whose hopes for the vice presidency in 1804 rested on the support of New York merchants and ship owners, had fought unsuccessfully for France to make good on its promise. Barbé-Marbois remarked wistfully that, "The American Minister at Paris had received orders to make this discontent known, and his notes were drawn up with a firmness to which Bonaparte was not accustomed. If one of the continental powers of Europe had dared to employ similar language, the invasion of its territory would have been the consequence."[46] The discussions on Louisiana provided an opportunity for Livingston to revive the question, and he pushed for a concession from

Barbé-Marbois to pay regardless of the outcome of the negotiation. The French minister, knowing the topic's importance to Livingston, insisted that the two were now linked. Monroe complained he "was constantly having to overrule the American Ambassador, who kept returning to 'the claims, the claims,'"[47] and Barbé-Marbois became concerned the issue would cause the negotiation to collapse. Livingston finally relented. "The moment was critical," he reported, "the question of peace or war was in the balance; and it was important to come to a conclusion before either scale preponderated. I considered the convention a trifle compared with the other great object, and as it had already delayed us many days, I was ready to take it under any form."[48]

Early on the afternoon on April 27, Barbé-Marbois brought two proposals to Monroe and Livingston. The first, which he claimed Napoleon had drafted, contained severe terms: a cash payment of one hundred million francs, the American assumption of the twenty million franc debt, and French navigational rights and commercial outposts on the Mississippi in perpetuity. The second, more lenient proposal, composed by Barbé-Marbois, outlined a sixty-million-franc payment plus the debts, and more limited navigational and commercial privileges. Barbé-Marbois acknowledged that the first proposal was "hard and unreasonable,"[49] and although Napoleon had not seen the second, Barbé-Marbois felt he could coax Napoleon into accepting it.

The Americans took both versions, each titled "Project of a secret convention," and spent April 28, Monroe's birthday, poring over them. Price remained an obstacle. However, as Monroe and Livingston worked through the articles, the structure of an agreement took shape. Using Barbé-Marbois's document as a template, the American negotiators prepared their own draft. The substantive changes included assuring French assistance in any future negotiation with Spain regarding Florida, and reducing French exclusive commercial rights on the Mississippi to a period of twelve years. They presented this to the French finance minister on April 29. He read it in front of them, and when he reached the article on price he declared that he would not proceed in the negotiation on an amount less than eighty million francs. This time the Americans could tell he meant it. Faced with the prospect of losing everything, they folded. "On this . . . explicit declaration on his part," Monroe wrote, "we agreed to accede to his idea and give eighty millions."[50]

Napoleon Bonaparte in 1804. (*Library of Congress*)

The rest fell quickly into place. Out of a sense of propriety, they thought it best to separate the agreement into three treaties. "The first," Barbé-Marbois explained, "related to the payment of the price of the cession. This instrument was made separate from the [others], as some embarrassment was felt in mentioning, at the same time, the abandonment of the eminent right of sovereignty and the sale for money of the . . . territory."[51] The second document transferred the territory, its government buildings, records, and archives, and articulated the extent and duration of the French commercial privileges and navigational rights. Barbé-Marbois persuaded Monroe and Livingston to abandon the clause regarding France committing to use its influence with Spain over Florida. "These stipulations of good offices," he wrote, "are not rare in treaties, but their execution is almost always attended by embarrassments; and I induced the Americans to be satisfied with the assurance that, should the occasion arise, [Napoleon] would afford them all the assistance in his power."[52] The final instrument provided for the payment of the French debts, and the establishment of a tribunal to adjudicate the claims as protection against speculators and opportunists. Since the government of the United States could not pay the purchase price in cash, the negotiators created a stock instrument redeemable over fifteen years payable to two investment banks that would advance the money. The banks were Hope and Company, of Holland, and Baring Brothers, of England. The use of a British financial firm must have been particularly satisfying to Napoleon. It was understood that he intended to use the funds for an invasion of England, and it was quite an accomplishment to arrange for British money to finance it.

The afternoon of April 30, Barbé-Marbois presented the document to Napoleon at St. Cloud. Barbé-Marbois returned to Paris that evening and called Monroe and Livingston to his office in the French treasury to tell them of Napoleon's acceptance of the arrangement. The next day, Livingston let Talleyrand know that Monroe had recovered sufficiently to be presented to Bonaparte at the monthly diplomatic reception. Monroe and Livingston dined with Napoleon before returning to meet with Barbé-Marbois at his home at eight thirty, where they reviewed and edited the final draft. With them unwilling to lose a day, Barbé-Marbois promised to "see [Napoleon] next morning, fix the points in question, and come prepared sometime in the course of that day to conclude and sign the treaty."[53]

On May 2, Barbé-Marbois, Monroe, and Livingston signed the treaty transferring Louisiana to the United States. They then rose and shook hands. "We have lived long," Livingston declared, "but this is the noblest work of our whole lives. The treaty we have signed has not been obtained by art nor dictated by force; equally advantageous to the two contracting parties, it will change vast solitudes into a flourishing country. Today the United States takes its place among powers of the first rank."[54]

The government in Washington knew nothing of the direction the talks had taken, and on the day of the signing in Paris,

The signatures and seals of Francois de Barbé-Marbois, James Monroe, and Robert Livingston on the final Louisiana Purchase agreement. (*National Archives*)

President Jefferson wrote candidly to a friend, "I am not sanguine in obtaining a cession of New Orleans for money."[55]

When told of the signing, Napoleon said, "The negotiations leave me nothing to wish. Sixty million for an occupation that will not last perhaps a day!"[56] Napoleon had reason to be pleased, having never relinquished control of Tuscany, which he had promised to Spain in return for Louisiana. He noted that, "By this increase in territory, the power of the United States will be consolidated forever."[57] War erupted in Europe two weeks after the treaty was signed, and France spent every penny it received from the purchase on preparations for an invasion of England that was never launched.

Several weeks later, Ambassador Livingston asked Talleyrand for further guidance regarding Louisiana's borders. "You have made a noble bargain for yourselves," Talleyrand replied cryptically, "and I suppose you will make the most of it."[58] In avoiding a war with France for New Orleans, which President Jefferson estimated would have taken seven years and cost over a hundred thousand lives, the United States instead gained a region larger than the combined area of France, Spain, Portugal, Italy, Germany, Holland, Switzerland, and Great Britain, containing just under a million square miles, or over five hundred million acres. The territory acquired in the Louisiana Purchase forms part or all of Arkansas, Colorado, Iowa, Kansas, Louisiana, Minnesota, Missouri, Montana, Nebraska, North Dakota, Oklahoma, South Dakota, and Wyoming.

In some quarters the purchase faced resistance. Senator Samuel White of Delaware declared, "I believe it will be the greatest curse that could ever befall us. . . . I would rather see it given to France, to Spain, or to any other nation . . . upon the mere condition that no citizen of the United States should ever settle within its limits."[59]

The U.S. Senate ratified the treaty on October 20, 1803 by twenty-four to seven, followed by the House of Representatives, which appropriated the funds five days later. Later that year, President Jefferson sent out the Lewis and Clark expedition to survey the new acquisition, which ushered in an era of exploration and mass western migration that would continue for the next century.

The United States fought several border wars with Spain over Florida before finally annexing it in 1819. James Monroe never recovered financially from the personal debts he incurred in order to undertake the negotiation, and after serving as secretary of state and two terms as president of the United States, he died in penury in his daughter's home in New York City on July

4, 1831. Disposal of the claims for the French debt to American ship owners proved more troublesome than expected, and the debts transferred to the American government as part of the Louisiana Purchase were not fully settled until 1925.

A cartoon celebrating Napoleon's exile to the island of Elba. (*Library of Congress*)

Chapter 3

The Congress of Vienna

1814–1815

IN 1814, after raging across Europe for twenty years, the Napoleonic wars ended with France's defeat by the great powers. Following Napoleon Bonaparte's disastrous retreat from Moscow and the fall of Paris to the Quadruple Alliance of Great Britain, Russia, Prussia, and Austria, the victorious powers exiled Napoleon to Elba and restored the deposed Louis XVIII to the French throne. A peace treaty signed in May of that year extended generous terms to France, restored its pre-Napoleonic boundaries of 1792, and returned French territories captured by Britain during the war. It called on "all of the powers engaged on either side" of the conflict, which included virtually every nation in Europe, to send representatives to a conference to be held in Vienna that would decide all outstanding territorial questions and establish a balance of power to keep future rivalries in check.[1] The heads of Europe gathered in Vienna to divide up the continent and construct a framework to restore order amid the wreckage and confusion Napoleon had left behind.

The foreign ministers of the four primary powers and France arrived several weeks before the scheduled opening of the congress. British Foreign Minister Viscount Castlereagh joined Prussian Chancellor Prince Karl August von Hardenberg,

Russia's foreign minister, Count Karl Nesselrode, French Foreign Minister Charles Maurice de Talleyrand-Perigord, and Austrian Chancellor Prince Klemens von Metternich. Tsar Alexander of Russia and King Frederick William of Prussia made their entrance to Vienna a week later to a thousand-gun salute lasting over an hour on a sunny afternoon on September 25. In their train followed a legion of Europe's statesmen. Vienna, the capital of the Austrian Empire and the cultural and intellectual capital of central Europe, hosted 215 heads of state, including principalities and the smaller grand duchies, and over one hundred thousand attendants, servants, and hangers-on.

On September 29, with the congress due to begin in two days, the four great powers appointed themselves as a directing committee to decide all important questions. As a courtesy, they would inform France and Spain of their decisions once they were made, and the full congress would then be assembled to endorse the settlement. "They had formed a league," Talleyrand complained, "to make themselves masters of everything, and constitute themselves supreme arbiters of Europe."[2] As the representative of the defeated power, Talleyrand was in an unenviable position. He naturally objected to the victors' excluding France from the major decisions, but he also felt that such a structure would rob any outcome of lasting credibility. "It is to be hoped," Talleyrand told them, "that in Europe force will no longer be transformed into law, and that equity, not expediency, will be made the rule."[3]

Talleyrand's argument, which coincided with France's interests, was that a balance of power alone was not sufficient. What Europe needed was a lasting peace, requiring the additional element of legitimacy to endure the storms of European politics. At a minimum, this demanded the concurrence of all the great powers, which meant including France as an equal partner in the new system. "I ask for nothing," Talleyrand told them, "but I bring you something important–the sacred principle of legitimacy."[4]

Talleyrand preferred that they convene the full congress at once and put the questions before it directly, but Castlereagh and Metternich insisted that would lead to chaos. "The intervention of Talleyrand," Friedrich von Gentz, Metternich's lieutenant and the secretary of the congress, complained, "has hopelessly upset all our plans."[5] Unable to agree on a plan or a structure, they postponed the opening of the congress until November 1.

British Foreign Minister Viscount Castlereagh. (*National Portrait Gallery*)

The first question was the future of Poland. In the late eighteenth century, Poland had been steadily carved up by its powerful neighbors Prussia, Austria, and Russia until it disappeared entirely in 1796. Tsar Alexander intended to revive a nominally independent puppet state of Poland out of the former Prussian, Austrian, and Russian parts of Poland. He argued that Russia, having suffered the burning of its capital during Napoleon's occupation, and having played a key role in the decimation of Napoleon's army in his disastrous retreat from Moscow, was entitled to compensation, which he demanded in the form of a reconstituted Kingdom of Poland with him at its head. Austria and Prussia would be compensated for their loss of Polish lands by territory taken from elsewhere. The tsar reminded his fellow statesmen that the Russian army, with six hundred thousand men the largest and most powerful in Europe, was already in possession of the areas he sought.

Castlereagh welcomed the restoration of Poland but made it clear that Great Britain would oppose uniting it under the tsar. Castlereagh argued that they had fought the war against Napoleon for the benefit of Europe and to rid the continent of a tyrant and a threat to freedom, not to increase their holdings. Protected by the English Channel and the Royal Navy, Great Britain asked for no continental territories but sought to avoid the emergence of a dominant power on the continent and desired to create a balance of power that would leave England free to use its control of the seas to expand its colonies and overseas trade. Castlereagh feared that a Russian annexation of Poland would concentrate too much power in the tsar's hands and leave the Austrian heartland strategically vulnerable to attack, and he warned the Russian foreign minister that the tsar's ambitions would ignite another war. He told the tsar the choice was his whether "the present Congress shall prove to be a blessing to mankind, or only exhibit a scene of discordant intrigue, and a lawless scramble for power."[6] The tsar responded coolly that "the question could only end in one way, as he was in possession,"[7] and declared his willingness to go to war to achieve his ambition. "I have two hundred thousand men in the duchy of Warsaw," he said. "Let them put me out of that."[8] The tsar dismissed Talleyrand's talk of legitimacy and international law. "What do you suppose I care for all your parchments and treaties?"[9]

Castlereagh approached Hardenberg on October 9 to bring Prussia, a large and rising power in northern Germany that sought territorial gains that would establish it as the dominant power in Northern Europe, into alliance with Austria and Britain against the Russian plan. As part of his Polish vision, the tsar had promised Prussia Saxony, a large, ancient Germanic kingdom whose ruler had allied himself with Napoleon, for Prussia's support and as compensation for giving up Prussian possessions that would form part of the tsar's new Kingdom of Poland. Hardenberg agreed to join Castlereagh's coalition against the tsar but in return demanded support for Prussia's bid to acquire Saxony. Castlereagh wanted a large, powerful Prussia to serve as a counterweight with Austria to France and Russia in Central

Europe, and was willing to sacrifice Saxony to achieve it. Hardenberg and Castlereagh asked for Metternich's approval, which the Austrian chancellor reluctantly gave. While Austria could satisfy its territorial ambitions in the south without infringing on the other great powers, it needed to prevent unacceptable concentrations of power on its borders. Austria was competing with Prussia for dominance over the German principalities, and allowing Prussia to absorb Saxony would make Prussia a major rival in Central Europe.

Austrian Chancellor Prince Klemens von Metternich. (*Kunsthistorisches Museum*)

With Prussia's and Austria's support, Castlereagh felt able to stand against Alexander's ambitions on Poland. Castlereagh offered him an ultimatum of three choices: he could re-create a free and independent Poland with its original borders; he could reconstitute a smaller version with less territory; or he could consent to a division of Poland among those three powers, leaving Russia bounded by the Vistula River. If the tsar could not accept either of these, the matter would be put before the full congress for a decision.

Metternich's personal life intruded. His mistress, Duchess Wilhelmina Sagan, had spurned Metternich in favor of a young cavalry officer, Prince Alfred Windischgraetz, plunging Metternich into an all-consuming despair. "You have done me greater harm," he wrote her, "than can ever be compensated by the whole universe—you have broken the springs of my soul, you have compromised my existence at a moment when my destiny is linked to questions which will decide the fate of whole generations to come."[10] Meanwhile the other countries were kept

in almost complete darkness. "Our existence here is very pleas-
ant, but we are told nothing of what is going on or of what will
happen to us,"[11] wrote a puzzled King Maximilian of Bavaria.
They occupied themselves instead with lavish entertaining.
Every Monday Metternich hosted a seated dinner in his residence for 250 people. Each night was filled with parties, salons,
concerts, and balls so elaborate (including a masquerade ball for
ten thousand) that the Austrian Empire was forced to institute a
fifty percent income tax to pay for them. In early October,
Emperor Francis I gasped, "If this goes on I shall abdicate. I can't
stand this life much longer."[12]

Emperor Francis brought the tsar and the king of Prussia on
a week-long tour of Hungary on October 30. The tsar, who had
a powerful personal hold over the weak and impressionable
Frederick William, reminded the Prussian king over dinner of
their friendship, how much he valued it, and the importance to
him of the reestablishment of a Kingdom of Poland. "Now that
he was on the eve of the accomplishment of his desires,"
Alexander asked, "was he to have the grief of counting his dearest friend among those who opposed him?"[13] The king, swayed
by the tsar's personal appeal, swore to support Alexander over
Poland and immediately ordered Hardenberg to withdraw from
Castlereagh's coalition against Russia. On the monarchs' return,
Castlereagh learned that his coalition had failed. "The hopes,"
Talleyrand reported, "which they had built upon the cooperation
of Prussia have been of brief duration."[14]

Castlereagh found the ground cut from under his feet. "You
will see," he complained to the Duke of Wellington, "we are at
sea and we have only to pray for favorable winds and cur-
rents."[15] Talleyrand hoped that confronting Russia with a
Europe unified in opposition would be sufficient, but he
believed that giving "dominion of Russia over the whole of
Poland would threaten Europe with so great a danger, that if it
were to be avoided by force of arms only, there must not be a

moment's hesitation in taking them up."[16] With the prospects for successful diplomacy fading, each of the great powers prepared for war. At Talleyrand's urging France called up its army, mobilizing nearly a half million troops. Austria drew up war plans and deployed four hundred thousand soldiers to its borders, and Russian forces were already in the field. Castlereagh insisted that if the emperor would not back down from his position, "he must be forced to do so by war."[17] The Austrian secret police reported to Metternich that "things are pointing toward a general war which will not long delay in breaking out."[18] The only step ever taken toward convening the congress came on November 1, the official day it was to open, when a committee was formed to receive, inspect, and verify the credentials of the representatives who had arrived in Vienna. The only meaningful deliberations would be among the representatives of the primary powers.

To Talleyrand's dismay, France was still left in the cold. "The role of France," Talleyrand observed, "was singularly difficult. It was very tempting and very easy for the Governments which had so long been hostile to keep her excluded from the major questions affecting Europe."[19] The French foreign minister watched for any opening to join the decision-making inner circle, and waited patiently on the sidelines.

Knowing that without Prussia behind them there was little the British could do, the tsar brushed off Castlereagh's ultimatum, and on November 10, in a coordinated move, Russian forces in Saxony pulled out and Prussian troops marched in. "Things in general," Austrian chief of staff Field Marshal Karl Schwarzenberg told Alexander, were "in a position which would render war inevitable."[20] Most of the statesmen and spectators at Vienna considered the diplomacy at Vienna to have failed and the negotiations to have broken down. Gentz wrote: "magniloquent phrases about 'restitution of the social order,' 'the recovery of European politics,' 'enduring peace based on a just apportionment of power,' and so on were trumped up only to quiet the masses and to confer on the Congress some semblance of import and dignity. But the real sense of the gathering was that the victors should share with one another the booty snatched from the vanquished."[21] Wrote a Russian delegate, "They've wandered into a bog, and they have no idea how to get out of it."[22]

Searching for a compromise, Hardenberg and Metternich presented the tsar with a proposal to establish a smaller Kingdom of Poland that left Austria a secure border defended by the strategic strong points of Krakow and Zamosc, and allowed Prussia to keep a substantial portion of its Polish territory. Alexander refused to moderate his demands and replied that he intended to hold on to the entire Duchy of Warsaw. However, he offered the token concession of making Krakow and Thorn free cities. Since Prussia would not be able to recover its former Polish territories, when Hardenberg showed the tsar's reply to Metternich on December 3, the Prussian chancellor asked that Prussia be allowed to absorb all of Saxony. The king of Saxony would be given a rump state made from other parts of Prussia. Metternich rejected the proposal. But since Prussia had acquiesced to Russia's designs on Poland, Metternich was no longer bound by his obligation to Hardenberg to help Prussia acquire Saxony.

The negotiators had reached a deadlock. Castlereagh wrote British Prime Minster Lord Liverpool that Russian, Prussian, Austrian, and French armies had been mobilized, and that the cost of keeping them fielded made their governments more inclined to use them sooner rather than later. Hardenberg reflected the Prussian preference for war if its demands were not met when he wrote, "It were better to have a new war than that Prussia, after such glorious deeds and so many sacrifices, should come out of the affair badly."[23] Castlereagh informed Liverpool on December 5 that "in the present extremely tangled state of

affairs"[24] war could erupt at any
moment, and he expected Britain to
be drawn in.

In a turning point, in response to
opposition attacks in Parliament and
growing public outrage over
Prussia's move to swallow Saxony,
the British cabinet ordered
Castlereagh to reverse himself and
work to keep Saxony intact. This
reversal raised Saxony to the forefront
and laid the groundwork for a
realignment of the forces at the table.

Prussian Chancellor Prince
Karl August Fürst von
Hardenberg. (*Schloss
Glienicke, S. 294*)

On December 10, Metternich made
a new offer in response to Hardenberg
and Alexander's proposition. Austria
would go along with Russia on Poland with minor adjustments,
although it drew the line at the annexation of Saxony by
Prussia. Instead Metternich proposed that Prussia take only a
part of Saxony, with 432,000 residents. Along with other territories, Prussia was also gaining Westphalia, land along the
Rhine, and what it would receive from Russia in Poland. That
would be sufficient to restore Prussia to its size before the
Napoleonic wars. Metternich insisted that Krakow be given to
Prussia and Thorn to Austria. He argued that a Prussian annexation of Saxony would throw the balance of power in Europe
out of sustainable proportion and create a perpetual threat to
peace. "The Congress," he argued, "must not degenerate into the
sad spectacle of a fight between the two powers which are the
most concerned with establishing peace in Europe. Germany
must become a political entity; the boundaries between the
great intermediate powers must not remain uncertain. The harmony between Austria and Prussia must, in short, be perfect, in
order that the great task may be completed. It is as a hindrance

to that harmony, an insurmountable obstacle to the pact of federation, that we object to the total incorporation of Saxony in
Prussia."[25] The two great powers of Central Europe, which
anchored the constellation of German-speaking states that had
once composed the Holy Roman Empire, would be forced into
open rivalry with each other. This would destroy the project of
German federation that relied on stable relations between them,
and it would place a hostile divide between the two states needed to hold the center of Europe together to form a secure buffer
against an engorged Russia. "All the Prussians and their supporters screamed murder,"[26] Metternich recorded.

Three days later, Alexander's dispute with Metternich turned
personal, and Alexander, accusing Metternich of insulting him,
threatened to challenge him to a duel. A shaken Metternich
offered his resignation to Emperor Francis, which he wisely
rejected. News of the event caused quite a stir with the delegates
and statesmen at Vienna, but the outburst appeared to have had
a cathartic effect. "The whole, as you may imagine, made for
two days a great sensation," Castlereagh wrote on December 17,
"but the result perhaps may serve to prove what I have ventured
before to allege, that the climate of Russia is often more serene
after a good squall."[27] The next day Alexander went to Francis
in a much more conciliatory mood, and Russia made its first real
concession. Although unwilling to surrender his claim to
Krakow, he offered to return the Polish region of Tarnopol with
a population of four hundred thousand, which Austria had lost
in 1809. That allowed Austria to back off of its demand over
Poland. "Austria, having reached the conclusion that she could
not save both Saxony and Poland," Metternich wrote, "decided
to drop the latter."[28] This allowed a shift in focus from the Polish
question, which now appeared solved, to the Saxony problem.

Talleyrand met with Metternich on December 14. With the
great powers divided, France's position as an outsider allowed it
to throw its weight behind either camp and suddenly made it a

surprisingly powerful player. Talleyrand maneuvered to place France closer to the center of the deliberations by cracking what remained of the unity of the former allies against France. He did this by asking Metternich, who had told Talleyrand of the new Austrian position on Poland, to make an official transmission to him in writing of the note stating Austria's new position, the diplomatic equivalent of including France in his confidence. "My particular motive for insisting on a formal disclosure lay in the fact that this

Tsar Alexander I of Russia. (*Royal Collection*)

would mark the real date of the rupture of the coalition,"[29] he wrote. Recognizing France's value as a potential future ally, after hesitating briefly, Metternich handed Talleyrand the note along with a personal message, which ended: "I am happy to find myself in agreement with your Cabinet on a point which is so nobly defensible."[30] "Such men as M. de Talleyrand," Metternich observed, "are like sharp-edged instruments with which it is dangerous to play. But for great evils drastic remedies are necessary and whoever has to treat them should not be afraid to use the instrument which cuts the best."[31]

Talleyrand rushed to exploit the rupture of the coalition. On December 19, he wrote an open response to Metternich's note outlining his philosophical views on the situation, which reframed the question as one over the nature of the future course of Europe. To recognize the Prussian seizure of Saxony as legitimate, he argued, would require conceding "that the practice of confiscation, which enlightened nations have banished from their code, is in the nineteenth century to be sanctioned by the public law of Europe . . . ; that peoples have no rights, and can be treated like a dairy herd; that sovereignty can be lost and gained by a single fact of conquest; that the nations of Europe are bound . . . only by the law of nature, and that what is called the public law of Europe does not exist; . . . in a word, that all is legitimate for him who is the strongest." Talleyrand insisted that not only would giving Saxony to Prussia upset the balance between Prussia and Austria and the general stability in Europe, but the structure underpinning the new European order also had to rest on the bedrock of moral legitimacy, which was impossible if small, vulnerable Saxony were allowed to be swallowed by Prussia. "In no other question today," Talleyrand wrote, "are the two principles of legitimacy and balance so involved at one and the same time and to such a great extent."[32]

On December 20, Talleyrand reported to King Louis XVIII, "The equilibrium of Germany would be destroyed if Saxony were sacrificed, and it is evident that she could not then contribute to the general balance of power. . . . Lord Castlereagh is like a traveler who has lost his way, and does not know how to find it. He is ashamed of having narrowed the Polish question, and, after having expended all his efforts on that question in vain, being duped by Prussia, in spite of our warnings, into giving up Saxony to her. He knows not what to do."[33] Hardenberg's deputy, Wilhelm von Humboldt, confided to his wife on December 20, "A second war is necessary, and it must take place sooner or later."[34]

As the alliance of the big four disintegrated, the French became the only ones the British felt they could trust. Liverpool described the situation by December 23 in a letter to Wellington. "The more I hear and see of the different Courts of Europe, the more convinced I am that the King of France is (amongst the great powers) the only sovereign in whom we can have any real confidence," he wrote. "The Emperor of Russia is profligate from vanity and self-sufficiency, if not from principle. The King of

Prussia may be a well-meaning man, but he is the dupe of the Emperor of Russia. The Emperor of Austria I believe to be an honest man, but he has a minister in whom no one can trust; who considers all policy as consisting in finesse and trick; and who has got his government and himself into more difficulties by his devices than could have occurred from a plain course of dealing."[35] Castlereagh reported to Liverpool on Christmas Day, "France is now a principal in the question."[36]

On December 23, Castlereagh and Talleyrand struck a bargain. When Hardenberg reiterated, with the tsar's support, the Prussian demand for all of Saxony, Talleyrand suggested to Castlereagh that together with Metternich they join in publicly announcing their defense of the rights of the king of Saxony and their commitment to defending them. Castlereagh asked whether Talleyrand proposed an alliance. "I think as you do," Talleyrand replied. "We must do everything [to maintain peace] except sacrifice honor, justice and the future of Europe." Talleyrand reported to his king: "I told him that I had no objections against that; but that, if we handled it in the same way that we have handled so many other matters up till now, by trusting to luck and following neither principles or rules, we should come to no decision; that we should therefore begin by laying down principles."[37] They agreed to support Saxony's sovereignty, and to form a statistical commission to calculate and adjust borders in the territories previously conquered by Napoleon according to their populations.

The statistical commission was given authority to settle disputes. After the introduction of mass conscription and national mobilization during the Napoleonic wars, national strength was measured in population, rather than geographical size or wealth. Talleyrand took Prussian consent to the formation of the statistical committee as a promising sign. "The Prussians," Talleyrand wrote on December 28, "have evidently subordinated their claims upon Saxony and their hopes to the result of the labors of the Commission, and that result will, most probably, be favorable to Saxony. Thus, the affair of Saxony is in a better position than it has yet been. That of Poland is not concluded, but its termination is talked of. It has been resolved that a thoroughly official character shall be given to these conferences. As boundaries only are to form the subject of this negotiation, the matter ought to be arranged in a few days."[38]

On December 29, Hardenberg reiterated Prussia's claim to all of Saxony and declared that any delay in transferring Saxony would be interpreted as a declaration of war. Castlereagh called this a "most alarming and unheard-of menace." He rejected the premise that fear of war could influence Britain's position on Saxony, declaring that "such an insinuation might operate on a Power trembling for its existence, but must have the contrary effect upon all that were alive to their own dignity," and adding, "if such a temper really prevailed, we were not deliberating in a state of independence, and it were better to break off the Congress."[39] Hardenberg was breaking down under the strain. He was unable to sleep and would pace his rooms at night. "He is upset beyond measure by everything that is going on, and dismayed that all his hopes have been dashed, and this affects him and his body,"[40] his deputy, Humboldt, wrote.

Hardenberg was on weak ground. Despite its belligerent posture, the Prussian military relied heavily on Russian support, and the tsar, faced with the imminent prospect of war, appeared to be having second thoughts. In a conference the day before with King Frederick William, the tsar gave an "ambiguous"[41] response when pressed on what he would do if war broke out over Prussia's demand for Saxony. Alexander seemed aware that Castlereagh, Metternich, and Talleyrand were moving toward an alliance, and confronted with a united Britain, France, and Austria, he grew unsure. Britain, which had provided much of the financing for the war against Napoleon, was still advancing the cost of keeping Russian troops in the field, so the tsar faced a financial as well as a military disaster. While Hardenberg was acting more belligerent, the tsar began searching for a peaceful way out.

Hardenberg backed down. But the skirmish showed how critical the situation had become and prompted Castlereagh to turn to Talleyrand for support. "Under these circumstances I have felt it an act of imperative duty to concert with the French and Austrian Plenipotentiaries a Treaty of Defensive Alliance,"[42] he reported.

Russia made a countermove on December 30, in a last effort to rally and unify its former allies. Hoping to move past the impasse and reach resolution on Saxony and Poland, Alexander offered a smaller Kingdom of Poland that allowed Prussia to hold on to the principalities of Gnesen and Posen, and part of western Prussia, with 850,000 inhabitants, and also allowed Austria to keep land on the right bank of the Vistula and Tarnopol, with a population of 400,000. Krakow and Thorn would become free, independent cities. Prussia would receive all of Saxony, and the Saxon king would receive a new state with a population of 700,000 made from territory on the right bank of the Rhine. The Prussians were thrilled by the proposal and relieved by Russia's apparent fresh show of support for Prussia's desire for all of Saxony. But Prussia and Russia increasingly operated from a position of weakness. Austria was willing to accept the Polish element of the proposal but would not agree to the Saxony arrangement.

New Year's Day brought word of the signing on Christmas Eve of the Treaty of Ghent, ending the War of 1812 between Great Britain and the United States. "The news of the American peace came like a shot here," wrote one of the British delegates. "Nobody expected it." By freeing troops and removing the possibility of the United States becoming a potentially valuable ally of Russia and Prussia, the announcement left Britain in a much stronger position. "We have become more European and by the spring we can have a very nice army on the Continent,"[43] observed Castlereagh.

Talleyrand moved to complete his goal of restoring France to the center of European great power politics. To establish a firm front that could answer the Russo-Prussian alliance and return the direction of Europe to a balance of power system founded on legitimacy while rescuing Saxony, on January 3, at Talleyrand's suggestion, Castlereagh, Metternich, and Talleyrand signed a secret document that pledged Britain, France, and Austria to come to each other's assistance if threatened with attack, and committing forces of one hundred fifty thousand men each. "France is no longer isolated in Europe," Talleyrand declared in a letter to King Louis XVIII the next day. Europe, he reported, now had "a federal system which fifty years of negotiations might not have constructed."[44]

In January, at Castlereagh's suggestion, the great powers formed a committee to take up the question of abolishing the slave trade, an important issue for the English public and a priority for Castlereagh. England offered the Caribbean island of Trinidad in exchange for French support, but Talleyrand instead demanded British assistance in replacing the king of Naples, a high French priority as the king was one of Napoleon's former generals and therefore considered a threat to the Bourbon dynasty. Castlereagh agreed, and secured the acquiescence of Portugal with a payment of three hundred thousand pounds sterling, and Spain with an additional four hundred thousand pounds. On February 8, the great powers produced a joint declaration calling the international slave trade "repugnant to the principles of humanity and universal morality"[45] and agreed to abolish the practice that had "desolated Africa, degraded Europe and afflicted humanity."[46] They agreed to include the abolition as part of the general settlement of Europe, with France allowed to phase it out over five years, and Spain and Portugal over eight.

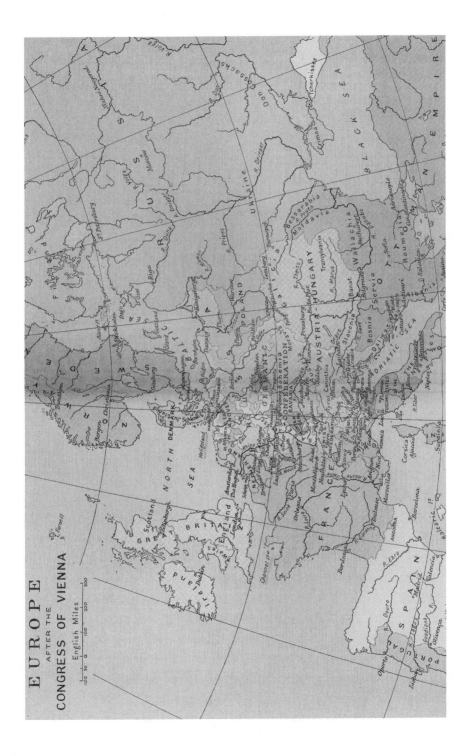

At six in the morning on March 7, an urgent dispatch for Metternich arrived from the Austrian Consulate in Genoa, Italy, with news that Napoleon had slipped out of his island prison at Elba. "Bony's conduct is very extraordinary," Wellington, who had just taken Castlereagh's place as England's representative at the congress, wrote on hearing of the escape, adding that he found Napoleon's actions worthy of "one fit for Bedlam."[47] Napoleon, who had with him about a thousand men, declared on landing at the southern coast of France: "The Congress is dissolved."[48] Wellington left immediately to take command of British forces stationed in Belgium. Six days later, the congress declared Bonaparte an outlaw, having "placed himself beyond the protection of the law and rendered himself subject to public vengeance."[49] Napoleon returned triumphantly to Paris, where he reclaimed his throne and defied the rest of Europe for one last time, and on March 25, Great Britain, Austria, Prussia, and Russia agreed to provide one hundred fifty thousand men each to defeat him. Before long a million men were on the march. Napoleon's return changed surprisingly little at Vienna. With the most challenging questions already settled, the negotiations continued uninterrupted during the fighting, and the representatives of the great powers worked to finalize the details of a comprehensive agreement.

The final acts of the Congress of Vienna were signed on June 9, 1815, nine days before Napoleon's defeat at Waterloo. The agreement restructured the borders of Europe and established a framework that provided a durable peace in Europe. By driving a wedge between the victorious great powers and exploiting their differences, Talleyrand was able to gain a seat at the table and to ensure that despite France's military defeat, its interests were protected as Europe's borders were redrawn. Austria emerged almost twice its previous size, adding Dalmatia on the Adriatic and control of much of northern Italy, including Parma, Modena, and Tuscany. Prussia, though disappointed, emerged as the dominant power in Northern Europe, while France surrendered its conquests and returned to its "ancient frontiers" before the rise of Napoleon.

The Congress of Vienna consolidated over three hundred pre-Napoleonic German kingdoms and principalities into thirty states joined in a loose German confederation that covered most of present-day Central Europe and extended from the Baltic to the Adriatic. The congress established Switzerland as a neutral, independent state, re-created a nominal Kingdom of Poland and made it subject to Russia (which soon absorbed it entirely), gave Norway to Sweden, and abolished the international slave trade. Saxony remained independent and kept three-fifths of its territory and two-thirds of its population. The Kingdom of the Netherlands, which Great Britain sought to strengthen and enlarge as a buffer on the coast, received Belgium, Luxembourg, and adjacent territory. The balance of power largely held, and Europe would not see a major, continent-wide conflict until World War I, nearly a hundred years later.

A commemorative postcard of the Portsmouth Treaty. (*Library of Congress*)

Chapter 4

The Portsmouth Treaty

1905

WITH the balance of power holding Russian ambitions in check in Europe in the late nineteenth century, Russia turned its attention eastward. The lack of effective central governments in China, Korea, and Manchuria created a vacuum that enabled Russia to extend its influence deep into the Far East, carving out exclusive trading zones and occupying a large swath of northern China and Manchuria. Japan, an emerging industrial power recently awoken from two hundred years of feudal isolation, had its own designs on the region and its raw materials, and saw Russian expansion as an intrusion into its sphere of influence and a strategic threat.

In February 1904, Japan launched a surprise attack against Russian forces in Manchuria and inflicted humiliating losses on the larger but poorly led Russian army. Russian troops dug in, reinforced by fresh soldiers brought over the Trans-Siberian Railway, and by early 1905, the war had cost more than one hundred fifty thousand lives, with no end in sight. Russia and Japan both rejected mediation efforts, each believing that continued fighting would work in its favor. The Japanese public, intoxicated by victories, demanded more, while Tsar Nicholas II placed his confidence in Russia's bottomless reserve of men and material. Nevertheless, American President Theodore Roosevelt saw an opportunity.

The United States, an ascendant power, also lay at a turning point. With the Civil War behind it and the taming of the West complete, the United States consolidated its position as a continent-wide power. Between the Civil War and the turn of the century, America's population doubled, and by 1900 the United States was producing a third of the world's cotton, corn, and oil, and half of its manufactured goods. U.S. victory in the Spanish-American War and the annexation of Hawaii in 1898 broadened American horizons, and the American public became interested in the United States playing a more assertive role on the world stage. While President Roosevelt's experience in international diplomacy was limited, his irrepressible confidence and sharp political instincts led him to believe he could bring Russia and Japan together and secure peace. At stake lay the future of the Far East, and Roosevelt worried that if war continued, Japan's and Russia's ties with other European powers would draw them in and ignite a global conflict.

Roosevelt suspected both parties were in worse shape than they admitted. Russia had suffered savage losses, and the Japanese, despite their unbroken string of victories, felt the strain of fighting an enemy three times their size. Worldwide public opinion, appalled by the scale of bloodshed, had turned against the war, and this had begun to affect the belligerents' ability to raise money for supplies and ammunition.

President Roosevelt faced two serious obstacles. First, he believed correctly that the Russian secret service had broken the American diplomatic code, compromising his overseas communications. Second, John Hay, his secretary of state who in his younger days had been President Abraham Lincoln's personal secretary, was incapacitated by an illness that would soon take his life. As Hay put it: "There is nothing the matter with me except for old age, the Senate, and two or three mortal maladies."[1] Roosevelt would be on his own.

Russia and Japan at first were cold to the president's advances. Secretary Hay complained in his diary that the Russian ambassador in Washington "throws a pink fit"[2] at any reference to peace. The Japanese, although polite, were no less adamant. Roosevelt nevertheless believed continuing the war was folly. He felt that protracted fighting "would be a very bad thing for Japan, and an even worse thing for Russia."[3] He wrote that Japan had "nothing further to gain from continuation of the struggle; its continuance meant to her more loss than gain even if she were victorious,"[4] while Russia, "in spite of her gigantic strength was . . . apt to lose even more than she had already lost."[5]

After a year of fighting, the break Roosevelt hoped for came on May 27, 1905, when the Russian fleet met the Japanese navy in the Strait of Tsushima. With a torrent of two thousand shells a minute, the Japanese annihilated the Russian fleet, sending twenty-two Russian ships to the bottom of the Sea of Japan, and with them the tsar's hopes for a quick victory. Roosevelt, a former assistant secretary of the Navy, remarked, "Neither Trafalgar nor the defeat of the Spanish Armada was as complete."[6] He told the Japanese now was the time for them "to build a bridge of gold for the beaten enemy,"[7] and sent a telegram to both parties stating that "The President feels that the time has come when in the interest of all mankind he must endeavor to see if it is not possible to bring to an end the terrible and lamentable conflict now being waged."[8] He asked them "not only for their own sakes but in the interest of the whole civilized world to open direct negotiations for peace,"[9] and offered his good offices to help.

Tentative indications of interest from the Japanese led Roosevelt to cut short a five-week bear hunt in Colorado to return to Washington in pursuit of bigger game. With the

Japanese in play, Roosevelt concentrated on finding a way to bring the Russians to the table. He considered his approach carefully. His concerns about the Russian ambassador in Washington, Count Arturo Cassini, whose unreliability in passing on messages to his government and tendency to "lie when he knows perfectly well that you know he is lying"[10] led Roosevelt to shift his focus to St. Petersburg and to direct George von Lengerke Meyer, his trusted ambassador there, to approach the tsar directly.

Meyer, an old friend of Roosevelt's who had been in the class ahead of him at Harvard University, had previously been the U.S. ambassador in Italy. Meyer had been in St. Petersburg only seven weeks when Roosevelt asked him to set up a meeting with the tsar. "The trouble with our Ambassadors in stations of real importance," Roosevelt wrote in his instructions, "is that they seem to think that the life of an Ambassador is a kind of glorified pink tea party. Now, at St. Petersburg I want some work done, and you are the man to do it."[11] In an audience at the Imperial Summer Palace, Meyer read the tsar a brutally frank letter from Roosevelt: "It is the judgment of all outsiders, including all of Russia's most ardent friends, that the present war is absolutely hopeless and that to continue it will only result in the loss of all of Russian territory in Asia. To avert trouble, and, as he fears, what is otherwise inevitable disaster, the President most earnestly advises that an effort be made by . . . representatives of the two powers in order to terminate the present hostilities and prevent the grand-scale calamity which the President greatly fears."[12] Roosevelt concluded: "The President seriously wishes to receive his early approval for this proposition in order to avoid further bloodshed and catastrophe."[13] Meyer told the tsar that if he agreed it would save "possibly hundreds of thousands of lives"[14] and win the respect of the world. As the audience drew to a close, the Tsar agreed to send a Russian delegation.

The Russian warships *Pallada*, left, and *Pobieda*, right, wrecked below Golden Hill, Port Arthur. (*Library of Congress*)

Russia and Japan each had a great deal to gain from a negotiation and a great deal to lose. Japan's victories had thrown the Russians on the defensive, but its military pace was unsustainable. A diplomatic solution could secure the gains already won and bring further concessions as the price of peace, but if the Japanese negotiators overplayed their hand and the negotiation failed, Japan risked famine and economic collapse. Russia was in the embarrassing position of being larger, stronger, and richer, but with an unbroken record of defeats. Although it was able to threaten a prolonged war, that might only deepen its losses. The negotiation table was the best chance to achieve what the Russian army had failed: to stop the Japanese advance and regain lost territory. There was little room for error. Russia faced domestic pressures and simmering unrest that foretold revolution, and the Russian state was unlikely to survive either a humiliating peace or an open-ended string of costly defeats.

In a sign of difficulties to come, it took over two months for Russia and Japan to agree on a location. Angling for a home-field advantage, Russia preferred Paris, the capital of its closest ally, while Japan for similar reasons favored Chefoo in China.

Roosevelt proposed The Hague in the Netherlands, which both promptly rejected, as Europe's history of opportunistic meddling in the Far East raised legitimate doubts about its disinterestedness. The only actor both sides felt they could trust was the United States, so Washington, D.C. emerged as the obvious choice. Roosevelt, though, had misgivings about holding the talks in Washington. A British cabinet report called it "probably the most difficult theatre in the world for carrying on delicate negotiations."[15] Washington's sweltering climate and intrusive, gossipy culture were invitations to trouble, so Roosevelt began looking for an appropriate place nearby where cooler heads could prevail without distraction. He was hoping for "some cool, comfortable and retired space, with as much freedom from interruption as possible."[16]

He found it in the small coastal town of Portsmouth, New Hampshire. Located on the Maine-New Hampshire border a little more than fifty miles north of Boston, it offered a quiet spot secluded from outside pressures, while the large Navy base just across the Piscataqua River provided a secure location for the representatives to meet and a full complement of modern communications facilities. The people of Portsmouth were delighted, and extensive preparations were made. Western Union laid extra telegraph lines to connect the hotel and Navy Yard with the transatlantic trunk cable in nearby Rye Beach. Washington sent a twelve-man Secret Service contingent to provide security, and ten French waiters arrived from the Waldorf-Astoria Hotel in New York to attend to the Russian delegation in case its members had difficulty ordering in English. A simple, two-story brick naval stores warehouse on the Navy base was chosen to house the talks, and two hundred men worked around the clock to prepare the building. Within two weeks they constructed a large central conference meeting room, a three-room suite on either side for each delegation, a dining room for lunch between meetings, and a reception room for visiting American dignitaries.

Russia and Japan had difficulty finding representatives, because insiders on both sides considered it a political suicide mission. After his top three choices declined, the tsar with great reluctance turned to Sergei Witte. When his name had been raised earlier as a potential envoy, the tsar replied firmly, "Anyone but Witte."[17] A former finance minister, Witte had served for many years under the tsar's father, but had clashed with Nicholas II, whom he described as, "A well-intentioned child, whose actions were entirely dependent upon the character of his counselors, most of whom were bad."[18] Witte had long opposed the war, but he saw appointment as chief delegate to the peace conference as a political death sentence. After his appointment on July 13, he told a close friend:

> Now this is what I think: I have been chosen not so much to render a service to my country as—figuratively speaking—to stumble and break my neck. They really want to go on with the war. It is calculated that the chances of my striking up a peace on really acceptable conditions are superlatively slight, and that in all probability, therefore, I shall fail. Then I shall be dead and buried. But my "well-wishers" go farther and argue that if I should succeed in ending the war on the terms that unfortunately are congruous with the military situation, my name will become odious to every self-respecting Russian.[19]

Sergei Iulievich Witte was born in 1849 to minor nobility of Dutch descent in the town of Tbilisi in southern Russia, now the capital of the Republic of Georgia, nestled in the Caucasus Mountains along the Turkish border. His family was moderately well-to-do, his father having begun as a storekeeper and built a successful enough banking business to serve as an adviser to the regional viceroy. Witte's first job was as a porter and ticket clerk for the Odessa railway. He rose quickly as his superiors recognized his native intelligence and aptitude for logistics. The Russo-Turkish war of 1877 allowed him to prove himself under the needs and disciplines of war, and he so outshone his corrupt and incompetent colleagues that he was swiftly promoted to division superintendent, and then in 1889 to minister of railways.

Witte's facility with organization, his despotic energy and his obsession with efficiency brought such order to the railroad tariffs that he was elevated to minister of ways and communications, and then, after only a year, to minister of finance. His rapid rise to the inner sanctum of the Russian elite brought him the mistrust of the upper nobility, and his ordering an investigation of Rasputin earned him the lasting hatred of the tsarina. Witte's industriousness, however, made him indispensable, and with a mad enthusiasm he threw himself into the role of finance minister. He monopolized the government manufacture and distribution of vodka, rebuilt the industrial base, doubled the national revenue, established the gold standard, and amassed such quantities of gold in the Imperial Treasury that he was able to make the currency redeemable at par. His crowning achievement was the construction of the Trans-Siberian Railway, which he organized and directed almost single-handedly. Still, for all Witte's accomplishments, his domineering intensity and contemptuous treatment of the aristocracy returned to haunt him. Because of his resistance to the war, after eleven years as finance minister, having established himself as the most powerful man in Russia next to the Emperor, he was promoted upstairs into obscurity as president of the Council of Ministers. It was from this political exile that he was recalled to lead the Russian delegation.

Six-and-a-half-feet tall, Witte was a commanding figure. His long, taciturn face partly covered by a mustache and graying beard conveyed a gruff, electric intensity. There was a hypnotic quality about him, and one journalist wrote how "his great, earnest, eloquent eyes held you."[20] Witte's character was complex. Respected for his honesty and ability, qualities in short supply in Russia at the time, he was moody and could be haughty and abrasive. The English ambassador in St. Petersburg was struck by his "rough manners, brusque speech and overpowering presence."[21] Witte was not easily impressed with anyone besides himself, and as is often the case with sensitive egos, he was unforgiving of the faults of others.

Witte's deputy in the negotiation, Baron Roman Romanovich von Rosen, had recently replaced Count Cassini as the Russian ambassador in Washington. A genteel man, and a talented musician, he spoke several languages fluently, including Japanese. He had been the Russian ambassador to Japan and was highly regarded by the Japanese, and it was hoped that his engaging personality and urbane manners would prove a useful contrast to Witte's blunt style. Sharply dressed, with warm but weathered features, Baron Rosen was the picture of diplomatic propriety. His skill lay in his methodical reliability, and an observer wrote, "He is incapable of a brilliant diplomatic stroke, but on the other hand he is incapable of making a grave diplomatic blunder."[22]

The Japanese also struggled to recruit a chief envoy. The mission was considered so toxic and unlikely to succeed that Japanese politicians jostled to propose their rivals for the job. One of the most promising candidates withdrew after remarking that "the position of the Japanese plenipotentiary was to be compared to that of a poker-player possessing an extremely doubtful hand."[23] For lack of a willing alternative, Prime Minister Katsura Taro sent his foreign minister, Baron Komura Jutaro. Forty-eight years old, Komura was a veteran diplomat and an early supporter of the war who had been Japan's ambassador to Korea, China, Russia, and the United States. As a boy he had been sent to America to Harvard, where he studied law and was a contemporary of Theodore Roosevelt's. After graduating in 1877, he took a junior position in the Ministry of Justice, where he displayed such promise that he was made secretary of the Foreign Office at the tender age of twenty-nine.

Ambitious and headstrong, Komura's methodical mind and tenacious drive were joined with a gracious spirit. He took naturally to diplomacy and proved himself in a series of increasingly demanding positions. After a brief stint as assistant director of the Translation Bureau, he was sent by the Foreign Ministry to China as secretary of the legation. He was charge d'affaires in Peking at the outbreak of the Chinese-Japanese War before running a province in Japanese-occupied territory and then serving as ambassador in Seoul. From there he was sent to be the Japanese representative to the United States. After Washington, Komura was entrusted with the delicate positions of Japanese ambassador to Russia and then China before his appointment as foreign minister in 1901.

Komura's chief deputy in the negotiation would be Takahira Kogoro, Japan's ambassador to the United States. One of Japan's most senior diplomats, he had been ambassador to Italy and the Austro-Hungarian Empire, and vice foreign minister. During his time in Washington, Takahira had impressed Roosevelt with his reliability and integrity. Komura and Takahira were supported by a team whose members included the director of the Foreign Ministry's Political Bureau, the private secretary to the foreign minister, as well as secretaries and political and military advisers, including the naval attaché to the Japanese Embassy in Washington, who was also President Roosevelt's private judo instructor.

The Japanese had one other unique human asset whom they employed vigorously as part of the negotiation, although he was not officially a member of the delegation: Baron Kaneko Kentaro, a prominent Japanese aristocrat who served as their cat's paw when they needed a direct and confidential channel to the president. Kaneko, a former member of the Japanese cabinet, was highly regarded by the emperor and Japan's governing elite. He had been a classmate of Roosevelt at Harvard, and through the years they had developed a close friendship. As a stealth intermediary, Kaneko would prove invaluable.

Roosevelt tried hard to secure a truce during the negotiation. The Russians were eager for an armistice, but the Japanese saw no reason to surrender their advantage in the field. "I did my best to get the Japanese to consent to an armistice," Roosevelt wrote, "but they have refused, as I feared they would. . . . The Japanese are entirely confident that they can win whatever they wish by force of arms, whereas they are deeply distrustful of Russia's sincerity of purpose in these peace negotiations."[24] Although unwilling to declare an armistice, the Japanese military halted its advance on the main front to give the negotiation some breathing room.

After an audience with the emperor, the Japanese delegates boarded the SS *Minnesota* on the afternoon of July 8, 1905, bound for the United States. Over five thousand people gathered to see them off. The jubilant crowd shuddered in unison with shouts of "Banzai," and the Tokyo *Asahi Shimbun* wrote that "the excitement of the people was . . . beyond description."[25] But the delegates were in a more sober mood. In the midst of the excitement, Komura turned to Prime Minister Katsura and predicted that "The peoples' reaction will have changed completely when I return."[26]

Two weeks later the Russian delegates boarded the German steamer *Kaiser Wilhelm der Grosse* bound for New York. Witte used the voyage to get acquainted with his team and to plan his strategy, as only two weeks had passed since Witte's sudden appointment. "During that time," he wrote, "there had been so much excitement that I had been unable to organize my thoughts and prepare for the dreadful diplomatic battle I would soon face."[27] The Russian negotiators were in a precarious position. Japanese forces lay within striking distance of Russia's heartland. If the Russian negotiators were to keep Russia from catastrophe, they would have to find a way to make the Japanese agree to terms acceptable to the tsar and to the war party in St. Petersburg. With little of value to offer, the negotiators would have to improvise.

In his instructions to Witte, the tsar said he did not feel that Russia's position required her to make peace, and made it clear that if Japan insisted on unforgiving terms he would resume the war. "I am ready to terminate by peace a war which I did not start," he wrote, "provided the conditions offered us befit the dignity of Russia. I do not consider that we are beaten; our army is still intact, and I have faith in it."[28]

The delegates arrived in Portsmouth on August 8. "I have brought them to a cool spring," Roosevelt told a friend. "It remains to be seen whether they will drink of it or not."[29] The president observed, "I know perfectly well that the whole world is watching me, and the condemnation that will come down on me, if the conference fails, will be world-wide too. But that's all right."[30] The town of Portsmouth was draped with banners, and people crowded around the delegates' carriages. Over one hundred and twenty news organizations from around the world were represented, and one delegate complained the reporters were like "mosquitoes from which there is no escape."[31] The delegates stayed at the Hotel Wentworth, a grand Victorian summertime resort on the crest of a hill overlooking a bay that had recently been renovated and expanded with the addition of a golf course, tennis courts, and a swimming pool. The hotel was full with over five hundred guests, so the Russian and Japanese representatives were spread out on different floors, mixed in with the tourists, journalists, and vacationers.

Witte described his feelings the evening they arrived: "It was an agonizing and depressing time. I felt myself under a heavy responsibility, understanding full well that if I did not return to Russia with an olive branch, fighting would be resumed. And I knew from official sources that if fighting were renewed we could expect new disasters. All Russia would condemn me if I did not make peace."[32]

On Thursday, August 10, two days after both delegations arrived at Portsmouth, Witte and Komura held their first meet-

The Hotel Wentworth, New Castle, New Hampshire, where the Russian and Japanese representatives stayed during the treaty conference. (*Library of Congress*)

ing. The participants rose early that morning, surrounded by journalists and well-wishers who had gathered to see them off for the short trip from the Wentworth to the Navy Yard. After the formalities, an "ominous silence"[33] came over both sides. With a Sphinx-like expression, Komura took out a paper containing the Japanese terms and declared that they had come hoping "to restore peace between Japan and Russia for the sake of world peace and humanity,"[34] and expressed the hope for a lasting peace "which will preclude future conflicts."[35] That depended on the terms, Witte replied. If they were reasonable, he wished to see a "firm friendly relationship established between our two countries," but if Japan's terms were "motivated merely by the desire for a temporary settlement," he felt "it would rather be desirable not to reach agreement, since a continuation of hostilities would most likely bring about a situation for the establishment of better relations between the two countries."[36]

There were twelve articles, which called for Russia to recognize Japanese dominion over Korea, relinquish its holdings in Manchuria along with railways and the strategic city of Port

Arthur, grant Japan fishing rights along Russia's coast, surrender Russian warships that had been interned in neutral ports, permanently limit its navy in the Pacific, surrender Sakhalin Island, and reimburse Japan for the cost of fighting the war. Before leaving Tokyo, Komura had received instructions that ranked the Japanese opening terms according to three categories: items that were indispensable, those that were desirable, and the rest, which were opportunistic and essentially disposable. The first category included Japanese control over Korea and the removal of Russian forces from Manchuria, which were Japan's original war aims. The second consisted of granting fishing rights to Japan along the Russian coast, the surrender of Russian naval vessels that had fled to neutral ports, the payment of a large war indemnity, and the transfer to Japan of Sakhalin Island. Last were throwaway terms, points of nominal value to be bargained away for other concessions, including a permanent reduction of Russian naval forces in the Pacific and the demilitarization of Vladivostok. Believing that the government's instructions fell short of what Japan deserved, on their own initiative Komura and Takahira had made several decisive changes, resolving to make Sakhalin Island and a cash indemnity nonnegotiable, even at the price of renewed war. The severity of the terms shocked the Russians. "The Japanese conditions," lamented Anton Planson, a junior Russian delegate, "were more heavy than anything it was possible to suspect."[37]

Witte believed that Komura and Takahira were bluffing. He was convinced the Japanese could not afford to let the war continue and were in a much weaker position than they appeared. In this, Witte was largely alone. The consensus among the popular media as well as disinterested observers such as President Roosevelt was that Russia would have to come to terms with Japan's superiority on the ground. In the teeth of the Japanese victories and prevailing opinion, Witte adopted a posture of brinksmanship and defiance.

The Japanese grew impatient, and on August 12 the *New York Times* ran an article under the headline "Oyama Awaiting Order to Strike," describing preparations for an assault led by the Japanese commander in chief, Field Marshal Oyama Iwao, against the main Russian front. Six hundred thousand Japanese troops faced a slightly larger number of Russian soldiers across a distance in some places of only a thousand yards, spread out over a line stretching almost a thousand miles from Korea across Manchuria to Vladivostok. The *Times* reported that "The battle which, it seems likely now, will be fought will unquestionably be the greatest in the history of the world." According to the article, it was in the hands of the negotiators: "The plans of the Japanese Commander in Chief are perfected, his armies are ready, and he only awaits the news that a rupture has occurred at Portsmouth to launch his attack."[38]

Witte and Komura at first made headway. In the smoke-filled conference room, as electric fans hummed in the background they methodically worked their way through the Japanese points, disposing of the first four articles and building momentum. They promised to respect the principle of open commerce and agreed to Japanese control over Korea, which it already occupied, with a guarantee protecting Russian interests there. Control of Korea was vital to Japan's security and had been one of the main reasons Japan started the war. They agreed mutually to withdraw their forces from Manchuria, which had been the center of so much of the fighting, and return it to Chinese sovereignty.

The first obstacle they faced concerned the fate of Sakhalin, a barren, mountainous island brimming with natural resources. Roughly the size of Ireland, covering almost thirty thousand square miles, it lies at the mouth of the Amur River, five miles off the Russian coast, separated from the northernmost island of Japan by a thirty-mile strait. In addition to a commanding strategic position, it contains extensive forests and fisheries, significant deposits of coal and iron, and some of the largest untapped reserves of oil and natural gas on Earth. Russia and Japan had long held competing claims over the island, and Japanese forces had seized it in the opening days of the peace conference. Witte refused to recognize Japanese ownership, asserting that under international law, occupation did not confer rightful title, and reminding Komura that Japan had given Sakhalin Island to Russia thirty years earlier in exchange for the Kurile Islands, a chain of smaller islands off the Japanese coast. "I cannot agree to the deprivation by force of territory which Russia has possessed for a long time based on a legitimate treaty right," he insisted.[39]

Komura responded that Sakhalin was uniquely important to Japan: "Its possession is for Japan essential for her security but for Russia it is merely of colonial and economic interest. . . . For Japan it is indispensable to her national security."[40] He pointed out that Russia had only to acknowledge an accomplished fact, but Witte replied that he viewed the Japanese occupation of Sakhalin as a circumstance of fact and not of right. Neither would yield, and after several days they agreed the differences appeared irreconcilable. They moved on to the other articles.

In the meantime, the mood was changing in St. Petersburg. The war party had grown in Witte's absence and its stiffening resolve had influenced the tsar. Across Russia outrage swelled as the people learned about Japan's terms from newspaper reports. Ironically, Witte had leaked the Japanese terms to the press in order to influence American opinion by showing how unfair they were, but the Russian press picked it up, and the harshness of the terms quickly fueled indignant disbelief among the Russian people. The British ambassador in St. Petersburg reported that "the publication of the Japanese demands had aroused a storm of protest and that public opinion appeared unanimous that it would be preferable to continue the war than to submit to such humiliating demands."[41]

Russian and Japanese representatives at the negotiating table during the Portsmouth conference. Witte is the center figure on the left while Komura sits opposite on the right. (*Library of Congress*)

With the discussion on Sakhalin stalled, the negotiators made progress on other questions, agreeing to transfer to Japan the portion of the Manchurian railway it already held, to refrain from using their railroads in China for military purposes, and to recognize the Japanese occupation of the strategic city of Port Arthur. But these were minor points.

One of Komura's central demands was for a large war indemnity, which Russia categorically refused. Two factors drove this contention, one financial and the other cultural. Japan had exhausted its resources to pay for the war and gone heavily into debt. Taxes and inflation had spread the effects across all segments of Japanese society, and politicians had encouraged a widely held belief that much if not all of the war cost would be reimbursed by Russia as a condition of peace. Naturally Russia had no such intention, and it did not occur to the Japanese government that the conflict had left the Russian treasury just as empty as its own.

At a deeper level, the problem stemmed from cultural differences. In Asian diplomacy indemnities were common, and the Japanese were keenly aware that in every major war in East Asia in the previous century the losing party had paid an indemnity. Given the course of the conflict and the facts on the ground, the Japanese expected an indemnity as their right according to the customs of war, and from where they stood, the Russians' refusal to pay, given Japan's victories, was an unspeakable insult. The Russians held a different perspective. Until the recent construction of the Trans-Siberian Railway, Russia had been oriented westward and drew its experience from Europe, where indemnities were rare and humiliating events that occurred only when a country had been overrun and its capital occupied. Russians saw themselves not as defeated, but as having suffered a series of losses in a remote theater far from home. Russia had spent more on the war than Japan and saw no reason it should pay for the conflict twice.

More than a week of meetings failed to produce movement. The negotiators returned to the same points over and over, but neither Witte nor Komura gave ground. President Roosevelt grew anxious. "I wish to heaven," he wrote his sister, "I could make these peace conferences meet under my immediate supervision, or else turn the matter over to me."[42] He blamed Witte's unwillingness to compromise and noted tartly in a letter to a British friend, "The Russians, having been unable to make war, seem now entirely unable to make peace."[43]

With the negotiation going nowhere, Komura cabled Prime Minister Katsura that he planned to make minor concessions and asked Baron Kaneko to meet at once with President Roosevelt. Kaneko rushed to Sagamore Hill, the president's summer home in Oyster Bay, Long Island, the next morning. He showed Roosevelt a telegram from Komura explaining where things stood and asked the president's opinion. "According to the latest developments, the situation appears to have become extremely difficult," Roosevelt told him. "One cannot tell whether the peace negotiations will fail or not. If you should have any idea as to how this difficulty might be overcome, I should like very much to hear it." Kaneko replied, "Komura will not withdraw his demand for the cession of territory and the reimbursement of war expenses, while Russian Plenipotentiary Witte will insist on his position and will not give way. In the present situation there seems to be no way out than to ask Your Excellency to turn to his last resort." Roosevelt agreed. "I feel the same way," he told the Japanese representative. "My last resort would be to dispatch a personal telegram to the Tsar of Russia. However, before I go that far I must urge Witte to make concessions to Japan. Witte is the Tsar's special delegate. If I were to address a telegram directly to the Tsar, without having first made any approach to Witte, his feelings would be hurt. Therefore, I should like first to telegraph Rosen or some other person in Witte's confidence to come here so that I might make recommendations to him."[44]

Roosevelt summoned Baron Rosen, who caught a morning train to Boston on Saturday, August 19, and made it to Oyster Bay early that afternoon. Rosen found the president in white flannels on the tennis courts in the middle of a game. Between volleys, Roosevelt traced out the contours of a compromise. If Russia would not surrender its claims to Sakhalin perhaps it might consider paying a negotiable amount to Japan for the northern half. The reparations question could be referred later to international arbitration. This would allow some cover for Russian pride while offering Japan the cash it needed to break the logjam. Witte rejected Roosevelt's compromise outright, arguing that the tsar would never accept it.

At the Wentworth, Witte received unwelcome news. A telegram from Foreign Minister Vladimir Lamsdorff informed him of a State Council meeting in St. Petersburg presided over by the tsar at which it was decided unanimously to reject the

Japanese terms. Instructions for ending the negotiation were to be transmitted the following day. Dumbfounded, Witte played for time.

Roosevelt worked to get Japan to back off its indemnity demand and told Kaneko, "I do not think her case for indemnity a good one. She holds no Russian territory except Sakhalin and that she wants to keep." Russia would not agree to pay and "the sentiment of the civilized world . . . [would] back her in refusing to pay."[45] If war resumed it would cost Japan millions more, spill an immense amount of blood, occupy Siberia, which it had no interest in, and still not gain any payment from Russia. "Every interest of civilization and humanity forbids the continuance of this war merely for a large indemnity,"[46] he wrote. The president also instructed Ambassador Meyer to call on the tsar, but the earliest Meyer could arrange an audience was August 23. "Dealing with Senators," President Roosevelt wrote a friend on August 21, "is at times excellent training for the temper; but upon my word, dealing with these peace envoys has been an even tougher job. To be polite and sympathetic and patient in explaining for the hundredth time something perfectly obvious, when what I really want to do is to give utterance to whoops of rage and jump up and knock their heads together—well all I can hope is that the self-repression will be ultimately helpful for my character."[47]

Witte received his final instructions from Lamsdorff. Without a substantive change in the Japanese position, he was to break off the negotiation. Witte stalled, asking to wait until the tsar had a chance to receive Roosevelt's overture.

On Wednesday, August 23, the parties, deadlocked, adjourned for three days to consult with their governments and await the outcome of Meyer's meeting with the tsar. Roosevelt appealed again to Kaneko for the Japanese to moderate their demands. Another year of war, he emphasized, would simply "eat up more money than she could at the end get back from Russia."[48]

Roosevelt continued "Ethically it seems to me that Japan owes a duty to the world at this crisis. The civilized world looks to her to make peace; the nations believe in her; let her show her leadership in matters ethical no less than matters military. The appeal is made to her in the name of all that is lofty and noble; and to this appeal I hope she will not be deaf."[49]

Meyer met the tsar at the imperial palace in St. Petersburg at four in the afternoon on August 23 to present Roosevelt's plan. The American ambassador again began by reading aloud a letter from Roosevelt. "I find to my surprise and pleasure that the Japanese are willing to restore the northern half of Sakhalin to Russia, Russia of course in such case to pay a substantial sum for this surrender of territory by the Japanese and for the return of Russian prisoners," the president wrote, before warning, "If peace is not made now and war is continued, it may be that, though the financial strain upon Japan would be severe, yet in the end Russia would be shorn of those east Siberian provinces which have been won by her by the heroism of her sons during the last three centuries." The president stressed the generosity of the Japanese offer given the circumstances: "As Sakhalin is an island it is, humbly speaking, impossible that the Russians should reconquer it in view of the disaster to their Navy; and to keep the northern half of it is a guarantee for the security of Vladivostok and eastern Siberia to Russia. It seems to me that every consideration of national self-interest, of military expediency and of broad humanity makes it eminently wise and right for Russia to conclude peace substantially along these lines, and it is my hope and prayer that Your Majesty may take this view."[50]

The audience lasted almost three hours. When Meyer had finished, the tsar told him he would sooner appeal to all the Russian people and march to Manchuria himself at the head of the Russian army than agree to Roosevelt's plan, but he offered to pay "a liberal and generous amount"[51] to reimburse Japan for the care and maintenance of Russian prisoners and entertained letting Japan keep "that portion of the island she had once had clear title to."[52]

Still, the failure of Roosevelt's compromise revealed a crack in the Russian position. On August 24 the Russian foreign minister cabled Witte that Russia was willing to accept a division of Sakhalin provided it did not have to pay for the return of the northern half. This, Lamsdorff said, would be Russia's final proposal. Roosevelt also pressed Komura through Baron Kaneko to cut in half their money demand for northern Sakhalin.

The pressure began to take its toll among the delegates. "Our nerves are strained, each of us is awaiting the issue of the diplomatic struggle, and watching the others," wrote one of the Russians. "On the whole, we are all sick of Portsmouth, or rather of the Wentworth hotel, with its monotony and isolation from the rest of the world."[53] A reporter wrote of the "peace conference face," a "haggard, bewildered, dubious and anxious look."[54] Komura faced his own pressures. A visiting member of the Japanese Parliament told reporters in Portsmouth that "Public sentiment was such in Japan . . . that Baron Komura would be murdered upon his return home if he yielded."[55]

With the talks a hair's breadth from breakdown and the fate of both countries in the balance, at their afternoon meeting Witte and Komura stared at each other in icy silence for eight minutes, smoking one cigarette after another. Roosevelt tried to stave off collapse. To make matters worse, it seemed that the tsar had backed down from his concession to Meyer, as his foreign minister gave a statement to the Associated Press returning to Russia's original position that it would neither pay money nor give up territory. "I cannot help offering Your Majesty some additional advice," Roosevelt wrote the tsar. "Count Lamsdorff is said to have stated that Russia would never be able to approve of reimbursements and the cession of territory. I cannot but regard this as a clear notice of the continuation of war. I fear that if war continues, Japan will no doubt experience difficulties, but the catastrophe for Russia will reach unprecedented proportions." He added, "I beg His Majesty to consider that such an announcement means absolutely nothing when Sakhalin is already in the hands of the Japanese."[56] Roosevelt knew it was unlikely to have any effect.

However, there was movement beneath the surface. Komura had received orders that day by cable from Prime Minister Katsura directing him to go with Roosevelt's compromise, and a member of the Russian delegation wrote in his diary, "We have evidently given up our former irreconcilability, and are ready to give up the southern half of Sakhalin."[57] Underscoring the depth of public sentiment against continued fighting, Jacob Schiff, a major financier and backer of Japanese war bonds, paid a visit to Takahira to tell him that the American, British, and German financial markets were no longer willing to support Japanese debt unless the war came to an end.

On Saturday, August 26, Roosevelt's telegram from the previous day was shown to the tsar, who responded simply, "I remain with my views."[58] Komura cabled Tokyo that he had decided to terminate the negotiation at the next session. He wrote his prime minister:

> It now seems that Russian determination has grown even firmer. . . . From what Witte told me in today's secret meeting, I cannot help but conclude that there is no hope at all that the Tsar will change his mind. He seems to believe . . . that his Manchurian army is now superior to ours and that there is a good chance that Russia can bring about a drastic change in the military situation in Manchuria. Thus, we must conclude that at this time he has no intention of concluding peace. Therefore . . . I consider that there is no longer any alternative but to cut off the negotiations.[59]

The telegram reached Tokyo on Sunday, August 27, at about 8 p.m. local time. Alarmed, the Japanese government ordered

Komura to postpone the next session for a day, then called a cabinet meeting that lasted well after midnight and reconvened first thing the next morning.

On Monday, August 28, Witte received the tsar's final order to "end discussion tomorrow in any event. I prefer to continue the war than to await gracious concessions on the part of Japan."[60]

In Tokyo, the Japanese cabinet assembled, while in the streets outside people celebrated in the belief that the meeting meant that the peace conference would be terminated and the war resumed. At the end of the meeting, after receiving the emperor's sanction, the Japanese government sent an instruction to Komura at 8:35 p.m. Tokyo time: "In view of the fact that through your negotiations we have already solved the more important questions of Manchuria and Korea, which were our objectives in the war, we have decided to reach an agreement in the negotiations at this time even if it means abandoning the two demands for indemnity and territory."[61] He was authorized as a last concession to "withdraw completely the demand for repayment of war expenses on the condition that Russia recognize the Japanese occupation of Sakhalin as a fait accompli . . . and even if the Russian plenipotentiaries should persist in their stand, you should not immediately break off negotiations. In that case, you will attempt to persuade the President to recommend to us, as his last effort for peace, that we withdraw the territorial demand and accept his recommendation for the sake of humanity and peace. If the President should refuse to take this role of mediator, you are instructed to withdraw, as a last resort and our Imperial government's final concession, the territorial demand. In short, our Imperial government is determined to conclude peace by any means necessary during the present negotiations."[62]

After these final instructions were transmitted to Portsmouth, new information arrived in Tokyo that completely changed the picture. The British had a well-placed spy in the Russian Foreign Ministry, and in a chance encounter with a British Embassy official in Tokyo, the head of the telegraph section at the Japanese Foreign Ministry, Viscount Ishii Kikujiro, learned of the results of the meeting between Meyer and the tsar on August 23 and of the tsar's willingness to accept a partition of Sakhalin island. On reporting this to the prime minister, Ishii was thanked and told that if he was wrong he would be expected to commit hara-kiri. The government then dashed off a revised set of instructions to Komura rescinding the concession of all of Sakhalin and replacing it with one relinquishing only the northern half of the island.

Sergei Iulievich Witte leaving the Wentworth Hotel. (*Library of Congress*)

"The day before we were to resume negotiations was a very tense one for me," Witte wrote. "All Portsmouth knew that the tragic question of whether or not blood would continue to flow on the fields of Manchuria would soon be decided. When I went to bed that night I did not know what tomorrow would bring, what instructions the Japanese would receive. . . . When I went to bed that night my soul was torn. . . . I spent a restless, nightmarish night, sobbing and praying."[63]

The atmosphere was strained as the representatives arrived at the Navy Yard on the morning of August 29. Both delegations had packed their bags and paid their hotel bills, and President Roosevelt was preparing a statement to issue to the press informing them of the conference's failure and the resumption of war.

In defiance of his orders, Witte met once more with the Japanese. He placed on the table a sheet of paper which he told them contained Russia's final concessions. Less generous than previous terms, Russia would pay no indemnity for Sakhalin. Komura told him that Japan would withdraw its demands for an indemnity if Russia abandoned its claims to Sakhalin. Witte refused. For several seconds silence filled the room as Witte blankly tore at bits of paper and Komura sat expressionless. Then Komura broke the silence and in a calm voice announced the Japanese would withdraw the indemnity and cede half of Sakhalin. Witte accepted. His gamble had worked.

Tsar Nicholas received word the following evening. He wrote in his diary, "This night there came a telegram from Witte with the news that the negotiations about peace have been brought to an end. All day after that I went around as if in a trance."[64] Count Witte and Baron Komura signed the treaty six days later on September 5, in a small ceremony with both delegations and a few assembled dignitaries. It was ratified by the Russian and Japanese emperors on October 14, and the ratifications were exchanged in Washington on November 25.

Witte's tenacity had paid off. Standing up to Komura's bluff and not backing down under pressure, Witte had barely skirted renewed war. But his boldness had been rewarded. In the end the deal that was struck was more favorable than Russia had reason to expect.

It is estimated that the agreement reached at Portsmouth saved at least a quarter of a million lives. The treaty awarded Japan control over Korea, the Liaodong Peninsula, and the southern half of Sakhalin Island in addition to railroads and fishing privileges in Russian waters along the northern Pacific coast. Both Russia and Japan agreed to withdraw their forces from Manchuria. The agreement spared Russia a lengthy and

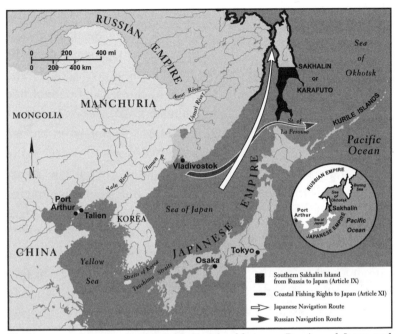

The Portsmouth Treaty divided Sakhalin Island between Russia and Japan and awarded Japan control of Korea, fishing privileges along Russia's northeastern coast, and other concessions.

potentially devastating war and it gave up little more than Japan already possessed. Although Japan sacrificed a number of its goals at the negotiating table, the Treaty of Portsmouth sealed Japan's status as a great power and established it as the dominant power in Asia.

When Roosevelt heard of the signing he thundered, "This is magnificent! It's a mighty good thing for Russia, and a mighty good thing for Japan, and a mighty good thing for me too!"[65] Praise and congratulations flooded in from all over the world. On hearing the news, Pope Pius X declared, "This is the happiest news of my life. Thank God for President Roosevelt's courage."[66]

In Japan the reaction was different. In Tokyo, black flags of mourning crepe were hung in the streets. The Japanese stock market plummeted, and the Osaka *Mainichi Shimbun* wrote in an editorial "the struggle of eighteen months and the sacrifice of a hundred thousand lives" had been "made worthless by the diplomacy of a fortnight."[67] Japanese newspapers called on the Emperor to renounce the peace and for the army in Manchuria to keep fighting. Newspapers and politicians openly advocated the assassination of the cabinet ministers.

Riots engulfed Japan. Thirty thousand rioters rampaged through Tokyo for three days as the violence quickly spread to other major cities. The authorities imposed martial law across the country and arrested several thousand people before the unrest quieted down. As an immediate consequence of the peace and its aftermath, the government fell in January 1906.

The Russian response was more muted. After recovering from the shock of being disobeyed by his representative, the tsar presented Witte with the title of count for his skill in winning "rightful concessions" from the Japanese and for securing an "all-advantageous peace."[68]

Tsar Nicholas II ruled until Russia's entry in World War I nine years later brought about the Russian Revolution. He abdicated in March 1917, and was executed along with his immediate family on the morning of July 17, 1918, in the basement of a house in Yekaterinburg in the eastern Ural Mountains. Witte was made Russia's prime minister on his return from Portsmouth. He survived an assassination attempt in 1907, and died of natural causes eight years later. After the fall of the Japanese government following the riots, Komura became Japan's ambassador to Great Britain and later served a second term as foreign minister.

Roosevelt's success at Portsmouth brought him the title "the greatest herder of Emperors since Napoleon."[69] The press called him "the grand victor in this battle of giants."[70] One of the Russian delegates later wrote of his experience with Roosevelt during the conference:

We Russians had come to Portsmouth without taking anything that he had said seriously, and yet when we left the United States it was with the knowledge that, all through our stay there, we had been brought in close proximity with one of the most powerful personalities now alive in the whole world. The man who had been represented to us as impetuous to the point of rudeness, displayed a gentleness, a kindness, a tactfulness mixed with self control, that only a truly great man could command.[71]

For his work in bringing about the peace, Roosevelt became the first American to win a Nobel Prize, winning the Nobel Peace Prize in 1906 for "sheathing the swords of a million men."[72] He accepted the award but refused the money because it was for work he felt he had performed as a result of his position as president. He wrote to his son: "I hate to do anything foolish or quixotic, and above all I hate to do anything that means the refusal of money which would ultimately come to you children. But Mother and I talked it over and came to the conclusion that . . . I could not accept money given to me for making peace between two nations, especially since I was able to make peace simply because I was President."[73]

President Roosevelt predicted that removing Russia as Japan's natural rival in the Pacific would eventually lead to war between Japan and the United States. He believed America would win, but "it will be one of the most disastrous conflicts the world has ever seen." However, he wrote, "My duty is to secure peace. . . . We'll have to let the future take care of itself."[74]

An American army field hospital in a ruined church in France. (*Library of Congress*)

Chapter 5

The Paris Peace Conference

1919

O N November 11, 1918, an armistice between Germany and the Allied Powers of England, France, Italy, and the United States brought the fighting of the First World War to an end. In its five years, the war had spread to every corner of the earth and bled Europe dry with forty million casualties, and the desolation it left behind caused people to look to the peace negotiations with a blend of euphoria and anticipation. British Prime Minister David Lloyd George captured the prevailing sentiment as he announced the armistice: "I hope that we may say that thus, this fateful morning, comes to an end all wars."[1]

The scope and ambitions of the peace conference went beyond anything that had come before. Geographically, politically, socially, and economically, it was to redraw the boundaries of the known world. The collapse of the Russian, German, Austro-Hungarian, and Ottoman Empires washed away the imperial system that had dominated Europe since the Middle Ages, and in its place long-suppressed nationalistic ambitions, encouraged by wartime promises from the Allies, rose and took hold from the Baltic to the Middle East.

Economically, both the victors and the defeated were ruined. The subjugation of industry to military needs, the loss of working-age populations to the front, and the ravages of war had led to a breakdown in production. Germany and Central Europe were in the early stages of mass starvation, and France was only months behind. Across the continent, nation after nation was reduced to famine and despair.

In January 1919, the leaders of Europe and their allies gathered in Paris to hammer out the terms of peace and build a new order out of the ruins. Twenty-seven nations were invited to participate, representing three quarters of the world's population. The major powers came full of expectations. The sacrifice in blood and treasure spent in subduing Germany weighed heavily on them and hardened them against compromise. Below the surface, though, lurked important differences. The wartime pressures that had bound them together so effectively had dissipated and would reveal competing interests and visions for the future.

The size of the delegations and the prominence of their members reflected the ambition of the undertaking. Britain, France, and Italy were represented by their prime ministers, and the English and American delegations each had several hundred members.

President Woodrow Wilson's decision to attend was resisted by his closest advisers. The day after the cessation of hostilities against Germany, Wilson's secretary of state, Robert Lansing, wrote in his diary:

> I had a conference this afternoon with the President at the White House in relation to the Peace Conference. I told him frankly that I thought the plan for him to attend was unwise and would be a mistake. . . . I pointed out that he held at present a dominant position in the world, which I was afraid he would lose if he went into conference with the foreign statesmen; that he could practically dictate the terms of peace if he held aloof;

that he would be criticized severely in this country for leaving at a time when Congress particularly needed his guidance; and that he would be greatly embarrassed in directing domestic affairs from overseas.[2]

Lansing also wrote, "I am convinced that he is making one of the greatest mistakes of his career and will imperil his reputation. . . . I prophesy trouble in Paris and worse than trouble here. I believe the President's place is here in America."[3]

The American government had prepared well in advance. In the autumn of 1917, it organized a secret project called "The Inquiry" consisting of one hundred and twenty-six geographers, historians, economists, scientists, and lawyers brought together to anticipate issues likely to come into play once the war was over. Their conclusions convinced Wilson to embark on a new course that would challenge the foundations of traditional diplomacy.

Ten months before the armistice, President Wilson laid out his vision for peace in a speech before a joint session of Congress. Intended to rally the American public and the Allies and to restore their sense of moral purpose after bloody years of war, Wilson proposed a plan in which the defeated powers would be invited to join a new society of nations based on openness, equality, and collective security. His Fourteen Points described the creation of an international body to settle disputes, open navigation of the seas, universal free trade, mutual disarmament, and the disposal of territorial claims according to the wishes of their inhabitants. The speech established the American position based on moral grounds rather than territorial interests.

The American delegation arrived in Paris on December 14, 1918, led by President Wilson. It was the first time a U.S. president had traveled overseas, and a hundred thousand people turned out to greet him.

Despite their grasp of the issues, the Americans had given

surprisingly little thought to what they were to do once they reached Paris. Members of the American delegation received only a single instruction before leaving. They "must be on board [the USS *George Washington*] at Hoboken by 10:15 of the evening of December 3, 1918. The President would embark the following morning at 9:00 and the ship would sail immediately."[4] At sea, the secretary of state addressed the American negotiators and confessed that "he knew of no plan of organization nor schedule of procedure,"[5] inspiring one to describe the American effort as "a magnificent improvisation." Concern over the absence of a strategy was widespread. One of the principal American delegates, General Tasker Bliss, wrote, "I am disquieted to see how hazy and vague our ideas are. We are going up against the wiliest politicians in Europe. There will be nothing hazy or vague about their ideas."[6] He was right.

The men Wilson faced were well prepared and had a clear sense of what they wanted and how to get it. They did not share Wilson's lofty idealism and were suspicious of his proposals. The European powers were driven by a desire for reparations from Germany and the fear that Germany would rise again if it were not properly shackled, impoverished, and dismembered. Lloyd George had just won election by a popular vote larger than any recorded in English history by campaigning that England would have "the uttermost farthing" from Germany and would "search their pockets for it."[7] One of his ministers had bragged, "We shall squeeze the German lemon until the pips squeak,"[8] while the French finance minister promised to balance France's budget and pay off the national debt with payments from Germany.

In French Prime Minister Georges Clemenceau, Lloyd George, and Italian Premier Vittorio Orlando, Wilson faced seasoned politicians who were well-informed, confident, sophisticated, and headstrong. Clemenceau, known as the Tiger by his countrymen, was a fighter. As a young man he had spent time in

European representatives to the Paris Peace Conference included, from left to right, Marshal Ferdinand Foch, French Prime Minister Georges Clemenceau, British Prime Minister David Lloyd George, Italian Premier Vittorio Orlando, and Italian Foreign Minister Baron Sidney Sonnino. (*Library of Congress*)

prison for dueling, and although he was a medical doctor by training, he had spent most of his career editing radical newspapers and honing his political instincts as a member of the National Assembly. Before he came to power he was famous as a political spoiler and was able to boast that in his career he had overthrown eighteen cabinets. This was Clemenceau's second time as prime minister, having first served from 1906 to 1909. Praised as "the Father of Victory," he was at the height of his powers and had just been reelected by a landslide of three-to-one in the Chamber of Deputies. Although eighty years old, Clemenceau was a tireless worker and would wake up during the peace conference every day at three o'clock in the morning and would often work until eleven at night. Secretary of State Lansing wrote of the French leader:

> Of the four heads of States Mr. Clemenceau . . . was, in my judgment, the dominant figure and the strongest man of the many strong men who participated in the negotiations at Paris. . . .

Clemenceau possessed a strength of character and a forcefulness which would have raised him above his colleagues. Persistent though patient, he was always ready, when the moment arrived, to use all his skill and cleverness in debate to obtain a decision which would be in the interest of his country. Every question was viewed by him in the light of how it would affect France.[9]

Lloyd George had been the youngest member of Parliament when he was first elected in 1890, and had held several cabinet positions, including chancellor of the exchequer, minister of munitions, and war secretary. He lacked Wilson's gravitas and Clemenceau's guile, but he had powerful charisma. The other delegates soon found that "it was simply impossible not to like him. His cheerfulness, his vivacity, his never-failing good nature, and his delightful humor"[10] quickly won them over and made him remarkably effective.

Rounding out the Big Four was Orlando. Of the heads of state, his strength lay in oratory and clarity of thought. None of the others was his superior in presenting a clear, concise, and comprehensive argument in an extemporaneous debate. Unfortunately, he spoke no English, which largely limited his participation to issues that affected Italy directly.

Italy had come to Paris to collect on promises made years earlier by the Allies to entice it to switch sides and join them in the war. In the 1915 Treaty of London, Italy had been assured parts of Austro-Hungary, holdings on the Adriatic (including the Dalmatian coast), Germany's African colonies, and portions of the Ottoman Empire. Orlando was there to see that this was not forgotten. Beyond what they had been offered, Italy also had territorial designs down the coast as far south as Albania. Italy saw this as a chance for economic and territorial gains that would finally allow it to dominate the Adriatic, extend its reach across the Mediterranean, and make it a great power.

The city that hosted them was a battered shell of its former self. In Paris there was hardly any coal or fuel, butter was unknown, and prices for basic necessities were beyond the reach of most Parisians. Transportation, when it could be found, was three to four times the normal cost, and the price of a hotel room doubled and tripled during the conference. The delegates lived in luxury (in the midst of the deprivation, one American negotiator wrote to his wife, "I am living more luxuriously than I ever did in all my life before."[11]), and accommodating them became such major business that expenditures by delegates and visitors during the negotiations surpassed France's revenue from foreign trade. Australian Prime Minister Billy Hughes wrote, "We are here in this ancient and most wonderful city of Paris— a motley band of high brows, more or less high brow, gathered together for the most amiable purpose of settling the peace of the world."[12] The fact that much of the war had been fought within a day's drive of Paris and their French hosts had a visible stake in the outcome was not lost on the delegates. "We felt," a member of the British delegation wrote, "like surgeons operating in the ballroom with the aunts of the patient gathered all around."[13]

The Americans settled in offices above the cabaret Maxim's. The delegation of several hundred included personal aides and assistants for the five commissioners, as well as technical advisers on international law, economics, finance, food, labor, shipping, and military and naval affairs. The American delegation stayed at the palatial Hotel Crillon. A symbol of eighteenth century Parisian decadence, it was built by King Louis XV in 1758 in the heart of Paris at the front of the Champs-Elysees on the Place de la Concorde. It had been a favorite of Marie Antoinette, who had often entertained there, and its grand salons were decorated with seventeenth-century tapestries, gilt and brocade furniture, and Louis XVI chests and chairs. Its 103 guest rooms and 44 suites accommodated the American delegates in a style far removed from the realities of postwar Paris. The British occupied the equally exclusive Hotel Majestic, one of the largest hotels in Paris, and made their offices in the adjacent Hotel Astoria, and the other delegations took up residence in various hotels and buildings throughout the city.

More than a month passed between the negotiators' arrival and their first meeting. The delegations took time to settle into their quarters, but the delay was also intended by Clemenceau to let the fever of popular sentiment surrounding Wilson's arrival die down. Wilson's impassioned advocacy for a just peace had made him an international celebrity, and British economist John Maynard Keynes remarked, "When President Wilson left Washington he enjoyed a prestige and a moral influence throughout the world unequalled in history."[14]

The major players began to size each other up the moment they reached Paris. The time between Wilson's arrival and the start of negotiations was filled with a shadow dance between Lloyd George, Clemenceau, and the president. Wilson was a powerful, unknown quantity, and the British and French prime ministers were eager to learn what they were up against. "All the European delegates," Lloyd George wrote, "were especially concerned to discover what President Wilson was like, what he was after and what he meant to insist on."[15]

Clemenceau, who had had the least exposure to Wilson, was especially wary. Lloyd George described how "Clemenceau followed his movements like an old watchdog keeping an eye on a strange and unwelcome dog who has visited the farmyard and of whose intentions he is more than doubtful."[16]

The Allies had originally intended to invite Germany to join the discussions once they had decided on terms for a preliminary settlement, but the challenges of reaching agreement among themselves proved greater than anyone expected. The Allies had also drawn their own lessons from France's diplomatic victory at the Congress of Vienna and had no inclination to give Germany a chance to do the same in Paris. Having brought Germany to concede to an armistice, the Allies saw themselves

The American delegation to the Paris Peace Conference included, from left to right, Colonel E. M. House, Secretary of State Robert Lansing, President Woodrow Wilson, Henry White, and General Tasker H. Bliss. (*Library of Congress*)

as victors. But though Germany was broken, it was not defeated. Although by all accounts its ability to prosecute the war was exhausted, its forces and borders remained intact and its people defiant.

Because it would be too unwieldy for all twenty-seven nations to meet, decision-making authority was vested in a Council of Ten, composed of the heads of state and foreign ministers of the four principal allies and Japan. Their secret meetings were held at the French Foreign Ministry on the Quai D'Orsay in French Foreign Minister Stephen Pichon's majestic private office. A high-domed ceiling supported a heavy chandelier, the walls of the room were lined with heavy oak Doric paneling that framed Rubens' tapestries copied from the Marie de Medici paintings in the Louvre, and carvings of cupids at play crowned the main door. Two large windows bordered by heavy green silk curtains looked out over a sculpted garden outside. At the center of the room was a plain empire table, where Clemenceau sat with his back to a massive fireplace crackling with great logs. Huddled around him were the other heads of state and foreign ministers, and a parade of experts, assistants, and secretaries.

The dizzying array of issues before the peace conference was too great for the Allied leaders to explore in detail themselves. A more systematic approach was needed, and reflecting the fever for mechanizing war and peace in the modern era, the negotiators arrived at an industrial solution. Questions were parceled out to panels of experts that in turn delegated subcommittees to hear testimony and produce reports. Fifty-eight commissions were formed during the course of the conference, which would hold over sixteen hundred official meetings.

Of the Fourteen Points, the creation of a League of Nations was dearest to Wilson's heart. In it he saw the philosopher's stone of international affairs, a device that would harmonize relations between states, resolve territorial disputes, and address frictions before they erupted into conflict. Wilson also looked to the League of Nations to make up for weaknesses in other areas of the peace, as it would allow flaws in the treaty to be corrected later. As he told his wife, "One by one the mistakes can be brought to the League for readjustment, and the League will act as a permanent clearinghouse where every nation can come, the small as well as the great."[17] Calling it "the key to the whole settlement,"[18] Wilson insisted that the League of Nations take precedence above all territorial, economic, military, and other issues before them and be incorporated into the peace treaty with Germany. Wilson saw the League, in the words of one member of the American delegation, as "the distinctive achievement differentiating this peace settlement from those of the past, which had invariably resulted in nationalistic rivalry and war."[19] It was to be a new constitution for mankind.

Others were more skeptical. When asked his opinion, Clemenceau said, "I like the League, but I do not believe in it."[20] Even Wilson's own secretary of state wondered if it made enough room for the darker parts of human nature. "There is in it too much altruistic cooperation," Lansing wrote. "No account is taken of national selfishness and the mutual suspicions which control international relations. It may be noble thinking, but it is not true thinking."[21]

The League was the first order of business, and on January 25, the full conference established a commission headed by Wilson on the League of Nations. It had nineteen members, two each from the Big Four and Japan and nine from the smaller countries. Their first meeting was on February 3 and they met every day on the third floor of the Hotel Crillon in the residence of the president's adviser, friend, and confidant, Colonel Edward House, seated around a large wooden table in his dining room covered with red cloth, with interpreters seated behind. Wilson and House worked day and night to prepare a draft before Wilson's scheduled return to the United States for a month on February 14. It was an impossibly short time.

President Wilson, House wrote, had one of the "most difficult and complex characters I have ever known."[22] He was famously stubborn, and capable of deep moral insights but also of vindictiveness and terrible personal grudges. He had presided over the entry of the United States into the war, which he convinced both himself and the nation could be justified only by upending the traditional balance of power system and replacing it with one governed by universal principles of ethical behavior.

After Wilson, the animating force behind the League of Nations was House, whose low profile concealed the fact that he was a master behind the scenes. One of his principal roles was to make sure there were no surprises. "I try," he said, "to find out in advance where trouble lies and to smooth it out before it goes too far."[23] An honorary Texas colonel, House was one of a curious breed of powerful presidential advisers apart from the official hierarchy who from time to time appear in American history. When Wilson was elected, House was offered the choice of any cabinet position he wished. He turned them all down to serve "wherever and whenever possible." With no official post, his power derived solely from his influence with Wilson, which was so complete that House was provided his own living quarters at the White House.

For such an audacious undertaking, the negotiators were surprisingly unprepared. Wilson had only the vaguest outline of a proposal, and when he presented his first draft to the commission, Lloyd George dismissed it as "crude and undigested."[24]

They worked feverishly. House wrote in his diary on February 2, "David Miller [the American legal adviser] brought me the revised Covenant for the League of Nations. He was up until four o'clock this morning and was at it by 8:30 again in order to get it finished and printed to present it to the President and me this afternoon, so we might look over it before tomorrow's meeting."[25] Their hopes were high. The following day House wrote, "The full committee met in one of my salons. . . . I could not help thinking that perhaps this room would be the scene of the making of the most important human document that has ever been written."[26]

The French representatives were particularly troublesome. They did not trust the League to protect them and found little comfort in Wilson's breezy assurances. Their tactics of obstruction and delay puzzled Wilson, who told his doctor, "The French delegates seem absolutely impossible. They talk and talk and talk and desire constantly to reiterate points that have already been thoroughly thrashed out and completely disposed of."[27] Clemenceau saw the League largely as a source of favors to trade for issues of more immediate interest to France. "Let yourselves be beaten," the French premier instructed his delegates on the League Commission. "It doesn't matter. Your setbacks will help me to demand extra guarantees on the Rhine."[28]

On February 9, Wilson—concerned that a number of "speechmakers" on the panel, especially many of the French and

Italians, were wasting time and slowing things down—devised an ingenious solution of setting up a "clarification committee" composed of the most verbose members of the commission to meet separately and talk to each other to their hearts content, freeing the rest to focus on the drafting. This improved the pace considerably.

The French pressed for the League to have its own standing army to give its decisions teeth, but the British and Americans bristled at the thought of placing a part of their armed forces under foreign control. "Unconstitutional and also impossible,"[29] was Wilson's reply.

On February 11, Wilson again firmly declined the French demand for an international force under the executive control of the League of Nations. He reiterated that the United States Constitution did not permit such an infringement on its sovereignty; and the British member, Lord Robert Cecil, said the same applied to the United Kingdom. The French stood their ground in the belief that it alone could give the League of Nations life and relevance. They ended the meeting shortly before midnight with the atmosphere tense.

They met again two days later, on the afternoon of February 13. It was the day before Wilson was to leave Paris, and only six articles out of twenty-six had been approved. That evening House wrote:

> This has been a memorable day. The President could not come in the afternoon, and I asked Lord Robert Cecil to take the chair. We agreed to try and make a record and, much to our gratification, we finished the other twenty-one articles by half-past six o'clock. . . . Lord Robert took several votes this afternoon and in this way stopped discussion. We had arranged to have another meeting tonight at 8:30. When I telephoned the President at seven o'clock that we had finished, he was astounded and delighted.[30]

After only ten meetings, the final draft was ready. The Covenant of the League of Nations had twenty-six articles that established a General Assembly composed of all the participating countries, an Executive Council with five permanent members (the United Kingdom, France, Italy, Japan, and the United States) and four members elected by the General Assembly for three-year terms, and an executive body led by a secretary general. The Executive Council had broad authority to raise any matter affecting world peace. Most significant decisions had to be unanimous. There was no League army, no mandatory disarmament, and no compulsory arbitration, but the covenant contained provisions for a permanent court of international justice, and formation of the International Labor Organization to improve working conditions.

On February 14, Wilson presented the draft Covenant of the League of Nations to the full body of the peace conference. The president was very satisfied. "Many terrible things have come out of this war," he said, "but some very beautiful things have come out of it."[31] Three hours after presenting it he was on his way to the United States.

"The actual time consumed in constituting the League of Nations, which it is hoped will be the means of keeping peace in the world, was thirty hours,"[32] reported the *New York Herald*. Many felt that the rush to get it done was too great. When Secretary Lansing had a chance to look at the proposal he wrote, "The more I studied the document, the less I liked it."[33] His disapproval opened a chasm between him and President Wilson that never closed. Lansing wrote:

> To believe for a moment that a world constitution—for so its advocates looked upon the Covenant—could be drafted perfectly or even wisely in eleven days, however much thought individuals may have previously given to the subject, seems on the face of it to show an utter lack of appreciation of the problems to be solved or else an abnormal confidence in the talents and

wisdom of those charged with the duty. If one compares the learned and comprehensive debates that took place in the convention which drafted the Constitution of the United States, and the months that were spent in the critical examination word by word of the proposed articles, with the ten meetings of the Commission on the League of Nations prior to its report of February 14 and with the few hours given to debating the substance and language of the Covenant, the inferior character of the document produced by the Commission ought not to be a matter of wonder. It was a foregone conclusion that it would be found defective.[34]

Five days later, on February 19, the negotiations suffered a tragic blow when a mentally unstable French anarchist fired seven bullets through the back panel of Clemenceau's car, hitting him once in the chest and missing his heart by inches.

The next day Clemenceau was out walking in his garden, and within two weeks the Tiger of France was back at work, the bullet still lodged in his body. While recovering, Clemenceau joked about his would-be assassin's marksmanship, "We have just won the most terrible war in history," he said, "yet here is a Frenchman who misses his target six out of seven times at point blank range. Of course this fellow must be punished for the careless use of a dangerous weapon and for poor marksmanship."[35] Still, it was a shock that underscored the instability of the environment and the narrowness of the margin for error. Clemenceau put on a brave front, but the injury had clearly taken its toll, and many observers, including Wilson and Lloyd George, felt he was never quite the same.

Lloyd George had left Paris briefly for London on February 10 to deal with labor unrest at home. With Clemenceau recovering and Wilson and Lloyd George away, major decisions were deferred until the leaders returned. In their absence, supporting figures such as British Foreign Minister Arthur Balfour and Colonel House stepped in and continued the discussions.

With the fighting over, the Allies were demobilizing as quickly as they could, reducing their ability to direct events on the ground. The United States alone was shipping home over three hundred thousand troops a month. With no one in control, uncertainty, anarchy, and chaos spread over Europe. "Hell was let loose," Lloyd George wrote, "and made the most of its time."[36] Revolution broke out in Hungary and Bavaria. Poland declared war against Russia, which was itself gripped by civil war. Romania went to war against Hungary. Scores of little wars erupted across the continent over petty vendettas and to grab territory to prejudice the outcome in Paris.

Shortages were everywhere. In Vienna, for lack of cotton cloth, the maternity hospitals put newborn babies in old newspapers. One of the British specialists recorded that in Bohemia "there is an absolute lack of milk and fats, with the result that something like 20 percent of the babies are born dead and something like 40 percent die within the first month."[37]

Wilson and House, in keeping with the Fourteen Points, sought a German peace without vengeance, but Clemenceau and Lloyd George had other priorities. The stage was laid for a defining battle between Wilsonian idealism and the hardened cynicism of European politics. The German treaty had three principle elements: disarmament, reparations, and territorial concessions. They began with disarmament.

The armistice stipulated steep reductions in German forces and equipment, and Germany had already surrendered much of its military hardware to the Allies, including its ships, airplanes, tanks, cannon, and machine guns. The German army had abandoned its positions in the field and demobilized, but the Allies made it clear they meant to go further and cut the sinews of German militarism so it could not grow back.

The military committee took three weeks to prepare draft terms. There was general agreement among the Allies on many points: Germany was stripped permanently of its air force, tanks, armored cars, heavy guns, dirigibles, and submarines. All fortifications west of the Rhine River and along its eastern bank were to be torn down, together with naval fortifications in the North Sea. Existing stocks of weapons and ammunition were to be destroyed, and only a few designated factories in Germany would be permitted to produce armaments.

French military advisers, led by Marshal Ferdinand Foch, suggested that the German army, which before the start of the war had over eleven million men, be cut to fewer than one hundred forty thousand based on universal conscription of service for one year. The chief British military adviser, General Henry Wilson, fearing that this system would produce a reserve of large numbers of trained men who could be mobilized on short notice, suggested instead a standing German army of two hundred thousand volunteers staffed by career soldiers. This in turn unsettled the French, who worried that a professional German officer corps might later be used as the backbone of a much larger force.

Lloyd George and Clemenceau fashioned a compromise that allowed Germany a volunteer force of one hundred thousand. General Wilson complained, "I got my principle but not my number, and Foch got his numbers but not his principles. An amazing state of affairs."[38] Germany's general staff was dissolved, its navy limited to six cruisers and some smaller vessels, and the country barred from possessing offensive weapons, including submarines, aircraft, tanks, and heavy artillery.

The negotiators looked next at the prickly question of German reparations. "The subject of reparations," said Thomas Lamont, an American banker who represented the Treasury Department in the discussions, "caused more trouble, contention, hard feeling, and delay at the Paris Peace Conference than any other point of the Treaty."[39]

The twin innovations of total war and industrialized warfare had multiplied the destructive potential of modern armies beyond anything before seen, and the war saw it employed without restraint against villages and cities across the continent. Rebuilding required massive amounts of capital that the financially exhausted Allies did not have, and there was universal agreement that Germany should pay. Even Wilson displayed uncharacteristic firmness toward Germany on the subject, explaining that "merely to beat a nation that was wrong is not enough. There must follow the warning to all other nations that would do these things that they in turn will be vanquished and shamed if they attempt a dishonorable purpose."[40]

The Allies presented eyebrow-raising claims. France and Belgium each asked for amounts that exceeded their entire pre-war wealth. The French demanded $220 billion, with payments lasting fifty-five years, which Lloyd George noted "would mean that for two generations we would make German workmen our slaves."[41] To his astonishment "the French professed to be confident that Germany was quite capable, given time, of paying the whole bill. Klotz, the French Finance Minister, evinced no doubts on the subject. He was of that hard, merciless type that gave no thought where money was concerned to anything except cash considerations. The prospect of the suffering inflicted, the old feuds kept alive, the new quarrels provoked, the unrest which would be fomented in Europe, in exacting the last penny, did not move him in the least."[42]

The French pointed with some justice to Germany's own record of imposing harsh terms. When Russia, consumed by revolution, had sued for peace less than a year before the Paris Peace Conference, Germany had given no quarter, extracting a large reparations payment as well as a third of Russia's population, half its industry, and nine-tenths of its coal mines.

No one knew the true value of the war's damage. The officer in charge of calculating the cost estimated it would take two years to make a proper assessment, but the Germans were expected in Versailles in a matter of weeks. The English, whose chief financial adviser at the conference was John Maynard Keynes, the founder of modern economic theory, suggested a total that was half of what the French proposed, and the American estimate was one-fifth of the British figure. It was clear, however, that Germany was unable to pay anything near the Allies' losses. The war had strained Germany beyond the breaking point, and it was unable to feed its own people let alone finance the reconstruction of Europe. "They play with billions as children play with wooden blocks," a journalist wrote of the Allies' demands, "but whatever we agree to will largely be a figure of speech, for the Germans will never be able to pay such a vast sum."[43] Lloyd George complained that in the economic discussions, Wilson "exercised no healthy influence at all, being, as he confessed, 'not much interested in the economic subjects.'"[44]

The French and British leaders found themselves in an impossible situation. Lloyd George admitted to House that he needed to present "a plausible reason to his people for having fooled them about the question of war costs, reparations, and what not."[45] He "admitted that he knew Germany could not pay anything like the indemnity which the British and French demanded."[46] A British negotiator described their predicament: "If too low a figure were given Germany would pay out cheerfully and the allies would get too little, while, on the other hand, if too high a figure were given, she would throw up the sponge and the Allies would get nothing."[47]

The closer they looked at the problem, the more complex it became. Germany's cash on hand was small. Even including confiscating art, rolling stock, overseas possessions, and other movables it was obvious that reparations would have to be paid out over time. To pay off its reparations debt, Germany would have to establish a large positive balance of trade with the Allies, and the more they demanded of Germany, the more it would displace their own domestic manufacturers and debase their currencies. Lloyd George, who had been chancellor of the exchequer and understood the circular nature of international finance, wrote "there was no experience to guide Governments as to the limit beyond which payments from one country to another could be extracted without harm to both."[48] It was a curious dilemma, and it conflicted with many Allies' desire to strip Germany of its more productive regions. One of the American representatives put it simply: "The only way in which Germany can pay is by exporting goods. She has got to be allowed to make money to pay over to the Allies. If a man owed you a million the last thing you would do would be to stick a knife in him."[49]

The armistice provided that Germany had only to pay for damage to civilian infrastructure and noncombatants, and the Allies were especially sensitive to how this was defined, as it affected how the benefits would be distributed among them. The Belgian delegate, for one, opposed the inclusion of full war costs by any of the Allies except Belgium. France had suffered the most extensive physical damage, but Britain had given over its industrial base to the war effort and felt that it justly deserved compensation. To secure a share of the reparations, Britain's representatives insisted on expanding the definition to include pension obligations Britain had made its soldiers and workers involved in the war effort.

The negotiators took care to keep their deliberations out of the public eye. Secretary of State Lansing complained, "Everybody seemed to talk in whispers and never to say anything worthwhile except in confidence. The open sessions of the Conference were arranged beforehand. They were formal and perfunctory. The agreements and bargains were made behind closed doors."[50]

Behind those closed doors the scene was chaotic, with as many as fifty people in the room including prime ministers, foreign ministers, assistants, and other officials. "Everything was very informal," an American delegate wrote, "each of the men speaking when they felt like it."[51] Lansing drew constantly during the sessions, mostly caricatures and grotesque figures. When he finished one he would drop it on the floor and begin another. "Lloyd George," one of the participants recalled, "was filled with admiration for the drawings: 'I say,' he said, 'could I have one of those; they're awfully good.' So Lansing gave him one and he folded it carefully and put it in his pocket with gratitude."[52] Italian Foreign Minister Baron Sonnino and Clemenceau would often doze off. The one source of lightness was the official translator, Paul Mantoux. "He puts more spirit into his translations than the principle puts into his original speech,"[53] remembered an American delegate.

By late February, widespread hopes had given way to confusion and delay, and the negotiators had yet to settle either reparations or the central question of territorial settlements. "The discouraging part of the conference," lamented an American delegate, "is that it seems so difficult to get an orderly program. Much matter which should be put before subordinates—details, technical disputes, etc.—comes before the Council of Ten, takes up their time, and perplexes them."[54] "A general feeling of impatience," British Foreign Minister Lord Balfour warned his colleagues, had taken root "in all countries on account of the apparent slow progress the Conference was making in the direction of Final Peace," and "it would be folly to ignore altogether the danger that feeling might produce."[55] The main cause was disorganization. "They are not getting anywhere, largely because of the lack of organization," House wrote in his diary in late February, adding that "the great fault of the political leaders was their failure to draft a plan of procedure." [56] They resolved to pick up the pace, and the Council ordered the committees to have their reports ready by March 8.

German boundaries were to Clemenceau and the French what the League of Nations was to Wilson. All else was secondary.

"As far as they were concerned," Lloyd George observed, "it represented the only fruit worth snatching from the tree of victory."[57] After suffering occupation twice in fifty years, the French had no illusions about Germany, and their cardinal demand was the establishment of a buffer state carved out of German territory along the left bank of the Rhine. This new state, to be called the Rhenish Republic, would be granted full autonomy but barred from joining any German confederation and occupied permanently by Allied forces. The French hoped that generous treatment, including an exemption from reparations, would pacify the inhabitants, who were mostly ethnic Germans. Clemenceau was quite open about his desire to dismember Germany, and candidly admitted that the more separate and independent republics that were established in Germany the better.

The British and Americans objected, pointing out that it would sever about four million Germans against their will from their native land, and it was a direct insult to Wilson's principle of self-determination. But the French took greater comfort in physical security than in Wilson's high principles. "The French," House wrote on February 9, "have but one idea and that is military protection."[58]

Clemenceau insisted also on coal deposits in the Saar valley, a fertile region near the French border which before the war had accounted for 8 percent of German coal production, as compensation for Germany's systematic destruction of the bulk of the French mines and to allow France to restart its economy. The British and Americans resisted, appalled by what they saw as a naked land grab.

Germany's eastern borders were also a focus of contention, intertwined with the perennial European question of resurrecting Poland. Poland's absorption by Russia, Prussia, and Austria at the Congress of Vienna in 1815 had erased it from the map for over a hundred years, but its culture and identity remained intact, and a few hardy patriots had kept alive the dream of reunification. An opportunity now presented itself to restore Poland to its rightful place in Europe and to grant freedom to the thirty million Poles living under foreign rule. Wilson had made reviving Poland one of his Fourteen Points, and France was excited by the possibility of a strong counterweight to Germany on its eastern border. "French foreign policy," Lloyd George observed, "has always been swayed by one paramount aim—the weakening of Germany and the strengthening of its political opponents."[59]

As with much of Central and Eastern Europe, the region was an amalgam of ethnicities without easily defined contours, and the landscape was mostly flat with few natural boundaries. Poland's ambitions extended over large areas of Russia, Germany, and Czechoslovakia, and the claims put forward by its representatives stunned even its supporters. "Drunk with the wine of liberty supplied to her by the Allies," Lloyd George complained, "she fancied herself once more the resistless mistress of Central Europe."[60] The Polish representatives brushed aside the principle of self-determination and demanded Galicia, much of the Ukraine, Lithuania, and parts of Russia. Wilson told the Council of Ten, "I saw [the Polish representatives] in Washington, and I asked them to define Poland for me as they understood it, and they presented me with a map in which they claimed a large part of the earth."[61]

Allowing Poland access to the sea was especially challenging. Nine-tenths of its exports went by water. Its natural outlet to the Baltic was Danzig, a major port city with a predominantly Polish population, surrounded by ethnically German territory. The only way to connect Poland was by cutting a deep swath through German provinces and the transfer of two million German speakers to Polish sovereignty.

President Wilson returned on March 14. Although no commitments had been made in his absence, he was shocked at how far the discussions had moved from the basis of his Fourteen Points and felt betrayed by House for concessions on Allied reparations, entertaining the possibility of a Rhenish Republic, and appearing open to further compromises. Wilson complained to his wife that "House has given away everything that I had won before we had left Paris. He has compromised on every side, and so I have to start all over again."[62]

Wilson's return and the need to pick up the pace prompted an important change in the format of the discussions. As the complexity of the questions multiplied and the tension rose, it became obvious that the Council of Ten was too large to make quick and decisive decisions. With up to fifty people in the room at any time, it was too cumbersome, and the potential for leaks made frank talk difficult. Harold Nicolson, a member of the British delegation, wrote his father, "The Conference is deteriorating rapidly . . . the Council of Ten are atrophied by the mass of detail which pours in upon them."[63] Wilson, Clemenceau, Lloyd George, and Orlando decided instead to meet alone without their foreign ministers in what became known as the Council of Four. The Japanese, as they were not represented by a prime minister or head of state, were excluded, except for questions that touched on the Far East.

Winston Churchill, who was part of the British cabinet and was present at the negotiations, wrote that Clemenceau for some time had been "ripening for a trial of strength,"[64] and with Wilson's return "the decks were cleared for action and the long looked-for conflict of wills could now at last begin."[65] The American position had in the meantime weakened. In Washington, President Wilson had discovered that serious changes had to be made to the League of Nations Covenant for it to be ratified by the Senate, in particular an amendment making special allowance for the Monroe Doctrine. It became clear that in return he would have to give way on many of his principles. Pressure was building to reach agreement, and House believed that if compromises had to be made it was better to make them sooner rather than later. "My main drive now," he wrote the day of Wilson's arrival, "is for peace with Germany at the earliest possible moment."[66] It would not come easily. On March 20, after a meeting of Wilson, Lloyd George, and Clemenceau, House asked Clemenceau how it had gone. He replied, "Splendidly, we disagreed about everything."[67]

Charles Seymour, one of the principal American representatives, saw the negotiation as a clash of competing perspectives: "It was not so much a duel as a general melee, in which the representatives of each nation struggled to secure endorsement for their particular methods of ensuring the peace. The object of all was the same—to avoid a repetition of the four years of world devastation; their methods naturally were different, since each was faced by a different set of problems."[68]

By the week of March 31 the conversations had taken on a "marked atmosphere of strain and tension,"[69] and relations between Lloyd George and Clemenceau had reached a point of crisis. One of the British representatives put it succinctly: "The French want the Rhine frontier as their bulwark against Germany. We refuse to give it to them."[70]

On March 28 Wilson rejected the French annexation of the Saar. For Clemenceau it was the straw that broke the camel's back. "It seems," House wrote, "that the long-expected row . . . had actually come."[71] Wilson told the French premier that no one had ever heard of the Saar until after the armistice, and Clemenceau responded by accusing the president of being pro-German. "Then," said the president, "if France does not get what she wishes, she will refuse to act with us. In that event do you wish me to return home?" "I do not wish you to return home," said Clemenceau, "but I intend to do so myself,"[72] and stormed out.

Wilson called the American delegates together the following morning and told them:

> Gentlemen, I am in trouble and I have sent for you to help me out. The matter is this: the French want the whole left bank of the Rhine. I told M. Clemenceau that I could not consent to such a solution of the problem. He became very much excited and then demanded ownership of the Saar Basin. I told him I could not agree to that either because it would mean giving 300,000 Germans to France. . . . I do not know whether I shall see M. Clemenceau again. I do not know whether he will return to the meeting this afternoon. In fact, I do not know whether the Peace Conference will continue.[73]

Clemenceau's temper soon cooled, and with all that France had in the balance, he rejoined the discussions and plunged back into the fray. In the first week of April all the issues came to a head at once. With the French and American positions dead-locked on the Saar and Rhineland, the French rejected an American attempt to limit reparations to what Germany could pay out over thirty years. The British, who had been coordinating with the Americans, changed sides and joined the French in opposition. Just when House had thought "agreement appeared imminent,"[74] it had slipped even further away. He fumed:

> We wasted the entire afternoon, accomplishing nothing, for the text when we finished was practically what it was when we went into the meeting. Any drafting committee could have done it better. This is what makes one so impatient at the whole procedure of the Conference. Instead of drawing the picture with big lines, they are drawing it like an etching. If the world were not aflame, this would be permissible, but it is almost suicidal in times like these to try to write a treaty of peace, embracing so many varied and intricate subjects, with such methods.[75]

Wilson and House were out of patience, and they feared that further concessions from the United States would only lead to new demands. Wilson, in bed with the Spanish flu, resolved with his advisers that unless the prime ministers agreed to make a peace in keeping with the principles of the Fourteen Points, the United States would pull out of the negotiations. "I went in and out of the President's room at various intervals," House wrote on the afternoon of Sunday, April 6, "to keep him informed as to the progress we were making. . . . I suggested that in the event there was no agreement by the end of next week, he draw up a statement of what the United States is willing to sign in the way of a peace treaty, and give the Allies notice that unless they can come near our way of thinking we would go home immediately and let them make whatever peace seems to them best. My suggestion was to do this gently and in the mildest possible tone, but firmly."[76] The following morning President Wilson sent a cable asking how soon the USS *George Washington* could be sent to France to pick him up to return to the United States.

Clemenceau and Lloyd George pleaded for him to stay, reminding him of what a disaster it would be if he left, and pledging to be flexible. It did not take much. With his League of Nations at stake, Wilson had too much invested in the outcome to walk away. Soothed by their assurances, Wilson returned to the Council of Four that afternoon and almost immediately began to back down on his previous positions.

The Allied leaders decided the reparations amount would be set at a future date by a committee with representatives from the major powers that Germany would have the right to petition for leniency. "Much to my delight," House wrote, "they came to a tentative settlement of the question of reparations. The President yielded more than I thought he would, but not more, I think, than the occasion required."[77] It was a fairly painless compromise for Wilson, but it left Germany in the position of having to sign a blank check and it represented an abandonment of a core principle in the first of what quickly became a cascade of concessions.

Wilson at first refused to discuss alienating the Saar from Germany. He went so far as to allow France to take over the

mines, but only if sovereignty remained under Germany. As a
compromise, Lloyd George proposed turning the Saar into a
neutral state, as, "A kind of Luxemburg," rather than annexing
it to France. Wilson in response suggested that rather than giving France administrative control over the region, German sovereignty be suspended for fifteen years, in which an administrative commission would exercise authority under the League of
Nations. After fifteen years a plebiscite would determine the
Saar's ultimate status.

While remaining firm against severing the Rhineland from
Germany, Wilson dropped his opposition to an occupation of
the Rhine by Allied troops for up to fifteen years. "The President
made a wry face over it," wrote House, "particularly the three
five-year periods of occupation, but he agreed to it all."[78] To
allay French concerns over leaving the Rhineland in German
hands, Wilson and Lloyd George extended an Anglo-American
guarantee to defend France in case of future attack by Germany.
This, together with German disarmament and the Allied occupation of the Rhine, was enough to satisfy Clemenceau. In return
Wilson received his coveted League amendments.

As Wilson gave way, his concessions led to widespread accu-
sations that he had abandoned the Fourteen Points. "He identi-
fied the Covenant of the League of Nations with this his central
impulse, and before the Ark of the Covenant he sacrificed his
Fourteen Points one by one,"[79] wrote one of the chief British
delegates.

It is impossible to estimate how many decisions were accepted,
how often obstruction was relinquished, how frequently errors
were passed over, under the aegis of that blessed Article XIX
[allowing adjustments to the settlement by the League of
Nations]. "Well," we were apt to think, "this decision seems foolish and unjust. Yet I shall agree to it rather than delay the Treaty
for a few days further. Its unwisdom will very shortly become
apparent even to those who are now its advocates. When that

day comes we can resort to Article XIX." I am convinced that practically all of President Wilson's own backslidings were justified in his own conscience by the thought that "The Covenant will put that right."[80]

More mundane influences also pulled Wilson toward the European position. One of the British representatives observed: "the collapse of President Wilson was due to little more than the continual pressure of ordinary courtesy: he disagreed with almost everything his colleagues suggested: they were fully aware of how painful to him was this constant disagreement: and inevitably—they exploited the situation thus created."[81]

Before the treaty was presented to the Germans, a last-minute crisis threatened to overturn what the Allies had struggled to produce. In a surprise, eleventh-hour extortion, the Italian representatives threatened to withhold their signature from the German treaty unless they were given additional territory in the Adriatic beyond what they had been promised in the Treaty of London. They demanded the vital Adriatic port of Fiume, which the Treaty of London had granted to Croatia. Croatia itself had been absorbed into the newly formed state of Yugoslavia, and Fiume was considered indispensable to this fragile new state's economic survival.

Wilson objected to the Treaty of London, which was signed before the United States had entered the war, and the notion of handing Fiume to Italy reeked to him of the Old World clubby dealing and spoils mentality that he meant to move away from. The president threatened to withdraw from the peace conference if Italy's demands were honored. The Italian representatives were indignant. After Wilson's concessions to the French and the British, the Italians felt entitled to a share in the feast, and they resented being singled out. Baron Sonnino complained, "America had given in in the case of France and Great Britain; because she had been immoral here she tried to re-establish her virginity at the expense of Italy."[82] Orlando rejected every attempt at compromise and threatened to withdraw from the peace conference if Italy's wishes were not obliged. "The whole world," House wrote, "is speculating as to whether the Italians are 'bluffing' or whether they really intend going home and not signing the Peace unless they have Fiume. It is not unlike a game of poker."[83] If the Italian delegates were not present when the German treaty was signed, Wilson and Lloyd George warned them, Italian claims to the German reparations would be forfeit. The Italian delegation, which withdrew in a huff, returned sheepishly the day before the German treaty was presented to the assembled peace conference.

On May 6, Clemenceau's chief adviser, Andre Tardieu, in a formal session read to the delegates of all the represented countries a summary of the completed German treaty, which most of them had never seen. The next day the German representatives, led by Count **Ulrich von** Brockdorff-Rantzau, received the treaty in a brief, awkward ceremony. The German delegation had been summoned only a couple of weeks before and kept under guard behind barbed wire until the final details of the draft were complete.

Far from Wilson's beacon of hope, it was described as "a peace with a vengeance." The Germans, who had placed their hopes in Wilson's Fourteen Points, were bitterly disappointed. "This fat volume," Brockdorff-Rantzau complained, "was quite unnecessary. They could have expressed the whole thing more simply in one clause—'Germany surrenders all claims to its existence.'"[84]

As they waited for the German response, the Allies turned to the Austro-Hungarian settlement. The Austro-Hungarian Empire, which had covered almost all of what is now known as Central Europe and traced its origins to classical Rome, had dissolved in the final days of the war, and its former possessions fell into near anarchy. Its sudden demise unleashed the aspirations of nations that had been suppressed for centuries, spurred by Wilson's promise of self-determination. Secretary of State Lansing worried early on about the dangers of disappointed expectations. "The phrase is loaded with dynamite," he wrote. "It will raise hopes which can never be realized."[85]

The aspiring nationalities came to Paris with hopelessly inflated expectations and conflicting territorial ambitions. Czechoslovaks, Hungarians, Yugoslavs, Poles, Serbs, and dozens of others vied for statehood and competed over choice bits of territory. The statesmen at Paris soon found themselves confronting a thicket of overlapping ethnicities. "These areas," Lloyd George marveled, "were the mangrove swamps where the racial roots were so tangled and intermingled that no peacemaker could move inside them without stumbling."[86]

The representatives of the smaller or nascent states first presented written petitions describing the territory they felt they deserved and why. After these had been reviewed by a subcommittee, the delegates were invited to argue their case before the Big Four in person. One of the British delegates observed:

> The smaller powers produced memoranda of claims which were far in excess of their real expectations. Inevitably in expounding these claims orally before the council they merely repeated what had been written in their Statements, and diminished the powers of resistance which these old gentlemen, in that hot and stuffy room, were able to maintain. . . . It gave to the members of the Supreme Council the impression that they were doing valuable and constructive work. Yet in fact they were doing nothing more than suffer, with varying degrees of courtesy, an exhausting and unnecessary imposition.[87]

This led to a sudden, explosive rush to finish as time grew short and decisions had to be made.

The decisive meeting on Central and Southern Europe of the foreign ministers of the Big Four came on May 8. As the chief British Central European expert described: "They begin with Transylvania, and after some insults flung like tennis balls between Tardieu and Lansing, Hungary loses her South. Then Czechoslovakia, and while the flies drone in and out of the open windows Hungary loses her North and East. Then the frontier with Austria, which is maintained intact. Then the Yugoslav frontier, where the Committee's report is adopted without change. Then tea and macaroons."[88]

The Allies carved the Austro-Hungarian Empire into Austria, Hungary, Czechoslovakia, Romania, and Yugoslavia, reducing Austria to little more than Vienna and the surrounding countryside. Hungary, which had split off from Austro-Hungary only days before the end of the war, was stripped of two-thirds of its territory and nearly two-thirds of its population. In the Balkans, a unified Yugoslavia grew out of the Slavic statelets of Serbia, Croatia, Macedonia, Bosnia-Herzegovina, and Slovenia.

France saw Czechoslovakia as a counterweight to Germany in Central Europe, and it emerged with large parts of what was formerly Hungary and over a million ethnic Hungarians. Lloyd George complained, "We won freedom for nations that had not the slightest hope of it—Czechoslovakia, Poland, and others. Nations that have won their freedom at the expense of the blood of Italians and Frenchmen and Englishmen and Americans. And we have the greatest trouble in the world to keep them from annexing the territory of other nations and imposing upon other nations the very tyranny which they themselves have endured for centuries."[89] The Austro-Hungarian settlement was approved on May 12.

The sullen, disillusioned German representatives returned to present their objections on May 29, but their protests had little effect. President Wilson was especially dismissive of the German complaints. "It is enough to reply," he said, "that we don't believe a word of what the German government says."[90]

Lloyd George, though, moved by the German response and seized by worries that they might refuse to sign, grew concerned that the Allies might have gone too far. He tried to revisit the

major provisions, petitioning his colleagues to shorten the duration of the military occupation of the Rhineland, to admit
Germany immediately into the League of Nations, and to revise
the reparations demands, but Clemenceau felt he had conceded
too much already, and Wilson turned a deaf ear. "It makes me a
little tired," the president told the American delegates, "for people to come and say now that they are afraid the Germans won't
sign, and their fear is based upon things that they insisted upon
at the time of the writing of the Treaty."[91] Wilson added sternly
that he felt Lloyd George had "no principles whatsoever of his
own, that he reacted according to the advice of the last person
who had talked with him: that expediency was his guiding
star."[92] The only change that resulted was the concession of a
plebiscite for the province of Upper Silesia to decide whether to
become part of Germany or Poland.

On June 16, the German delegates were given three days to
accept the treaty, extended to June 23—or else. Count
Brockdorff-Rantzau and his assistants returned to Germany that
night. He and the entire German delegation favored rejecting
the treaty.

The Allies were prepared to act. Clemenceau told the Council
of Four, "If Germany refuses, I favor a vigorous and unremitting
military blow that will force the signing."[93] With Wilson and
Lloyd George in agreement, the supreme Allied command
ordered preparations for a massive military thrust of forty-two
divisions into the heart of Germany. On June 20 the German
cabinet, unable to agree whether to accept the treaty, resigned.
At the same time Brockdorff-Rantzau stepped down as head of
the German delegation and retired to private life.

The deadline for German acceptance was seven o'clock in the
evening on June 23. German President Friedrich Ebert cobbled
together a new government on June 22, and the National
Assembly voted in favor of signing on June 23, just hours before
the deadline expired. The statesmen in Paris waited breathlessly

for word of the Germans' decision. "I am counting the minutes," Clemenceau said.[94] At 5:40 p.m., the German reply arrived.

The signing ceremony was held on June 28, a clear, beautiful day, in the Hall of Mirrors at Versailles. Germany was represented by Herman Muller, the new foreign minister, and Johannes Bell, the transportation minister. That night, after the conclusion of the ceremony, Wilson left to return to the United States. A sense of foreboding cast a shadow over the delegates as they returned home. Secretary Lansing wrote:

> The terms of peace were yesterday delivered to the German plenipotentiaries and for the first time in these days of feverish rush of preparation there is time to consider the Treaty as a complete document. The impression made by it is one of disappointment, of regret, and of depression. The terms of peace appear immeasurably harsh and humiliating, while many of them seem to me impossible of performance. The League of Nations created by the Treaty is relied upon to preserve the artificial structure which has been erected by compromise of the conflicting interests of the Great Powers and to prevent the germination of the seeds of war which are sown in so many articles and which under normal conditions would soon bear fruit. The League might as well attempt to prevent the growth of plant life in a tropical jungle.[95]

It would lead, Lansing wrote, "as surely as day follows night"[96] to another war. Marshal Foch agreed. "This is not Peace," he declared. "It is an armistice for twenty years."[97] His prediction was off by only sixty-five days.

The day after departing France to return home, House wrote in his diary:

> I am leaving Paris, after eight fateful months, with conflicting emotions. . . . While I should have preferred a different peace, I doubt very much whether it could have been made, for the ingredients required for such a peace as I would have were lacking at Paris. . . .

We have had to deal with a situation pregnant with difficulties and one which could be met only by an unselfish and idealistic spirit, which was almost wholly absent and which was too much to expect of men come together at such a time and for such a purpose. And yet I wish we had taken the other road, even if it were less smooth, both now and afterward, than the one we took. We would at least have gone in the right direction and if those who follow us had made it impossible to go the full length of the journey planned, the responsibility would have rested with them and not with us.[98]

President Wilson returned to the United States to face a hostile Senate. His failure to appoint Republicans among any of the American delegates had created resentment and suspicion, and opposition coalesced around Article X of the League of Nations. This bound its members to come to each others' aid in case of aggression, and many senators were concerned that it infringed on Congress's constitutional authority to declare war. Wilson's contempt for those who disagreed with him and his unwilling-ness to compromise played poorly in the Senate, and it refused to ratify the treaty by the two-thirds majority required. The United States later made a separate peace with Germany, Austria, and Hungary, but its refusal to join the League of Nations crippled the organization from birth.

China also refused to sign the final settlement with Germany, as a result of outrage over a clause granting Japan possession of Shantung, a Chinese province and former German colony that Japan had seized at the start of the war. China signed a sep-arate peace with Germany in September 1919.

The machinery of the conference continued its work until January 1920, but with the major issues settled and the return home of the principal actors, only relatively mundane details remained.

The treaty with Germany was just under one thousand pages long and contained 440 clauses. Germany was forced to accept responsibility for causing the war, and lost 13 percent of its territory, over 10 percent of its population amounting to seven million people, 16 percent of its coal fields, and half of its iron and steel production. It surrendered its colonies and merchant fleet, and the Polish Corridor cut off Germany from East Prussia. Efforts to enforce German disarmament were soon abandoned, and the amount of reparations was steadily reduced before being eliminated entirely. German reparation payments never totaled more than five billion pounds sterling, most of which the Allies loaned to Germany. While the Allies gained no real financial benefit from the reparations, it gave German extremists a political grievance to rally around and caused a great deal of embarrassment for the Allies. In 1921 the Reparations commission set the final amount at 132 billion gold marks, equal to 6.6 billion pounds sterling, or $33 billion. Germany actually paid out only 22 billion gold marks before finally defaulting in 1932.

The Paris Peace Conference drew most of the borders of Europe as we now know them. Lloyd George wrote, "The Treaties of Paris constitute the greatest measure of national liberation of subject nations ever achieved by any war settlement on record. . . . No peace settlement has ever emancipated as many subjugated nationalities from the grip of foreign tyranny as did that of 1919."[99] Poland was reunited into a sovereign nation with a population of thirty million and was given a mandate over Galicia for twenty-five years. Danzig was made a "free city" under the League of Nations. Poland also received Upper Silesia from Germany and the area surrounding Posen, creating the Polish Corridor to the Baltic. Austria's new borders contained only a quarter of its previous territory and only a fifth of its population. It was limited to an army of thirty thousand volunteers and a navy of three police boats on the Danube. Czechoslovakia became an independent state and was given a large territory, including much of the coal-rich Bohemian province of Teschen, which it and Poland had both coveted.

Czechoslovakia's robust territory, however, was a poisoned chalice, as almost a third of its population of fifteen million was neither Czech nor Slovak and included a large population of Sudeten Germans. Bulgaria was forced to give up four border provinces to Yugoslavia as a penalty for fighting on the side of the Central Powers and it was subjected to reparations payments equal to its entire national wealth. Hungary surrendered more territory to Romania than it retained, and it lost over three million ethnic Magyars, a fourth of its population.

Discussions begun at Paris among the Allies on the fate of the former possessions of the Ottoman Empire were concluded and formalized at the San Remo Conference in April 1920. Armenia was granted independence, and Greece and Italy received large portions of Asia Minor on the Mediterranean coast, although the Turkish national uprising led by Ataturk soon forced them out. In the Middle East the settlement played out largely along the lines of secret wartime agreements made between the French and British governments. Arab independence was granted in the mostly uninhabitable interior of the Arabian Peninsula, but the rest of the region was parceled out between France and Great Britain. Britain was given custody over Palestine and Mesopotamia in present-day Iraq, whose rich oil deposits were shared evenly with France. Syria and Lebanon were handed over to French control. The arrangement ushered in the birth of the modern Middle East, establishing Saudi Arabia, Syria, Iraq, Palestine, and eventually Lebanon and Jordan as separate nations, and laying the foundation for decades of continuing tension and conflict in the region.

In Europe the Paris Peace Conference failed in its central purpose of averting another major war. As Henry Kissinger observed, "the attempt to reconcile American idealism with France's nightmares turned out to be beyond human ingenuity."[100] The result was an uneasy compromise that left none of the major parties satisfied and sowed the seeds of conflict on two continents. Germany was left alienated, weakened, and embittered, but intact. It was surrounded by a constellation of weak, ineffective states that were internally divided and quarreled with each other. France, vulnerable and menaced by Germany, did not feel more secure. Italy's ambitions were frustrated. Great Britain failed to secure the relief it had promised its citizens for the war's financial burdens. The United States did not establish the Fourteen Points as the basis for international relations. Without the might of the United States to sustain it, the League of Nations flickered quietly into darkness, although its essence was revived after World War II and remains with us as the United Nations.

Still, the parties collected many prizes. France gained control over Syria and Lebanon, as well as Alsace-Lorraine, the use of the Saar coal mines for fifteen years, and half of the oil in Mesopotamia. The British Empire acquired over eighty million people and almost a million square miles, including Germany's former overseas colonies, Iraq, and Palestine.

President Wilson, frustrated and embittered by resistance to what he had worked so hard to achieve in Paris, gave way under the strain. Less than two weeks after returning to Washington his mental and physical health began to fail. He suffered a series of strokes that left him bedridden, and lingered for several more years before dying in 1924 at age sixty-seven. Wilson was awarded the Nobel Peace Prize in 1919.

Lloyd George remained influential in British politics for several decades and died in 1945 at age eighty-two. Clemenceau served as France's prime minister until 1920, when he was defeated in a run for the presidency for giving away too much at the Paris Peace Conference. Lloyd George wrote that the French political class "never forgave Clemenceau for what they regarded as his failure to take full advantage of the opportunity afforded by the victory to realize traditional French ambitions on the Rhine. They stigmatized it as a betrayal of France, and when the chance came they recorded their verdict on his conduct by intriguing a humiliating defeat of his candidature for the Presidency."[101] He died of natural causes on November 24, 1929.

Adolf Hitler's rise to power was fueled by the sense of injustice and humiliation that had festered in the German mind following Versailles. He seized on the grievances and the longing Germans felt for the territory they had been deprived of, and when he had taken control he used the German minority populations in the surrounding countries as stepping stones to conquest. In a dark irony of history, twenty-one years after the Hotel Majestic housed the British delegation at the peace conference, it was taken over to serve as the headquarters of the German forces occupying Paris. Lloyd George observed:

> When nations are exhausted by wars in which they have put forth all their strength and which leave them tired, bleeding and broken, it is not difficult to patch up a peace that may last until the generation which experienced the horrors of the war has passed away. Pictures of heroism and triumph only tempt those who know nothing of the sufferings and terrors of war. It is therefore comparatively easy to patch up a peace which will last thirty years. What is difficult, however, is to draw up a peace which will not provoke a fresh struggle when those who have practical experience of what war means have passed away.[102]

The original document signed by President Harry Truman declaring the United States recognition of Israel. (*National Archives*)

Chapter 6

The Egyptian-Israeli Armistice Agreement

1949

W HEN the mandate granted to Britain over Palestine as part of the Versailles settlement expired on May 14, 1948 after a UN-sponsored plan to divide Palestine into separate Jewish and Arab states failed, Israel declared independence, and its Arab neighbors, led by Egypt, invaded. Following fierce fighting with heavy casualties on both sides, the United Nations secured a four-week truce. Hostilities erupted again on July 11, and the United Nations Security Council, fearing the consequences of a wider conflict, imposed a second cease-fire on July 18. The UN sent a mediator, Swedish Count Folke Bernadotte, to the region to oversee the truce and lay the groundwork for negotiation. Bernadotte tried desperately to bring the two sides together, but in mid-September he reported:

> Since my arrival in Cairo . . . I have striven ceaselessly to find a common basis upon which peace negotiations between the two parties might be undertaken. I have tried to bring them together in my presence or without it. I have studied carefully their respective positions, claims, and contentions, and . . . have devised compromises . . . put to them either orally or in writing. I have employed abundantly both reason and persuasion, but to

date neither agreement between the parties nor a basis for agreement has been found.[1]

His assassination in Jerusalem the following day confirmed his point.

In mid-October fighting resumed, and the Israeli army launched Operation Yoav (Ten Plagues), a massive thrust in the south that broke the Egyptian lines. Within a week, the Israelis captured the Negev desert and southern Palestine except for the Gaza Strip, and surrounded an entire Egyptian division at al-Faluja, while a simultaneous Israeli drive in the north captured the Galilee. The UN Security Council halted the fighting again with resolutions in November and called on both sides to begin negotiation on an armistice. But the Arabs and Israelis were not done. On December 10, Egypt launched an attack hoping to rescue the al-Faluja division and recapture the Negev, a six-thousand-seven-hundred-square-mile desert extending from the Dead Sea to the Gulf of Aqaba. Israel's counteroffensive shattered the poorly equipped Egyptian army and threw it back into the Sinai Peninsula. Finally, on January 6, 1949, after the loss of more than ten thousand lives and creating over a half million refugees, under decisive pressure from the UN and the British and American governments, the parties consented to UN-sponsored armistice negotiation.

Israel's decisive battlefield victories smashed the opposing forces beyond repair, and it dictated events on the ground and controlled a much larger area than originally envisioned. As a new state founded largely under UN auspices, it hoped to consolidate its military triumphs into a diplomatic agreement. Israel also had a great deal to lose. It was vulnerable politically. Its new borders, acquired during UN-mandated cease-fires, were seen as illegitimate. If the United Nations withheld recognition or imposed sanctions and the great powers followed suit, Israel risked international isolation, a fatal prospect for the small, poor, and fragile young nation.

Egypt felt tremendous pressures as well. The defeats had taken their toll, the united Arab front had crumbled into suspicion and rivalry, and the United States leaned heavily on Cairo for a formal peace. Britain grew increasingly nervous that the violence would jeopardize the security of the Suez Canal, and rattled the Egyptian government with talk of bringing troops in to safeguard the area. Egypt also knew that the only hope of separating Israel from its newly won territories lay with a negotiated settlement or UN Security Council resolution accompanied by sanctions. But Egypt's greatest incentive to come to the negotiating table lay with the fate of two thousand seven hundred Egyptian soldiers (nearly a third of the total Egyptian forces) trapped by the Israeli military at al-Faluja, completely encircled, without hope of rescue or resupply and in danger of running out of food. Whatever the Egyptians' distaste for meeting with the Israelis, the al-Faluja issue simply had to be addressed, and this could only be done as part of a larger armistice negotiation with Israel. Still, the prospect of an armistice with Israel was a bitter pill to swallow. Egypt refused to recognize Israel or acknowledge its right to exist. Cairo insisted on UN involvement for fear that one-on-one negotiation would imply recognition of what it referred to as "the so-called State of Israel."[2] Egyptian leaders swore often and publicly that they would rather die than strike a bargain with Israel, and there was no shortage of assassins willing to keep them to their word.[3]

For the United Nations, established three years before, this was a defining moment. The armistice negotiation was its first major test in matters of war and peace, and the world waited to see if it could produce results or if it would fall prey to the same inaction and lack of resolve that doomed the League of Nations.

As a formal end to hostilities, the negotiation would address both the military issues concerning withdrawal and balance of forces and larger political questions of territorial boundaries and steps toward a permanent peace. The Egyptian delegation's ten

members included Colonel Seif El Dine, the head of the delegation; Dr. Abdul Mustafa, the chief political adviser; Colonel El
Rahmany; and Colonel Ismail Sherine, a cousin and brother-in-
law of King Farouk. Israel's delegation, headed by Walter Eytan,
the 39-year-old founder of the Israeli Foreign Service, included
Reuven Shiloah, Prime Minister David Ben-Gurion's foreign
policy adviser; Elias Sasson, the Syrian-born director of the
Middle East Division; and Shabtai Rosenne, the Foreign
Ministry's legal adviser. Colonel Yigael Yadin, chief of staff of
the Israeli army, led the small group of military advisers.

The negotiation was supervised by Ralph Bunche, a man
uniquely suited for the challenge. Orphaned as a young child,
Bunche was raised in the tough Watts section of Los Angeles by
his maternal grandmother, "Nana" Johnson, who had been born
into slavery. He could remember no time in his childhood when
his family lived in conditions other than those of extreme
poverty,[4] which imbued him with a toughness tempered by tolerance. "Life was no idyll," he remembered. "I was learning what
it meant to be a Negro, even in an enlightened northern city. But
I wasn't embittered by such experiences, for Nana had taught
me to fight without rancor. She taught all of us to stand up for
our rights, to suffer no indignity, but to harbor no bitterness
toward anyone, as this would only warp our personalities. She
instilled in us a sense of personal pride strong enough to sustain all external shocks, but she also taught us understanding
and tolerance. Be honest and frank with yourself and the world
at all times, she said. Never compromise what you know to be
the right. Never pick a fight, but never run from one if your
principles are at stake."[5]

Bunche earned his way through high school laying carpets,
and worked as a janitor to put himself through the University of
California at Los Angeles, where he excelled as a star athlete and
class valedictorian. On his graduation, the black community of
Los Angeles raised one thousand dollars for him to pursue grad-

uate studies at Harvard University, where in 1934 he became the first black American to receive a PhD in political science in the United States. With the advent of World War II, Bunche joined the Office of Strategic Services, the precursor to the CIA, where he headed the Africa section and played an important role in the Allied landings in North Africa. When the war ended, Bunche joined the State Department as its first black official and head of the Colonial Affairs Division. In April 1945, the State Department sent him to San Francisco, where he helped organize

Ralph Bunche (*Library of Congress*)

the founding of the United Nations and contributed in the writing of its charter. Bunche joined the United Nations as a specialist on colonialism, decolonialism, and trusteeship, and quickly became one of the UN's leading experts on Palestine. When his close friend and colleague Count Bernadotte was assassinated, Bunche was appointed in his place as UN mediator. UN officials made it clear to Bunche before he left for the negotiation that the outcome would determine not only prospects for the Middle East, but also the future of the United Nations.

The delegations arrived at Rhodes on January 12. An ancient Greek island off the Turkish coast, Rhodes was neutral, secluded, and conveniently close to Cairo and Tel Aviv. While architecturally beautiful, the majestic Hotel des Roses, which housed the delegations, had uncomfortable rooms, little or no heat, and inedible food. "Dr. Bunche and his staff," Eytan wrote, "had set up their headquarters and living accommodations in one wing of the spacious Hotel des Roses and had reserved the other for the Egyptian and Israeli delegations. Israel occupied the larger part of one floor, and Egypt the floor immediately above. It was an excellent arrangement. All the parties concerned in the negotiations were under the same roof, yet each enjoyed almost perfect privacy."[6]

They met the following day in Bunche's sitting room. "I can readily think," Bunche told them, "of a million ways to stall, delay, obstruct and stalemate these discussions should anyone care to do so. I trust there will be no tendency to be rigidly legalistic, picayunish about detail, or recriminatory. There are many eyes here, and motes can be readily found in them. The lives of many people and indeed the peace of the Near East hang in the balance while you meet. You cannot afford to fail. You must succeed. I have faith that you will succeed."[7] Bunche drafted a statement of basic principles to frame the discussion, which the two sides agreed to the next day. It called for "scrupulous respect for the injunction of the Security Council against the use of military force; no aggressive actions to be planned or executed by either party; respect for the right of each party to its security and to freedom from fear of attack; and the acceptance of the armistice as an indispensable step toward peace in Palestine." He also laid out the agenda: al-Faluja, then delineation of armistice lines, withdrawal of forces, and finally reduction of forces.[8]

Eytan reported to Israeli Foreign Minister Moshe Sharett:

We have been here for just over twenty-four hours, and I think the time has come to give you some first impressions. . . . Bunche himself is dead keen on achieving success, and, if the Egyptians are at all susceptible to a mélange of charm and high-pressure diplomacy, he may pull it off. . . . The formal opening meeting went off smoothly. Bunche told me afterwards that the Egyptians were pleasantly surprised at our appearance; they had apparently expected fierce, warlike persons to come exultantly to the table, with grim expressions on their faces. The Egyptians were visibly nervous, never quite sure whether they were doing

the right thing. [The Israeli representatives] agree that the thing
to do is to try to wear down their initial suspicion and caution.[9]

The first week was filled with challenges. When the negotiators passed each other in the narrow hallways they would avert
their eyes and turn away. The two sides refused to meet, forcing
Bunche to tell them, "It was my understanding that we had
come here to negotiate, and to do this, gentlemen, one side must
talk to the other."[10] The Egyptians and Israelis would not sit
down at working meetings with each other, forcing Bunche to
work separately with each side. He shuttled between the two
delegations, discussing the proposals and delivering the written
responses. After five days, Bunche had had enough. He told the
delegations that he was not there in the capacity of a high-class
messenger boy and asked them, "Can you give a single example
in history of a peace that has been concluded without the two
parties meeting?"[11]

They also confronted more fundamental obstacles. Along
with the normal pressures to bring home a respectable compromise able to withstand domestic opposition were unique con-
straints. To minimize political tensions with the Arab world, the
Egyptian government maintained the public fiction that the
negotiation at Rhodes did not involve direct talks with Israelis
and did not address the broader issue of peace. The Egyptian
leadership also placed itself in the awkward position of having
concealed the army's defeat from the Egyptian public. Outside
of the military and high-level politicians, Egyptians were under
the illusion that their army lay within striking distance of Tel
Aviv and hailed their returning soldiers as triumphant victors.
Thus any concession by Egyptian negotiators, even of territory
they no longer held, would be seen as treason.[12] Israeli interests
were more direct. In exchange for the release of the al-Faluja
division and concessions on territory still held by Egypt in the
Gaza Strip, they hoped to gain legitimacy for their control over
the Negev and greater political stability.

Eytan wrote to Israeli Foreign Minister Sharett on January 16:

> Reuven and I wish to place the following considerations before you and [Prime Minister] Ben-Gurion, though we are sure you are both well aware of them. The fact of signing this armistice with Egypt is in itself of far-reaching importance irrespective of the terms of the agreement. As we now know, Lebanon, Syria and Jordan are willing to sign an armistice if the negotiations with Egypt succeed. . . . A series of such armistice agreements would transform the political situation in the Middle East. They are possible only if the talks with Egypt lead to results. If we here fail, it sets back indefinitely the chances of armistice with all these countries. We consider, therefore, that the signing of an armistice agreement with Egypt in itself transcends in importance this detail or that. We have no hint yet as to what the Egyptians have in mind regarding armistice lines, withdrawal and reduction of forces, etc.[13]

Eytan worried that time was not on Israel's side. "In the changeable Middle East, with Egyptian Prime Ministers liable to be assassinated any day, we should in our interest clinch the matter as soon as we can."[14] He described the Egyptian delegation as "skillful, tenacious and well-briefed."[15]

The first item on the agenda was al-Faluja. Anxiety over the fate of the besieged division there was the principal reason for Egypt's presence at the talks, and the Israelis were well aware of its bargaining value. Bunche wanted the issue resolved early in the discussions in the hope of building momentum by removing this source of tension before moving on to the thornier question of demarcation lines. Bunche composed a plan that allowed the Egyptian division to evacuate under UN supervision, with its heavy equipment held in UN custody until a settlement was in place. The Israelis agreed at once to the unconditional evacuation of the sick and wounded, but they tried to hold half of the rest until the conclusion of an armistice. After prodding from

Bunche, who reminded them of their obligations under UN resolutions, and a hope that the talks would proceed quickly, the Israelis relented and agreed to an evacuation to take place on January 24, one week later. Both sides approved the plan at a formal joint meeting on the evening of January 17.

UN Secretary General Trygve Lie. (*United Nations*)

The quick agreement on al-Faluja generated a sense of optimism, and Bunche and the Israeli and Egyptian delegations predicted the talks would be finished within a week. With the al-Faluja issue ostensibly settled, the negotiators moved on to the meatier issue of boundary lines. "Armistice demarcation lines next—the crucial issue by which we succeed or fail,"[16] Bunche wrote in his diary. Here the negotiators ran aground. Eytan wanted the Egyptians all the way out of Palestine, arguing that armistice lines should be based on the fighting lines as they stood, while the Egyptians demanded the October lines, before UN cease-fire violations. Bunche cabled UN Secretary General Trygve Lie on January 20:

> Egyptians pressing for 4 November resolution and Memorandum of 13 November as basis for lines which would require Israeli withdrawal from Rafah–Bir Asluj area and Egyptian advance. I have informed Egyptians privately that miracles seldom happen. Israelis desire Egyptian-Palestine frontier as basis for lines with special arrangement for Gaza–Rafah coastal strip not involving Israeli occupation. Situation is toughest I have ever faced but no reason for discouragement yet since spirit remains good on both sides and there is no take it or leave it attitude. Israeli delegation becoming sensitive to time factor in view of imminence of election day and criticism in opposition Hebrew press. Egyptians in no hurry.[17]

While "neither side appears aggressive in its position," Bunche wrote, he found little room to maneuver as they stuck "stubbornly but not adamantly to their original positions."[18] Bunche believed he could reconcile Israel's security concerns with Egypt's desire to minimize its loss of territory. He worked to devise compromise formulas, drafting and meeting with the delegations until early each morning. But as the days wore on without movement, hopes began to fade.

Bunche rode both delegations hard. On January 23, he gave Eytan a stern lecture, telling him that in his view the Israelis were making no concessions of consequence while asking the Egyptians to sign a blank check. In his reply, Eytan dropped a bombshell. The evacuation of the al-Faluja division, scheduled to take place the following day, would not be allowed to occur. When they agreed to permit the evacuation on January 24, the Israelis had assumed the talks would be concluded by then. When it was clear that they were nowhere close to agreement, the Israelis began to suspect that Egypt was indifferent to an armistice and was concerned only with the release of its division. Once that happened, they feared, the Egyptians would renew fighting. Eytan blamed Bunche, claiming he had "seduced" them with the prospect of a quick settlement, but the results were disastrous.[19]

Bunche informed the Egyptians, who were "dumbfounded,"[20] while Eytan sent a cable to Tel Aviv warning that "we have more or less succeeded in antagonizing Bunche by what he considers our ungenerous attitude."[21] Bunche reported to Secretary General Lie that the Israeli cancellation of the evacuation had created a "sudden crisis which threatens the complete disruption of the negotiations on the question of good faith."[22]

That night, Bunche told the Egyptians to sleep on it, and sat down to try to salvage the talks. The lynchpin of his strategy having worked itself free, he needed a stopgap to keep the negotiation alive and buy time to find another way to move the two sides forward. The next morning he presented a three-point plan, consisting of (1) a strong and signed cease-fire of indefinite duration, (2) an undertaking by the Israelis to permit food and medical convoys through to al-Faluja exclusively under UN supervision, and (3) adjournment of the discussions for three days until Thursday, January 27, to allow some of the delegates to go home and consult with their governments. With minor changes, the proposal was accepted. [23]

The talks were saved, but barely. After two weeks of nonstop negotiating, the only tangible results were a reiteration of the cease-fire already in effect and a convoy of twenty-five tons of food and medical supplies for al-Faluja. Both sides remained as far apart as ever. While the parties adjourned to confer with their governments and reconsider their positions, Bunche continued working. "Spent the evening working on a draft agreement," he recorded, "but I doubt it will ever come near being signed."[24]

Bunche unwound by playing billiards, which he loved. "I never once saw him lose his temper," his secretary, Doreen Daughton, said later. "Whenever things got bad he simply took a few minutes off and went down and played billiards. Then he came back and got to work again."[25] Shabtai Rosenne offered a similar description:

> My most vivid recollection of this physically huge man—handsome and attractive in his own way, a soupcon of a smile on his lips, a bubbling sense of humor that never seemed to leave him, a healthy touch of cynicism—is with a half-smoked cigarette dangling from his lips, after dinner bent over the billiard table in the games room of the Hotel des Roses, vigorously playing a form of three-sided snooker with teams from the UN, Egypt, and Israel (possibly carefully choosing the winner for that night or at least ensuring that it would not be the UN). There were drinks around the table and the atmosphere became relaxed and human. At around 10 P.M. he would call a halt and summon

members of one delegation or of both to meet in his room, where he would patiently, firmly, and sometimes roughly give his analysis or hear reports from the delegations, probe reactions to this or that suggestion, first from one side and then from the other.[26]

Billiards also served a more subtle purpose. "Those games of snooker," Rosenne continued, "were, I often think, one of the keys to Bunche's success. Certainly they were the catalyst. They broke the ice. They showed us that the Egyptians were human like us, with similar emotions of pleasure when they were winning and of dismay when they were losing—Bunche insisted all the time on true sportsmanship in these games—and I hope and believe that the Egyptians observed the same human qualities in us."[27]

The talks resumed with the return of the delegates on January 27, but there was no movement. Bunche called for greater flexibility from both parties, and urged magnanimity from the Israelis. In his discussions with Eytan, Bunche appealed for "generosity toward what was at this stage, a beaten foe. . . . There was a real opportunity for great statesmanship on the part of Israel which in his purely personal view would pay handsome dividends in the future."[28] Eytan, while recognizing Egypt's need to "get out of Palestine . . . without dishonor," believed that rescuing the Egyptian government from its dilemma had "nothing to do with the armistice and was no concern of ours." Sharett wrote Bunche more directly that "the Egyptians are paying for their criminal invasion and its failure, and the Egyptian government must not expect Israeli assistance if it lacks the courage to admit its failure to the Egyptian people."[29]

Bunche wrote his wife Ruth, "There is a cat and mouse game going on here between each of them [Egyptians and Israelis] and me—they would be happy if I would terminate the negotiations and thus relieve them of any responsibility. But I am not going to take that rap. . . . It's like having a bear by the tail and being afraid to let go."[30]

The delegations were locked in an impasse. Neither side would change course, but neither wanted to take responsibility for terminating the negotiation. "Look," Bunche finally told an Arab delegate, "you or the Israelis will have to break off the negotiations—and take responsibility! As the U.N.'s representative, I am your servant, and I will stay out here as long as one or both of you stay. I'll remain ten years if necessary." "Ah," the Arab said, smiling. "Well, why not? What's the hurry?"[31] Bunche cabled Lie, "Following separate talks with each delegation conclusion is inescapable that prospects for an armistice are virtually nil. Each delegation is adamant on its position. Have exerted every possible effort to induce concessions from each side but to no avail."[32] Lie encouraged Bunche to "keep going and smiling,"[33] and U.S. Assistant Secretary of State Dean Rusk sent him a cable urging him to hold his course: "We have been much encouraged by your masterly direction of the Rhodes talks, and even though auspices may not now seem bright, we do hope you will stick by the job until it is finished. While fully conversant with your desire to return, we feel that no one but yourself should shepherd these delicate negotiations at this time."[34]

"Bunche was tough," Rosenne wrote. "He could be harsh; he cajoled, he threatened, and he charmed. If he twisted your arm, it hurt, and was meant to. But he was fair and open to argument and persuasion and to me was the incarnation of belief in the UN—not the United Nations as viewed through the rose-tinted spectacles of a wishy-washy ideology but the UN as a necessity for the preservation of mankind in the nuclear age. From perhaps an opposing point of departure I personally could meet him halfway, and I regard him as one of the greatest men I have ever had the honor to meet and to work with, and against."[35]

Bunche stepped up the pace. His efforts were going nowhere and he knew that he needed a more drastic approach. He understood that for all their bluff, the one thing that the negotiators feared more than making concessions was blame for scuttling the conference. On Sunday, January 30, Bunche threw down the gauntlet. He called in each delegation and told them he was increasing the pressure and his schedule called for agreement by Tuesday or disagreement by Wednesday. He promised them a meaty draft first thing the next morning.

Bunche composed a new proposal that put both sides on the spot by putting forward compromise formulas that were below their minimum demands on crucial points but reasonable enough that they could not be refused without embarrassment. The draft articulated the outline of the armistice agreement, stipulated the eventual release of Egyptian troops at al-Faluja, and made specific recommendations on demarcation lines and the reduction and balance of forces located near the border. He figured that neither side would like the proposal but they would find it difficult to reject. "With this agreement," he wrote, "both parties are trapped."[36]

The Egyptians took the draft back to Cairo for consultations with their government. With the Egyptians briefly gone, the Israelis shared their reservations with Bunche. They felt it set a floor below which the Egyptians would not go, whereas otherwise they might go all the way to accepting the Israeli position.[37] The Israelis particularly objected to a provision Bunche included as a concession to Egyptian demands that demilitarized the southern town of El Auja, which lay at the Egyptian border along a strategic road and which Israel had captured at the close of the conflict. Reuven Shiloah, speaking for the Israelis, told Bunche that the agreement would "cause trouble," and Bunche answered that "we already had plenty of trouble and a little more wouldn't hurt."[38]

Bunche wrote to Eytan:

> I recognize fully that in certain important respects this draft falls below the minimum demands of each delegation. . . . But

though positions are sacrificed on both sides, I am certain that no vital national interests on either side would be seriously jeopardized by an armistice agreement somewhat along these lines. My whole effort has been directed at trying to find some approach which could at once be considered moderately reasonable and fair while doing no gross injustice to the positions of the parties. . . . I honestly feel that the world would find it difficult to believe that two parties seeking peace could not discover it somewhere along the road thus outlined. I am sure the world will be seriously disturbed if agreement is not found, either along this road or some other. . . . Nothing could be clearer from these negotiations thus far than the fact that if peace is to be sought after, some sacrifices of significance must be made by those who seek it.[39]

On January 31, Eytan wrote Sharett that he worried that their unyielding position might lead to the failure of the negotiation, and the blame would fall on Israel. He thought the Egyptians wanted an armistice, but if Israeli conditions remained stiff they might be satisfied with the cease-fire agreement already signed, quit Rhodes, and take their case to the Security Council. He asked Sharett to find out the extent of the government's willingness to accept responsibility for failure of the talks and if the cabinet fully recognized the consequences to relations with the United States and the Security Council.

Outside of Rhodes, Bunche set larger forces in motion during the Egyptians' absence. The threat of UN Security Council sanctions invariably lay beneath Bunche's discussions, and as the talks dragged on this danger began to sink in with the Israeli delegation. Israel worried that if the matter went to the Security Council, it might well impose a harsher solution than what the Egyptians offered. Bunche maintained direct channels with the American and British governments that he used to bring pressure on the Israeli and Egyptian leadership over the heads of the delegations, which often resulted in fresh directions to the negotiators at Rhodes from their cabinets back home. President Harry Truman sent word to Bunche of his willingness to exert pressure where and when it would be helpful. This was one of those moments, and Bunche hoped British and American support for his draft proposal would help turn the corner for the two sides.[40]

Seif El Dine struggled to get the draft accepted in Cairo. The Egyptian military wanted an end to its troubles, but the politicians still preferred tough talk. With the support of the delegation and pressure from the Americans, the government finally went along. The Egyptians returned early on the morning of February 3. For once, Bunche felt, the Egyptians had shown clever tactics—they accepted the compromise draft with only minor modifications. In doing so, they put the Israelis on the spot.[41] The immediate Israeli response was subdued. Eytan told Bunche laconically that Egyptian thinking was "a puzzle" to him. But beyond the grumbling, the Egyptian acceptance brought new life to the negotiation and marked a turning point in the conference.[42]

Bunche called an informal joint meeting the next day, February 4. They made some progress, and prospects picked up. Bunche cabled Secretary General Lie, "Israelis have made no concessions of consequence since the compromise draft was circulated while Egyptians made very substantial concessions in accepting that draft. In view of all of us here provision for El Auja in compromise draft would afford fully adequate protection to security interests of both sides."[43] Seif El Dine suggested a meeting of the two military leaders to discuss specifics on the demarcation lines. "This gave things a shot in the arm and was quickly accepted," Bunche wrote.[44]

Because of the delicacy of the situation, Bunche took an incremental approach, breaking the issues into small, practical questions that both sides could address without involving matters of principle. Bunche, Eytan later noted, "took a realistic view of the situation throughout. He probably had fewer illusions than any of us. He not only preached the doctrine of 'one thing at a time,' but he practiced it."[45] A large number of issues had to be covered, and Bunche separated them into individual items. They included al-Faluja; demarcation lines along almost a thousand square miles of desert; provision for the withdrawal of over a hundred thousand troops; the status of dozens of towns in Israel, Gaza, and the Negev; and numerous derivative issues. He took each item to the delegations for talks—on the agenda for discussing the item. Then he would bring the two sides together to sign an agreement formally approving the agenda. Once they agreed on the agenda, they would then meet to discuss the item itself.[46] "There was a double purpose in this," Bunche explained:

> Primarily it was to get both sides to meet—but also, I wanted them both to get accustomed to taking formal action, and to signing something. That way, I figured, the next step might not be so difficult. . . .
>
> Whenever they got together, you'd always find that there was still a gap between them. It was always a matter of timing, always a matter of finding out when it would be appropriate to reduce a discussion to a formal, written draft of one point. We never would throw a whole draft at them at the beginning—that would've scared them to death. Finally, after we had gone pretty far along, we'd give them the first draft of a complete agreement [on that point.] That had to be modified over and over. It was just that you had to talk everything out with them beforehand, separately and together—a matter of their going back to consult with their governments, of compromises and more compromises.[47]

The atmosphere was so tense that according to Bunche, "every time you blew your nose you'd offend someone. There was a crisis every day."[48] The negotiators worked every angle to gain advantage. They employed "all kinds of ruses—guile, promises, wheedling, threats, suggestions that they were leaving Rhodes" in an attempt to win concessions from the other side.[49]

Bunche used creative language to bypass differences. "When the parties failed to agree," an Israeli delegate wrote, "he could draft a formula so that each could interpret it in his own way. When I questioned him on this approach, he said the basic aim at the time was to bring an end to the fighting. Later, when the parties would discover that on certain items they did not get what they expected, they would not renew the war on that account, but the realities of life would shape the appropriate arrangements."[50] Bunche also made time an ally, drawing out meetings with both sides until three or four in the morning, when fatigue would compel the weary representatives to concede agreement on a subpoint and sign to it.[51] One session lasted twenty hours: beginning at ten in the morning, without stopping for meals ("He lived on orange juice," Daughton said) or leaving his sitting room, he alternated between delegations until they came to an agreement on the point in contention at six the following morning.[52] His persistence won the delegates' respect. "Dr. Bunche," Eytan said, "never lost sight of the immediate goal, which, limited as it was, long seemed remote and perhaps unattainable. At the same time, he understood that the armistice was an essential step in the transition from truce to peace."[53] Another Israeli delegate wrote that "it was difficult not to be impressed by Dr. Bunche's handling of the sessions. . . . He spoke little and listened to others with intense concentration. It seemed as though he was trying not only to hear what was being said but also to penetrate the mind of the speaker to discover what lay behind his words."[54]

The heavy negotiating paid off, and the differences between the Egyptians and Israelis began to narrow. A remaining point of contention was the status of Beersheba, a large town in the center of the Negev halfway between Jerusalem and Egypt, captured by the Egyptian army in the early days of the war but retaken by the Israelis in October. A large Israeli force there would pose a continuing threat to the Gaza Strip and the Egyptian border, so the Egyptians asked to make Beersheba a demilitarized area. Egypt also insisted on an Egyptian civil administrator for Beersheba, a town whose strategic crossroads made it the key to the Negev.

Eytan resisted the demilitarization of Beersheba. The Israelis felt they needed a garrison there because they feared the presence of other Arab troops in the eastern Negev and British troops at nearby Aqaba. Also, by this point both the Israelis and Egyptians were negotiating with an eye to Israel's subsequent armistice talks with the other Arab states, and the Israelis worried that their concessions would be seen as weakness and make things more difficult for them in future discussions. Egypt, in rivalry with King Abdullah of Jordan for stature in the Arab world, sought to reduce his chances of gaining access to the Negev, which Jordan also claimed.

Bunche cabled the secretary general on February 5, "Egyptians announced at morning meeting they were prepared to sign the compromise draft today."[55] The next day he reported, "Israeli position unchanged. I had a long heart to heart talk with Eytan today and handed him a personal letter giving my full appraisal of situation. Egyptians conciliatory but are strongly resisting any further major concessions in absence of any concessions by Israelis."[56]

On February 7, Eytan wrote Sharett:

> The threat of Security Council action has of course lurked behind Bunche's conversations with us ever since we came here, but it has never come out so clearly before. The basic question which the Government has to ask itself is whether it is prepared to face the Security Council on these issues. I take it from your cable to Bunche that the answer is in the affirmative, though I do not for the life of me know what the Government would do if the Security Council, egged on by Bunche and fed up with our

failure to comply with orders, took a really strong line to force us to withdraw from Auja, return to November 13th lines, etc.— or be branded as violators of the truce and mockers of the U.N., with all that this would mean in respect of our chances of becoming members of that organization in the near future. For all the strength of our military case—and it is this of course that we have been pressing all along—we should have a very sticky time attempting to justify ourselves in terms of the international order as represented by Security Council decisions. . . . I am beginning to feel that unless there is some move on our part, the scene will soon shift from Rhodes to [the United Nations].[57]

Eytan believed that the Egyptians were certain that Israel would not resume fighting and that Egypt would be able to achieve its objectives with regard to Faluja and El Auja through the Security Council even if there was no agreement. The Israelis also knew that failure of the Egyptian negotiation would preclude agreements with other Arab states. The Israeli delegation cabled Tel Aviv that Israel must make substantial concessions if it wanted an agreement, since "all concessions made up to now are not really concessions, but rather retreats from exaggerated demands."[58]

Bunche sent a telegram to Lie asking him to speak with the British about removing their forces from Aqaba to relieve the pressure on Beersheba. Meanwhile, at Bunche's request, Truman ordered Secretary of State Dean Acheson to send a message to Prime Minister Ben-Gurion encouraging Israel to support the compromise proposal.[59] Bunche and his chief of staff and military adviser, Marine Corps General William Riley, held a long meeting with Eytan and Colonel Yadin. Bunche suspected that Yadin, who was "obviously holding up the agreement," really wanted a surrender. Bunche lectured him about impatience in negotiation and told him that the real test of the potential greatness of both a nation and a military leader was the ability to accept victory gracefully.[60]

The Egyptians introduced a new and unusual request. In addition to the demilitarization of Beersheba, they asked for a token Egyptian military governor there, in order to keep up appearances with the Egyptian public. After considerable argument, the Israelis persuaded the Egyptians that this request was absurd. The Egyptians then fell back on an alternative demand. A tiny village named Bir Asluj lay between Beersheba and the Egyptian border. As it was small and without strategic value, the Egyptians hoped the Israelis might allow them the fig leaf of an Egyptian military governor there. The thought of a military governor presiding over Bir Asluj, a gathering of mud huts along the road running from Beersheba to El Auja and Egypt, was surreal, but creation of the position "Military Governor of Bir Asluj" might have made for imposing headlines in Egypt and helped save face for the Egyptian government. "We talked them out of this," Eytan recalled, "mainly by ridicule."[61]

The Egyptians finally suggested a military governor at El Auja, nearer the Egyptian border. Eytan rejected this as well, insisting that Israel could not agree to an Egyptian military governor anywhere on territory it controlled. Bunche understood the Israeli reluctance, but he also felt that the Egyptian need to save face was genuine. He proposed instead that Israel refrain from keeping troops in El Auja, and that both this and a similar assurance from Egypt be included in the final agreement. The Israelis reluctantly agreed to consider the idea.

Bunche continued to draft potential compromises. He reported to the secretary general on February 10, "Negotiations proceeding with tortuous but steady progress toward agreement. Daily discussions and compromise drafts producing results, but continued pressure from all sources remains indispensable."[62] Sasson cabled Sharett on February 10 that he felt Egyptian statements threatening to terminate the negotiation over Beersheba were sincere and that they will regret the failure of the talks but are willing to return home empty-handed if necessary. Eytan reported to Sharett on February 10:

> I can see no way out of the impasse in the near future, except if our Government were prepared to make generous concessions, which I see it is not. I have been sitting in this place now for a month, and for all its scenic charm I am not at all sure that if I continue to reside here much longer I shall really be doing the most useful job of which I am capable. In the absence of concessions by us, I can see only two choices before us: either to break off (or "adjourn") the talks, or to leave here a purely nominal delegation, to sit in Rhodes and listen to anything new the Egyptians may have to say next week or next month or next year. . . . [T]he choice is really only between making further concessions or breaking off the talks. As we shall soon be forced by the Security Council to make these concessions anyway (and more), I am naturally in favor of making the concessions now and securing in return an armistice agreement and a good name at the U.N.[63]

When the discussions on Beersheba appeared stalemated, Bunche called both delegations to his room. He opened a chest of drawers to reveal two sets of beautiful decorated ceramic plates with the inscription: "Rhodes Armistice Talks 1949." "Have a look at these lovely plates!" Bunche told them. "If you reach agreement, each of you will get one to take home. If you don't, I'll break them over your heads!"[64]

On February 11, the British government gave an assurance to the United Nations that its force in Aqaba would never be used for offensive purposes, relieving pressure on the Israeli position. Bunche reported to Lie two days later, "Situation improved afternoon thirteenth when Israelis relaxed their position on El Auja and informed me they would withdraw their troops from El Auja and vicinity."[65]

Once the negotiation began to move slowly forward, especially on boundary lines, a handful of representatives from each side discreetly began direct talks. These one-on-one meetings—facilitated by an Egyptian on Bunche's staff and involving Egyptian political adviser Abdul Mustafa (whom the Israelis considered the "real boss of the Egyptian delegation"), Colonel Yadin, and Sasson—gave the Israelis the impression that the Egyptians were becoming more flexible. Sasson suggested the two delegations meet without UN oversight, "in order to remove the contradictions between us in a direct manner and in a friendly atmosphere."[66]

Eytan introduced fresh compromises authorized by Tel Aviv over the demilitarized zone in El Auja and positions elsewhere in the Negev, and the delegations became optimistic that an agreement was within reach. On February 16, Bunche cabled the secretary general that with the other issues either settled or on their way to solution, the remaining stumbling block to agreement appeared to be the demilitarization of Beersheba, which the Egyptians still pressed for and the Israelis still refused.

"The matter of Auja has been as good as settled, and this has transformed the whole atmosphere," Eytan wrote Sharett on February 16. "There now remains only the specific problem of what outposts we shall hold along the Gaza-Rafah front, and the more general question of Beersheba and the Eastern sector. We have used every device to make it clear to all concerned that Beersheba and the eastern sector cannot be touched by an agreement with Egypt and that we can agree to no diminution of our full rights and freedom there. I stated this emphatically to Bunche last night, Elias Sasson as emphatically to the Egyptians this morning, and for good measure Yadin rubbed it into Bunche again this afternoon."[67] Eytan cabled Sharett the following day, "Today has been devoted almost exclusively to Beersheba, for which the Egyptians are putting up a last-minute fight. . . . Incidentally, one of us asked Bunche yesterday evening: 'The Egyptians seem to be getting all the benefits from this agreement. What are *we* getting out of it?' Bunche replied without hesitation: 'the Negev.' I hope he is right. It will have made all these six weeks of trouble and endless discussion at Rhodes worth while."[68]

The Egyptians insisted the sole reason for their adamant position on an Israeli withdrawal from Beersheba was that such a gesture, which would not affect Israeli military domination of the town, was necessary to win acceptance of the modified agreement by some members of the Egyptian government. Bunche reported to Lie on February 19:

> Israelis stand firm on no withdrawal especially while British forces remain at Aqaba. Israelis fear any withdrawal from Beersheba now would weaken their future claim. It will be a major tragedy if either side prevents agreement on either of these flimsy grounds. Projected procedure is to have a revised draft agreement ready by Sunday with all articles agreed upon, if proves possible, except Article VII which includes Beersheba. An Egyptian representative will fly to Cairo with this draft on Sunday . . . . I can swing everything left but Beersheba. On that it seems I need help critically.[69]

Bunche met the next day with the Egyptian delegates until three in the morning, and worked until eight-thirty on a draft agreement that left out the demilitarization of Beersheba. The Israelis approved it, and although Beersheba remained an obstacle for the Egyptians, they agreed to take a copy with them for consultations with the Egyptian government on Monday. This was the last chance for an agreement. "If unfavorable," Bunche wrote, "negotiations will be adjourned. Our fingers are severely crossed."[70]

Bunche informed Lie that in his view the Israelis were not bluffing and would end the talks rather than concede on Beersheba, and asked the secretary general to intercede directly with the Egyptians. On February 20, Bunche cabled Lie:

> If you consider it advisable Fawzi Bey might be informed that in my view Israelis are not repeat not bluffing on issue of with-

drawal of their forces from Beersheba. If Egyptian delegation after consultations in Cairo Monday return to Rhodes and attempt to renew negotiations on Beersheba Israelis have advised me they will walk out of the conference. . . . This is a thoroughly honorable agreement for the Egyptians and in view of their military position a unique one. They will lose very much if they refuse to sign.[71]

Lie saw Egyptian Foreign Minister Mahmoud Fawzi three times in as many days to press the case. At Bunche's request, Lie explained that the Israelis were not bluffing over Beersheba and reminded Fawzi that the armistice agreement would accomplish for the Egyptians what the Security Council had been unable to do since November 4, 1948. "In view of the disastrous Egyptian military position, this was a unique opportunity and a thoroughly honorable agreement."[72]

On Wednesday, February 23, the Egyptians returned. They conceded Beersheba. They would sign the agreement. Yadin thanked Bunche for his efforts, noting that "patience pays."[73] The signing took place at a solemn ceremony on February 24, 1949, in the winter dining room of the Hotel des Roses. The delegations sat on either side of Bunche, around a large square table decorated with a simple white tablecloth and fresh flowers. As the five signature copies were being signed, Bunche looked over at General Riley, whose eyes were filled with tears. "It was the greatest moment of my life," Riley later told Bunche. "The first time I had helped to make peace, instead of war."[74]

That evening they held a party to celebrate the achievement, and relaxed and dined on food flown in by the Egyptians from the renowned Groppi's pastry shop in Cairo. Eytan sat with Seif El Dine, who showed him pictures of his family. Eytan observed:

It was an atmosphere as different as one could imagine from that of the first day in the corridor, with its averted heads. . . . In the course of the six weeks we spent together at the Hotel des Roses, we became quite friendly with the Egyptians. Their earli-

The signing of the armistice agreement. (*United Nations/Department of Special Collections, UCLA Library*)

er attitude may have been due to insecurity, or to shyness; I am certain it was not caused by any deep-seated hostility. . . . We felt that night, and I am fairly sure the Egyptians did too, that we had not only brought the fighting phase to a formal end, but had laid the foundations, if not of love and affection, at least of normal relations between our two countries.[75]

The armistice allotted about 135 square miles of the contested land to Egypt, while making roughly 100 square miles neutral territory and giving the remainder to Israel. The division at al-Faluja was successfully evacuated, and its deputy commander, Gamal Nasser, would later become president of Egypt. Until the Camp David Accords almost thirty years later, the armistice remained the most significant, and perhaps the only meaningful, diplomatic achievement in the Middle East.

The armistice was enthusiastically received in Israel, where the news dominated the press. Prime Minister Ben-Gurion called it "an historic triumph, no less than the military victories."[76] The reception was more muted in Cairo, as the government faced the challenging prospect of selling it to a surprised public. Prime Minister Ibrahim Abdel-Hadi issued a short statement stressing that the armistice had "no political character," dealt only with "purely military questions," and did not "in any way affect the political future of Palestine." Government censors prohibited the Egyptian press from printing copies of the agreement, concerned over the possibility of a "violent reaction," which never occurred.[77]

As expected, negotiation with Israel's other Arab neighbors went comparatively smoothly, although Bunche had by that time returned to New York. Israel signed armistice agreements with Lebanon on March 23, Jordan on April 3, and Syria on July 20.

After completing his term as director general of Israel's Foreign Ministry, Walter Eytan became Israel's ambassador to Paris in the 1960s. From 1970 until his retirement in 1978, he was chairman of

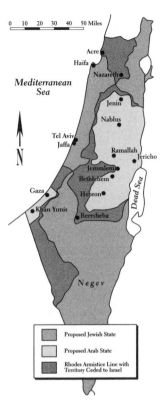

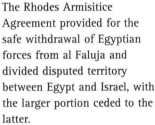

The Rhodes Armisitice Agreement provided for the safe withdrawal of Egyptian forces from al Faluja and divided disputed territory between Egypt and Israel, with the larger portion ceded to the latter.

the Israeli Broadcasting Authority. Yigael Yadin retired from the Israeli army in 1952 to study archeology at the University of Jerusalem, where he earned his PhD in 1955. He became a noted archeologist, leading prominent digs in Hazor, Masada, and Megiddo, and was one of the principal translators of the Dead Sea Scrolls. In 1970 he became head of the Institute of

Archeology at the Hebrew University, before returning briefly to politics as Israel's deputy prime minister from 1977 to 1981. Reuven Shiloah became the founder and first director of the Mossad, Israel's secret intelligence service. Yitzhak Rabin, who left the negotiation before it was concluded in protest over Israeli concessions, became Israel's prime minister and was awarded the Nobel Peace Prize in 1994 for his leading role in negotiation on the Palestinian issue. He was assassinated in 1995 for his attempts to establish peace in the region. Abdul Mustafa became the assistant secretary general of the Arab League and was a foreign policy adviser to the king of Saudi Arabia. In 1952, King Farouk of Egypt appointed Colonel Sherine as his minister of war. Objections to Sherine's lack of qualifications for the position by Egyptian army officers, already resentful of high-level corruption and the embarrassment of Egyptian defeats in the 1948 war, precipitated a coup that overthrew the monarchy and installed a military dictatorship.

For his efforts at Rhodes, Ralph Bunche received the Nobel Peace Prize in 1950, over other nominees that included Sir Winston Churchill and George Marshall. He was the first black American, and the youngest person ever, to receive the award. He initially turned it down, explaining in a letter to the Nobel Prize Committee, "You don't work in the [UN] Secretariat to win prizes," but relented when Secretary General Lie ordered him to accept it. Bunche, who would also be awarded the Presidential Medal of Freedom, sixty-nine honorary doctorates, and countless other honors, chose to remain at the United Nations where he became under-secretary general for special political affairs.[78] His fame was not universal, though. During one of many press interviews, a journalist noticed Bunche's five-year-old son playing in Bunche's office. The reporter asked the child if he knew what his father did. "Yes, of course," he replied. "He's a U.N. radiator."[79]

Bunche continued his work with civil rights in the United States, joining with his friend Martin Luther King Jr. in the 1963 March on Washington and again in Selma in 1965. Harvard University offered him a full professorship, and President Kennedy asked him to become his secretary of state, but Bunche remained at the United Nations until his death in 1971. When asked how he had managed through the successful negotiation, Bunche replied:

> Like every Negro in America, I've been buffeted about a great deal. I've suffered many disillusioning experiences. Inevitably, I've become allergic to prejudice. On the other hand, from my earliest years I was taught the virtues of tolerance; militancy in fighting for rights—but not bitterness. And as a social scientist I've always cultivated a coolness of temper, an attitude of objectivity when dealing with human sensitivities and irrationalities, which has always proved invaluable—never more so than in the Palestine negotiations. Success there was dependent upon maintaining complete objectivity. Throughout the endless weeks of negotiations I was bolstered by an unfailing sense of optimism. Somehow, I knew we had to succeed.[80]

A declassified map of the potential range of nuclear missiles launched from Cuba. (*National Archives*)

Chapter 7

The Cuban Missile Crisis

1962

T HE seeds of the Cuban Missile Crisis were planted on New Year's Day 1959, when an insurrection led by Fidel Castro replaced General Fulgencio Batista's dictatorship with a Marxist government that turned Cuba into a client of the Soviet Union. The United States, alarmed by the establishment of a communist beachhead in the Western Hemisphere just ninety miles from the Florida coast, tried to destabilize the Castro regime, and in April 1961 landed twelve hundred armed Cuban exiles on the Bay of Pigs in a failed attempt to spark an uprising. Nearly all were killed or taken prisoner.

Soviet Premier Nikita Khrushchev worried that sooner or later the United States would try again with better luck and preparation, and spent the next thirteen months searching for a way to protect his new and vulnerable Caribbean ally. While vacationing in Bulgaria in May 1962, he conceived an idea that with a single stroke could eliminate the possibility of future U.S.-backed invasions of Cuba and nearly double the Soviet offensive nuclear-strike capability against the United States. "Why not," Khrushchev asked, "throw a hedgehog at Uncle Sam's pants?"[1] By placing Soviet missiles on the island, he could bypass the Soviet Union's seventeen-to-one inferiority in strategic nuclear forces and reduce the warning time for incoming missiles from twenty minutes to less than three. "My thinking," Khrushchev explained, "went like this: if we installed the missiles secretly and then if the United States discovered the missiles were there after they were already poised and ready to strike, the Americans would think twice before trying to liquidate our installations by military means. I knew that the United States could knock out some of our installations, but not all of them. If a quarter or even a tenth of our missiles [in Cuba] survived—even if only one or two big ones were left—we could still hit New York, and there wouldn't be much of New York left."[2]

With Castro's consent, the operation, code-named Anadyr, began that summer. Over the course of five months, more than eighty ships, the entire sealift capacity of the Soviet Union, secretly transported forty-two medium-range missiles, forty-two long-range bombers, one hundred sixty-four nuclear warheads and fifty thousand troops, advisers, and engineers, along with fighter aircraft, surface-to-air missiles (SAMs), and support vehicles and equipment across the Atlantic.

Everything went according to Khrushchev's plan until an American U-2 spy plane returned on October 14 from a routine flight over western Cuba with photographs clearly revealing the outline of a nearly completed missile launch site. National Security Adviser McGeorge Bundy informed President John F. Kennedy of the discovery over breakfast on October 16, and the president immediately assembled an ad hoc crisis-management team. Known as the Executive Committee of the National Security Council, or ExComm, the group's fourteen members included the national security adviser, secretaries of state and defense, director of central intelligence, attorney general (The president's younger brother Robert), and a handful of other senior officials whose judgment and intellect the president respected. "In the Executive Committee," wrote presidential adviser Arthur Schlesinger, "consideration was free, intent and contin-

A U-2 survelliance photo of Los Palacios, Cuba, showing a Russian missile establishment. (*National Archives*)

uous. Discussion ranged widely, as it had to in a situation of such exceptional urgency, novelty and difficulty. . . . Every alternative was laid on the table for examination, from living with the missiles to taking them out with surprise attack, from making the issue with Castro to making it with Khrushchev. In effect, the members walked around the problem, inspecting it first from this angle, then from that, viewing it in a variety of perspectives."[3]

They winnowed their choices down to three: air strike, invasion, or blockade. An air strike had the advantage of a focused response, but as Khrushchev had predicted, with the targeting technology at the time, the Air Force could only be sure of destroying sixty to ninety percent of the missiles. The military preferred an air strike followed by an invasion, which would eliminate the threat and rid Cuba of Castro for good. But the situation was too volatile for such an escalation, and Kennedy wanted to give the Soviets a chance to back down before taking irrevocable action. A blockade leveraging the overwhelming American naval superiority in the region offered a graduated response and preserved American flexibility. "The blockade," Bundy explained, "would not remove the missiles; it would not prevent the Russians from completing their installations if they had all the necessary materials at hand, and while the evidence was incomplete, no one could assume they did not. A blockade might produce a deeply embarrassing counterblockade, most obviously in Berlin, and it might require deadly force in its application. But it did not begin with sudden death, and it was a first step, not a last."[4]

Kennedy and his advisers prepared for the worst. The president deployed three hundred Navy warships to the Caribbean and South Atlantic in preparation for the blockade; mobilized one hundred eighty thousand troops for a possible invasion of Cuba, the largest invasion force assembled since D-Day; and ordered U.S. missile forces to be ready to launch a full-scale nuclear strike within several minutes' notice. He ordered emergency supplies of food, water, and medicine sent to nuclear fallout shelters nationwide and prepared a speech to the nation for the evening of Monday, October 22, announcing the discovery of the missiles and his decision to impose a blockade of Cuba.

As the nation sat glued to its television screens, the president calmly delivered his speech from his desk in the Oval Office:

> Within the past week, unmistakable evidence has established the fact that a series of offensive missile sites is now in preparation on that imprisoned island. . . . We no longer live in a world where only the actual firing of weapons represents a sufficient challenge to a nation's security to constitute maximum peril. Nuclear weapons are so destructive and ballistic missiles are so swift, that any substantially increased possibility of their use or any sudden change in their deployment may well be regarded as

a definite threat to peace. . . . The 1930s taught us a clear lesson: aggressive conduct, if allowed to grow unchecked and
unchallenged, ultimately leads to war. . . . [O]ur unswerving
objective, therefore, must be to prevent the use of these missiles
against this or any other country, and to secure their withdrawal or elimination from the Western Hemisphere.[5]

The president warned that he had directed the armed forces
to prepare for any eventualities, and that "these actions may
only be the beginning. . . . We will not prematurely or unneces-
sarily risk the costs of worldwide nuclear war," he maintained,
"but neither will we shrink from that risk at any time it must be
faced." Kennedy further declared, "It shall be the policy of this
Nation to regard any nuclear missile launched from Cuba
against any nation in the Western Hemisphere as an attack by
the Soviet Union on the United States, requiring a full retalia-
tory response upon the Soviet Union." He called on Khrushchev
"to abandon this course of world domination, and to join in an
historic effort to end the perilous arms race and transform the
history of man." "This nation," he said, "is prepared to present
its case against the Soviet threat to peace, and our own proposals for a peaceful world, at any time and in any forum—in the
OAS, in the United Nations, or in any other meeting that could
be useful—without limiting our freedom of action." It "was not
the best speech of JFK's presidency," Kennedy speechwriter
Theodore Sorensen wrote, "but it surely was his most important."[6]

The Soviets responded immediately. Following Kennedy's
speech, Khrushchev activated the Soviet Union's strategic missile forces and ordered all Soviet ships bound for Cuba to maintain their course. Khrushchev convened the twelve-man
Presidium, the highest Soviet governing body, in the Kremlin
and told them, "This may end in a big war."[7]

Khrushchev composed a defiant letter to Kennedy, advising
him to "renounce the actions pursued by you, which may lead

to catastrophic consequences for world peace." He characterized Kennedy's actions as "undisguised interference in the internal affairs of the Republic of Cuba, the Soviet Union and other states," and accused the blockade of Cuba of violating the United Nations Charter and international norms of freedom of navigation on the high seas, calling it an "aggressive action" against both Cuba and the Soviet Union. Rejecting Kennedy's argument, he wrote, "And naturally, neither can we recognize the right of the United States to establish control over armaments which are necessary for the Republic of Cuba to strengthen its defense capability. We reaffirm that the armaments which are in Cuba, regardless of the classification to which they may belong, are intended solely for defensive purposes."[8] That night, Khrushchev recalled, "I slept on a couch in my office—and I kept my clothes on. I was ready for alarming news to come any moment, and I wanted to be ready to act immediately."[9]

Kennedy responded with a terse letter to Khrushchev:

Dear Mr. Chairman,
I have received your letter of October twenty-third. I think you will recognize that the steps which started the current chain of events was the action of your Government in secretly furnishing offensive weapons to Cuba. We will be discussing this matter in the Security Council. In the meantime, I am concerned that we both show prudence and do nothing to allow events to make the situation more difficult to control than it already is. I hope that you will issue immediately the necessary instructions to your ships to observe the terms of the quarantine, the basis of which was established by the vote of the Organization of American States this afternoon, and which will go into effect at 1400 hours Greenwich time October twenty-four.[10]

Following Kennedy's announcement, the Americans secured the backing of key allies and neighbors. In his briefing to the ambassadors of member states of the Organization of American States, Secretary of State Dean Rusk told them, "I would not be candid and I would not be fair with you if I did not say that we are in as grave a crisis as mankind has been in."[11] The OAS unanimously approved the quarantine, and its members offered naval ships to assist with the blockade. That night Harlan Cleveland, the assistant secretary of state for international organization affairs, said offhandedly to Rusk, "I'll see you in the morning." A weary, worried Rusk replied, "I hope so."[12]

Soviet Premier Nikita Khrushchev and President John F. Kennedy at their summit in Vienna, Austria, in June 1961. (*Library of Congress*)

The day after the speech, the president initiated regular low-level reconnaissance flights over Cuba and signed the order initiating the quarantine. At the White House, Kennedy and his advisers pondered the Soviets' next move. He had recently read Barbara Tuchman's book *The Guns of August*, which cataloged the errors that led to the start of World War I, and the risk of catastrophe from one side misinterpreting the other's signals haunted him. "We were not going to misjudge," Kennedy said, "or precipitously push our adversaries into a course of action that was not intended or anticipated."[13]

Both sides considered traditional channels inadequate for a situation that required speed, clarity, and candor, so the White House and the Kremlin opened a number of improvised and sometimes unorthodox avenues of communication with each other. At a minimum, each needed information on the other party's thinking, as both governments were flying blind. None of the KGB's four highly placed sources in the U.S. government had access to the deliberations, and several days before, the KGB had arrested Colonel Oleg Penkovsky, the CIA's only highly placed spy in Moscow.

As a trial balloon, Robert Kennedy asked Charles Bartlett—the Pulitzer Prize-winning Washington bureau chief for the Chattanooga Times and an old friend of the Kennedys' who had set John and Jackie up on a blind date—to meet with Georgi Bolshakov. Bolshakov, ostensibly a gregarious reporter for the Soviet news wire agency TASS, was in fact the deputy Soviet military intelligence station chief in Washington, and the Kennedys had used him as a secret conduit with the Kremlin to defuse a crisis over Berlin almost exactly a year before. Bartlett and Bolshakov knew each other through Washington journalism circles, and the two agreed to meet in Bartlett's office at the National Press Club. President Kennedy had sanctioned the meeting, Bartlett told Bolshakov. "He is very angry about what has happened in Cuba," he said. "It reminds him of the Japanese deception before Pearl Harbor." Still, "the President does not want to invade Cuba, he only wants to eliminate the medium-range ballistic missile bases."[14] Bartlett thought there might be a way to solve the problem through the United Nations and wanted to see if the Soviets would be willing to explore that possibility. To facilitate this he proposed the Soviets stop the convoys on their way to Cuba. Bolshakov listened attentively but gave no response. Robert Kennedy asked Bartlett to meet with Bolshakov again later in the day and gave him copies of the missile-site photographs to show the Soviet spymaster as a token of sincerity. As Robert Kennedy had hoped, the meetings alerted Moscow that despite the Americans' anger, the White House was open to the possibility of working with the Soviets to explore a way out of the crisis.

For the first time, the United States raised its nuclear strike forces alert level to DEFCON 2, one step short of all-out war, making a point of sending the message on an uncoded channel so the Soviets would pick it up and understand the seriousness of the American position. Tensions were high everywhere. "This could well be our last conversation," the press officer at the

Soviet mission to the United Nations told an American reporter. "New York will be blown up tomorrow by Soviet nuclear weapons."[15]

That evening at nine-thirty, Robert Kennedy went to see Soviet Ambassador Anatoly Dobrynin in his office on the third floor of the Soviet Embassy. He knew that Dobrynin had direct access to Khrushchev, and the two of them had worked discreetly together before to smooth over differences without involving the diplomatic bureaucracies. The attorney general, visibly tense and agitated, told the ambassador that he had come on his own initiative to communicate how deeply he and his brother felt deceived after accepting Khrushchev and Dobrynin's assurances that the Soviet Union would not place offensive missiles in Cuba, including a pledge relayed by Dobrynin from Khrushchev not to take any provocative actions before the midterm congressional elections. After berating the ambassador, Kennedy turned to leave. He paused at the door before turning to ask, "Can you say what instructions were given the captains of the Soviet ships after the President's speech last night and the signing of the quarantine proclamation today?" Dobrynin answered, "I do know these instructions, they must not submit to any illegal demands on the high seas, as these are in violation of the international norms of free passage." He added that the order, as far as he knew, had not been changed. As they parted, Kennedy said, "I don't know how all this will end, but we intend to stop your ships."[16]

In Moscow, Khrushchev dictated a spirited and unapologetic reply to Kennedy's letter from the previous day:

> In presenting us with these conditions, you, Mr. President, have flung a challenge at us. Who asked you to do this? By what right did you do this? Mr. President, if you coolly weigh the situation which has developed, not giving way to passions, you will understand that the Soviet Union cannot fail to reject the arbitrary demands of the United States. When you confront us

with such conditions, try to put yourself in our place and consider how the United States would react to these conditions. I do not doubt that if someone attempted to dictate similar conditions to you—the United States—you would reject such an attempt. And we also say—no. The Soviet government considers that the violation of the freedom to use international waters and international air space is an act of aggression which pushes mankind toward the abyss of a world nuclear-missile war. Therefore the Soviet government cannot instruct the captains of Soviet vessels bound for Cuba to observe the orders of American naval forces blockading that Island. Our instructions to Soviet mariners are to observe strictly the universally accepted norms of navigation in international waters and not to retreat one step from them. And if the American side violates these rules, it must realize what responsibility will rest upon it in that case. Naturally we will not simply be bystanders with regard to piratical acts by American ships on the high seas. We will then be forced on our part to take the measures we consider necessary and adequate in order to protect our rights. We have everything necessary to do so.[17]

The blockade went into force at 10 o'clock that morning with twenty-five Soviet cargo ships steaming toward the quarantine line. The blockade's military value was minimal, as most of the equipment was already on the island, and although deadly serious, the blockade was principally a diplomatic instrument, an announcement initiating the bargaining over the missiles. The U.S. Navy had orders to fire on any ship trying to cross, and every indication pointed to a Soviet intention to run the blockade. "We were close to war," Khrushchev later wrote, "standing on the very brink of war. Anything could have happened. Whether you wanted it or not, if one side fired, the other would have replied."[18]

In the White House, President Kennedy waited with his senior advisers as the ships approached. "This was the moment we had prepared for, which we hoped would never come," Robert

Kennedy wrote. "The danger and concern that we all felt hung like a cloud over us all. . . . These few minutes were the time of greatest worry by the President. His hand went up to his face & covered his mouth and he closed his fist. His eyes were tense, almost gray, and we just stared at each other across the table. Was the world on the brink of a holocaust and had we done something wrong? Isn't there some way we can avoid having our first exchange be with a Russian submarine—almost anything but that, he said. . . . We had come to the edge of a final decision—& the President agreed. I felt we were on the edge of a precipice and it was as if there were no way off."[19]

As the tension hung in the air, an assistant handed a message to CIA Director John McCone from naval intelligence that twenty of the inbound Soviet ships (presumably those carrying incriminating cargo) had either stopped in the water or reversed direction. Rusk turned to Bundy and said, "We're eyeball to eyeball, and I think the other fellow just blinked."[20]

"Everyone looked like a different person," Robert Kennedy remembered. "For a moment the world had stood still, and now it was going around again."[21] The ships' turnaround brought a pause in the confrontation at sea, but the central problem of the missile bases remained, and as work on them continued, the danger grew as more of the missiles already on the island became operational.

In Moscow, Khrushchev invited American businessman William Knox on short notice to a meeting at the Kremlin, hoping Knox, who was in the Soviet Union on business as president of Westinghouse International, would pass on a message to the American government. In his three-hour meeting with Knox, Khrushchev suggested a summit between Khrushchev and Kennedy to discuss the crisis. Khrushchev resented the "illegal" blockade and repeated several times during the meeting that he might choose to stop some of the Soviet ships or turn them around, but if Kennedy continued the quarantine he might take action against American shipping elsewhere, and "sooner or later," the Soviet premier warned the American businessman, "the Soviet Union would send its submarines to sink the ships enforcing the blockade."[22] Khrushchev for the first time privately conceded the existence of nuclear-armed Soviet ballistic missiles in Cuba. He pressed for a meeting with Kennedy, either in Washington, in Moscow, at sea, or elsewhere. He was interested in avoiding catastrophe, but "if the United States insists on war," he warned, "we'll all meet in Hell."[23]

At the United Nations, Secretary General U Thant called for a two-week pause to arms shipments to Cuba along with a simultaneous suspension of the American quarantine. The proposal, and the Soviet Union's immediate acceptance, put the Americans at a disadvantage. From their viewpoint it equated aggression and response, said nothing about the missiles already in Cuba, permitted work to go forward on the sites, and contained no provisions for verification. Undersecretary of State George Ball said the plan "was anything but helpful. For us to accept the proposal would so relieve Khrushchev of pressure that we would probably never be able to get the missiles out of Cuba."[24] He was right. A frustrated President Kennedy told his advisers, "We cannot permit ourselves to be impaled on a long negotiating hook while the work goes on on these bases."[25]

Kennedy decided that the UN moratorium plan was unacceptable unless the Soviets agreed to certain provisions, which Adlai Stevenson, the U.S. ambassador to the United Nations, submitted to U Thant that afternoon: the USSR would have to suspend all arms shipments, halt construction of the missile bases, and immobilize the missiles within forty-eight hours, subject to independent verification before the United States would lift the quarantine. "The existing threat," President Kennedy wrote in his letter rejecting U Thant's offer, "was created by the secret introduction of offensive weapons into Cuba and the answer lies in the removal of such weapons."[26]

In Moscow, Khrushchev proposed in a letter to philosopher Bertrand Russell a meeting of the two leaders to resolve the crisis. Kennedy and Khrushchev had met in Vienna four months before, and Kennedy, who by his own account had been bested by the Soviet leader at the summit, which he had described as "the roughest thing in my life,"[27] said, "I think it'd be useless."[28] The president realized the suggestion was a ploy by Khrushchev to buy time until the missiles became operational, and was not inclined to fall into the trap.

The first test of the quarantine came on Thursday morning, October 25, as the Soviet ship *Bucharest* neared the quarantine line. President Kennedy wondered, "Are we better off to make this issue come to a head today, or is there some advantage in putting it off till tomorrow?"[29] The Americans thought it was unlikely the ship carried contraband, and Kennedy decided to buy time by letting the ship pass after it responded to a hail by an American naval ship. "We don't want to push him to a precipitous action—give him time to consider," the president said of Khrushchev. "I don't want to put him in a corner from which he cannot escape."[30]

The American efforts seemed to be having little effect, and it sunk in that it would take more than a blockade alone to remove the missiles. "As the exhaustive and exhausting deliberations of that long October week went forward," presidential speechwriter Ted Sorensen wrote, "the limits of time did become more pressing. For all of us knew that, once the missile sites under construction became operational, and capable of responding to any apparent threat or command with a nuclear volley, the President's options would be drastically changed."[31]

Kennedy wrote to Khrushchev on October 25, "I have received your letter of October 24, and I regret very much that you still do not appear to understand what it is that has moved us in this manner." He ignored Khrushchev's offer of a summit and struck a firm tone. He gave a brief and straightforward defense of the American response in light of the deception and false assurances by the Soviet leadership prior to the discovery of the missiles, and concluded, "I ask you to recognize clearly, Mr. Chairman, that it was not I who issued the first challenge in this case, and that in the light of this record these activities in Cuba required the responses I have announced. I repeat my regret that these events should cause a deterioration in our relations. I hope that your Government will take the necessary action to permit a restoration of the earlier situation."[32]

At the United Nations, Stevenson made the American case in a speech that sealed world opinion against the Soviets. Challenging Soviet Ambassador Valerian Zorin in the Security Council, he declared, "Those weapons must be taken out of Cuba. . . . You, the Soviet Union, have sent these weapons to Cuba. You, the Soviet Union, have created this new danger—not the United States." In a dramatic face-off, Stevenson put Zorin on the spot under the glare of live television cameras.

"Do you, Ambassador Zorin, deny that the U.S.S.R. has placed and is placing medium- and intermediate-range missiles and sites in Cuba? Yes or no? Don't wait for the translation, yes or no?"

Zorin responded coldly: "I am not in an American courtroom, sir, and therefore I do not wish to answer a question that is put to me in the fashion in which a prosecutor puts questions. In due course, sir, you will have your answer."

"You are in the courtroom of world opinion right now," Stevenson replied, "and you can answer yes or no. You have denied that they exist, and I want to know whether I have understood you correctly."

Zorin said: "Continue with your statement. You will have your answer in due course."

Stevenson responded: "I am prepared to wait for my answer until hell freezes over, if that's your decision. And I am also prepared to present the evidence in this room."

Adlai Stevenson, U.S. Ambassador to the United Nations, left, and Valerian Zorin, right, Soviet Ambassador to the United Nations. (*Library of Congress*)

Stevenson finished by saying: "We know the facts and so do you, sir, and we are ready to talk about them. Our job here is not to score debating points. Our job, Mr. Zorin, is to save the peace. And if you are ready to try, we are."[33]

Meanwhile Khrushchev gathered the Presidium in Moscow at midday on October 25. He told them he saw no further advantage in continuing to trade "caustic remarks"[34] with Kennedy, as the president did not appear deterred by Khrushchev's threats. On the contrary, the information reaching the Kremlin from each of its channels confirmed the likelihood of an invasion of Cuba within the next several days. "Moscow will have to find another way to protect Fidel Castro,"[35] he told them. He suggested telling Kennedy, "Give us a pledge not to invade Cuba, and we will remove the missiles," [36] assuring his Soviet colleagues "by this we will strengthen Cuba"[37] and ensure its security. The Presidium unanimously supported Khrushchev's course, and Khrushchev, seeking to take the heat off the situation, told them, "Comrades, let's go to the Bolshoi Theater this evening. Our own people as well as foreign eyes will notice, and perhaps it will calm them down."[38] He later conceded, "We were trying to disguise our own anxiety, which was intense."[39]

On Friday morning, October 26, the U.S. Navy successfully stopped and searched its first ship, a Soviet-chartered Panamanian freighter. "We all knew," Undersecretary of State George Ball wrote, "that at some point soon we would have to stop a ship if our blockade were to be credible, so a Panamanian-owned ship, the *Marcula*, under Soviet charter, was chosen as the least provocative."[40] The boarding party encountered no resistance, the ship carried no weapons, and the Americans allowed it to continue on to its destination. The relief they felt was tempered by intelligence reporting that work on the missile sites was accelerating.

That afternoon the KGB station chief in Washington, Alexander Feklisov (known by his codeword "Fomin"), called his friend John Scali, the State Department correspondent for ABC, to meet for lunch. The Soviet agent, who as Julius Rosenberg's handler had stolen the secrets of the atom bomb from the Americans, warned that, "War seems about to break out. Something must be done to save the situation."[41] After Scali reminded him that the Soviets should have thought of that before placing the missiles in Cuba, Feklisov made a suggestion: "What would you think of a proposal whereby we would promise to remove our missiles under United Nations inspection and Khrushchev would promise never to introduce such offensive weapons into Cuba again? Would the President of the United States be willing to promise publicly not to invade Cuba?"[42] Over lunch they formulated a three-part plan to resolve the crisis in which Khrushchev would agree to withdraw the missiles from Cuba under UN auspices, Castro would declare that he agreed never to receive weapons of that kind again, and Kennedy would commit publicly not to invade Cuba. "Why they selected this means of communication," Robert Kennedy wrote, "was not clear, but an unorthodox procedure of this kind was not unusual for the Soviet Union."[43] When Scali returned and reported his meeting to the State Department, Rusk recognized it as a Soviet trial balloon.

The Americans were wary of using Feklisov as a channel, but they were encouraged by the news and decided the chance was worth it. "When you are in contact with the KGB," Rusk noted, "you have to be alert to the question as to whether the KGB is reinforcing the real view of the government in Moscow or whether the KGB is playing a game of some sort."[44] Rusk thought the plan was worthwhile and asked Scali to meet with Feklisov again that evening to bring him an official message. In a brief meeting at the Statler Hotel in Washington, Scali told the Soviet agent that he was authorized to say that there were "real possibilities in this proposal" and that "the representatives of the USSR and the United States in New York can work this matter out with U Thant and with each other,"[45] although time was short. Feklisov reported on the meeting to Moscow immediately after returning to his office that afternoon, but it did not reach the Kremlin until several days later. On the American side, however, word of the meeting caused tremendous excitement and deeply affected American thinking at this critical time.

Prompted by the United States, U Thant made a second, more modest proposal, asking the Soviets to stop their ships moving to Cuba for twenty-four hours "to permit discussion of the modalities of a possible agreement,"[46] and asking Kennedy to issue instructions "to United States vessels to do everything possible to avoid direct confrontation with Soviet ships in the next few days in order to minimize the risk of any untoward incident."[47] Kennedy answered that if the Soviet ships would "stay away from the interception area for the limited time required for preliminary discussion,"[48] U.S. vessels would oblige his request. Khrushchev told U Thant that the Soviets would also agree to his suggestion but warned that their restraint would not last long.

The wearing pace began to show within Kennedy's inner circle. "In one sense," Sorensen wrote, "the urgent pace of those thirteen days helped us all to cope emotionally with the crisis. We were simply too busy to be scared. But I still remember the night when the enormity of the crisis sank in. Looking up at the stars, and remembering the planetarium sky show I had seen several years earlier, I thought about those planets or stars that, at some unknown time in ages past, had been extinguished, blinked out, self-destructed. Were we about to join them?"[49]

With the failure of the blockade to remove the missiles and activity continuing on the bases, pressure rose in the White House to attack Cuba. McGeorge Bundy observed, "The blockade, the hawks insisted, had not worked; it had simply allowed the Soviets time to complete the missile emplacement."[50] The Pentagon pressed for an invasion, and Kennedy's advisers felt a rising need to take active measures to eliminate the threat. The Americans considered three choices: air strike, diplomatic solution, and an intensified blockade. Defense Secretary Robert McNamara wondered aloud, "I don't know what kind of a world we'll live in after we've struck Cuba. How do we stop at that point? I don't know the answer to this."[51]

On Thursday night, Khrushchev confronted a growing number of reports of an imminent American invasion of Cuba and received disturbing news from the Cuban leadership. In a chilling note, Castro urged the Soviet leader to launch a preemptive, full-scale nuclear strike on the United States if the expected invasion of Cuba took place. He reiterated his point in a private conversation with the Soviet ambassador in Havana. The message met with disbelief in the Kremlin. "When this message was read aloud to us," Khrushchev wrote, "we sat there in silence, looking at one another for a long time. It became clear at that point that Fidel absolutely did not understand our intentions."[52] Khrushchev decided the time had come to take action to avoid

The Gearing-class destroyer *Joseph P. Kennedy* (DD-850) intercepting the Panamanian freighter *Marucla* under Soviet charter during the Cuban blockade. (*Naval History and Heritage Command*)

a clash. In a rambling, emotional, twelve-page appeal, he wrote to Kennedy:

> You threaten us with war. But you well know that the very least you would get in response would be what you had given us; you would suffer the same consequences. And that must be clear to us—people invested with authority, trust and responsibility. We must not succumb to light-headedness and petty passions, regardless of whether elections are forthcoming in one country or another. These are all transitory things, but should war indeed break out, it would not be in our power to contain or stop it, for such is the logic of war. I have taken part in two wars, and I know that war ends only when it has rolled through cities and villages, sowing death and destruction everywhere. . . . You may regard us with distrust, but you can at any rate rest assured that we are of sound mind and understand perfectly well that if we launch an offensive against you, you will respond in kind. But you too will get in response whatever you throw at us. And I think you understand that too. . . . If people do not display wisdom, they will eventually reach the point where they will clash, like blind moles, and then mutual annihilation will commence. Let us therefore display statesmanlike

wisdom. I propose: we, for our part, will declare that our ships bound for Cuba are not carrying any armaments. You will declare that the United States will not invade Cuba with its troops and will not support any other forces which might intend to invade Cuba. Then the necessity for the presence of our military specialists in Cuba will be obviated. . . . If you have not lost command of yourself and realize clearly what this could lead to, then, Mr. President, you and I should not now pull on the ends of the rope in which you have tied a knot of war, because the harder you and I pull, the tighter the knot will become. And a time may come when this knot is tied so tight that the person who tied it is no longer capable of untying it, and then the knot will have to be cut. What that would mean I need not explain to you, because you yourself understand perfectly what dread forces our two countries possess. Therefore, if there is no intention of tightening this knot, thereby dooming the world to the catastrophe of thermonuclear war, let us not only relax the forces straining on the ends of the rope, let us take measures for untying this knot.[53]

The message arrived at the State Department Friday evening. Kennedy and his advisers found it encouraging, but wondered whether "the old fellow might be losing his cool in the Kremlin."[54] McNamara thought "it had been dictated by a man who was either drunk or under tremendous stress," but they decided there had been an important change in Khrushchev's position, and the shift brought renewed feelings of optimism. "Considered against the background of the Scali incident," Undersecretary of State George Ball wrote, "the Chairman's letter seemed to be the break in the clouds we had been waiting for."[55] The letter was "long, meandering, full of polemics," Sorensen wrote, "but in essence appearing to contain the germ of a reasonable settlement: inasmuch as his missiles were there only to defend Cuba against invasion, he would withdraw the missiles under UN inspection if the U.S. agreed not to invade. Similar talk came the same day in the UN from Zorin to U Thant and, through a highly informal channel, from Counselor of the Soviet Embassy in Washington Alexander Feklisov to the ABC correspondent covering the State Department, John Scali."[56] Rusk worried that this might be a trap to lead the Americans down "the path of talking, talking indefinitely while the missile sites come into full operation, including those in the intermediate range. And then we are nowhere."[57] They were informed the missiles could now be armed in less than eight hours.

Just as the White House felt a gust of relief, Moscow's attitude stiffened. On Saturday, Khrushchev sent a second, tougher letter to Kennedy, with no mention of his previous letter, that demanded America withdraw its missiles in Turkey as well as pledge not to invade Cuba. "You are disturbed over Cuba," Khrushchev wrote. "You say that this disturbs you because it is 90 miles by sea from the coast of the United States of America. But Turkey adjoins us; our sentries patrol back and forth and see each other. Do you consider, then, that you have the right to demand security for your own country and the removal of the weapons you call offensive, but do not accord the same right to us? You have placed destructive missile weapons, which you call offensive, in Turkey, literally next to us." The Soviet premier then outlined his new offer: "We are willing to remove from Cuba the means which you regard as offensive. We are willing to carry this out and to make this pledge in the United Nations. Your representatives will make a declaration to the effect that the United States, for its part, considering the uneasiness and anxiety of the Soviet State, will remove its analogous means from Turkey. Let us reach agreement as to the period of time needed by you and by us to bring this about. And, after that, persons entrusted by the United Nations Security Council could inspect on the spot the fulfillment of the pledges made."[58]

This sudden change in demands puzzled Kennedy's advisers. The shift in tone and language suggested confusion and possibly an internal struggle within the Soviet leadership. Bundy saw in the Turkish demand "the ordinary Soviet effort to sweeten any agreement by one last haggle,"[59] while Ball wondered whether the Saturday morning letter was "simply a kind of fishing expedition"[60] to see if the Soviets could get more than Khrushchev asked for in his previous letter. Khrushchev's second letter, broadcast in order to shorten communication time, brought a new dimension to the correspondence. The speed of transmission came at a price. Making the letter public marked the end of private negotiation and raised the stakes.

Ball wrote that the situation on Saturday morning "seemed darkly foreboding."[61] Maybe the Soviet leadership had decided the earlier proposal was too much of a setback for them and decided to go back on it? "How can we negotiate," McNamara wondered aloud, "with somebody who changes his deal before we even get a chance to reply and announces publicly the deal before we receive it?"[62] While Rusk thought Khrushchev had sent out the first letter "without clearance,"[63] Bundy, along with most of Kennedy's advisers, believed that Khrushchev was the author of the message on Friday, but felt that the Saturday morning letter was the result of "his own hard-nosed people overruling him . . . they didn't like what he said to you last night." "Nor would I," added Bundy, "if I were a Soviet hard-nose."[64]

President Kennedy said, "Most people will think this is a rather even trade and we ought to take advantage of it."[65] "This is a pretty good play of his," he said admiringly of Khrushchev's move. "Until we can get an agreement on the cessation of work, how can we possibly negotiate with proposals coming as fast as the wires will carry them?"[66]

"And the ships are still moving," Bundy added, "in spite of his assurances to U Thant."[67]

The president worried that Khrushchev would "hang us up in negotiations on different proposals while the work goes on."[68] Kennedy had previously intended to pull the Jupiter missiles out of Turkey and Italy as the fifteen vulnerable, obsolete, liquid-fueled missiles in Turkey were provocative but carried little military value. Their primitive design was based on the German V-2 rocket, and their above-ground firing position and long fueling times (before firing trucks had to pump in six thousand gallons of kerosene-based rocket fuel and twelve thousand gallons of liquid oxygen) made them vulnerable and limited their usefulness. "We are now in a position," Kennedy told his advisers, "of risking war in Cuba and in Berlin over missiles in Turkey which are of little military value. From the political point of view it would be hard to get support on an air strike against Cuba because many would think that we would make a good trade if we offered to take the missiles from Turkey. We are in a bad position if we appear to be attacking Cuba for the purpose of keeping useless missiles in Turkey."[69]

Further news added to the gloom. A Soviet antiaircraft battery shot down a U-2 over Cuba, killing the pilot. Two other reconnaissance planes were shot at over Cuba the same day, convincing Kennedy's advisers that the Soviets had decided to escalate the situation. "There was the realization," Robert Kennedy wrote, "that the Soviet Union and Cuba apparently were preparing to do battle. And there was the feeling that the noose was tightening on all of us, on Americans, on mankind, and that the bridges to escape were crumbling."[70] CIA Director John McCone also reported that work on the missile sites was proceeding day and night. "We were forced to confront the possibility," Bundy wrote, "that the Kremlin, or some part of it, was prepared to charge a price we could not pay, or to force a military test, or even conceivably both."[71]

In fact, Khrushchev was furious. A ground commander had acted in defiance of explicit orders from the Kremlin not to fire on American planes. In an effort to reassert control, he issued an order for his military forces to exercise restraint: "No independent initiatives. Everything is hanging by a thread as it is."[72]

Pressure mounted for military action as the Joint Chiefs of Staff and congressional leaders pressed for an air strike or invasion. After the U-2 pilot was shot down, the Joint Chiefs reiterated to President Kennedy "that they had always felt the blockade to be far too weak a course and that military steps were the only ones the Soviet Union would understand."[73] Preparations were almost complete, and the invasion force waited in Florida. At a minimum, ExComm had resolved firmly earlier that week that if a U-2 were shot down, the United States would retaliate by bombing a SAM site in Cuba, and if a second U-2 were attacked, the Air Force would eliminate all the SAM sites in Cuba.

Scali and Feklisov met again at just after four p.m. "I think it likely," Bundy wrote, "that a Saturday afternoon meeting between Scali and Fomin may have been particularly persuasive to Khrushchev. Scali was shocked by the Saturday proposal for a Turkish swap. He thought he had been made the go-between for a false lead. Rusk sent for him, asked him quietly what had happened, and sent him back to Fomin to see what he could find out."[74] Scali, furious, called the new Soviet demand for a Jupiter missile trade a "stinking double cross" and told Feklisov that a missile swap was and would remain totally unacceptable. "If you think the United States is bluffing," Scali continued, "you are part of the most colossal misjudgment of American intentions in history. We are absolutely determined to get those missiles out of there. An invasion of Cuba is only a matter of hours away." Feklisov insisted repeatedly that his suggestions from Friday "were still valid," and attributed the cause of any mix-up to cable delays. But Scali was unsatisfied, and the two left "on a frosty note."

During the 4 p.m. ExComm meeting, the news arrived in Washington that a U-2 had accidentally strayed into Soviet airspace across the Bering Strait while conducting a high-altitude air-sampling mission. U.S. F-102 fighters armed with nuclear-

An ExComm meeting on October 29,1962. (*National Archives*)

tipped air-to-air missiles scrambled to provide cover. Soviet MiGs sent to intercept were minutes away when the U-2 made it safely to international airspace. President Kennedy quipped calmly, "There is always some son of a bitch who doesn't get the word."[75]

Both sides worried that the situation was moving beyond their ability to contain it, and the events of the previous forty-eight hours led each side to fear the other had lost control of its government. "Our little group seated around the Cabinet table in continuous session that Saturday," Sorensen later wrote, "felt nuclear war to be closer on that day than at any time in the nuclear age."[76]

Sorensen and Robert Kennedy suggested to the president a creative response to Khrushchev's second, disappointing letter. Why not, they wondered, ignore the second letter and respond only to the positive elements in the first? The small chance it would work, the president thought, was worth delaying his response to Khrushchev's second letter for twenty-four hours. "The final draft of his reply," Sorensen wrote, "read into the Chairman's letter everything we wanted."[77]

As the letter was typed up, the Kennedy brothers sat in the oval office. "He talked about the miscalculations that lead to war," Robert Kennedy remembered. "War is rarely intentional. The Russians don't wish to fight any more than we do. They do not want to war with us nor we with them. And yet if events continue as they have in the last several days, that struggle—which no one wishes, which will accomplish nothing—will engulf and destroy all mankind. He wanted to make sure that he had done everything in his power, everything conceivable, to prevent such a catastrophe. Every opportunity was to be given to the Russians to find a peaceful settlement which would not diminish their national security or be a public humiliation."[78]
"If anybody is around to write after this," the president told his brother, "they are going to understand that we made every effort to find peace and every effort to give our adversary room to move. I am not going to push the Russians an inch beyond what is necessary."[79]

Kennedy issued his response to Moscow and released it to the press at eight o'clock that evening. "I have read your letter of October 26 with great care," he wrote, "and welcomed the statement of your desire to seek a prompt solution to the problem. The first thing that needs to be done, however, is for work to cease on offensive missile bases in Cuba and for all weapons systems in Cuba capable of offensive use to be rendered inoperable, under effective United Nations arrangements. Assuming this is done promptly, I have given my representatives in New York instructions that will permit them to work out this week and—in cooperation with the Acting Secretary General and your representative—an arrangement for a permanent solution to the Cuban problem along the lines suggested in your letter of October 26." Kennedy concluded by warning, "The continuation of this threat, or a prolongation of this discussion concerning Cuba by linking these problems to the broader questions of European and world security, would surely lead to an intensification of the Cuban crisis and a grave risk to the peace of the world."[80]

The president didn't expect the ploy to work. "We had not abandoned hope," Robert Kennedy wrote, "but what hope there was now rested with Khrushchev's revising his course within the next few hours. It was a hope, not an expectation. The expectation was a military confrontation by Tuesday and possibly tomorrow."[81] Secretary of Defense McNamara recalled, "I remember leaving the White House at the end of that Saturday. It was a beautiful fall day; and I remember thinking that I might never live to see another Saturday night."[82]

Shortly after the afternoon ExComm meeting, the president gathered Rusk, Bundy, Robert Kennedy, and two or three others to decide what to do next. Time was running out, and preparations were moving ahead for an air strike on Cuba on Monday to be followed by an invasion. Kennedy had signed and released the letter to Khrushchev drafted by his brother and Sorensen. But in light of the new demand, the president questioned whether a pledge not to invade Cuba would be sufficient for the Kremlin. President Kennedy asked his brother to approach Dobrynin in secrecy with an additional offer to help Khrushchev save face within the Kremlin. It was agreed that while a public quid pro quo was out of the question, he could tell Dobrynin that the president was willing to remove the missiles in Turkey once the situation in Cuba had been resolved. The attorney general was instructed not to lead with the offer of a trade, but if it was broached by Dobrynin he was to say that the missiles could be dismantled after four or five months. Bundy wrote:

> The proposal was quickly supported by the rest of us and approved by the President. It was also agreed that knowledge of this assurance would be held among those present and no one else. Concerned as we all were by the [political] cost of a public bargain struck under pressure at the apparent expense of the Turks, and aware as we were from the day's discussion that for

some, even in our closest councils, even this unilateral private assurance might appear to betray an ally, we agreed without hesitation that no one not in the room was to be informed of this additional message.[83]

Robert Kennedy phoned Dobrynin at quarter past seven on Saturday night and asked him to come to his office at the Justice Department. Dobrynin arrived at a quarter to eight. "Robert Kennedy looked exhausted," Dobrynin reported to the Kremlin. "One could see from his eyes that he had not slept for days. He himself said that he had not been home for six days and nights."[84] The president's brother began by telling Dobrynin that the Cuban crisis continued to quickly worsen. The White House knew that work continued on the missile bases. It had also learned in the last two hours that an unarmed American plane was shot down while carrying out a reconnaissance flight over Cuba and that the pilot was killed. The U.S. military was demanding that the president retaliate and respond to fire with fire. "This was an extremely serious turn in events," Robert Kennedy reported telling the Soviet ambassador. "We would have to make certain decisions within the next 12 or possibly 24 hours. There was very little time left. If the Cubans were shooting at our planes, then we were going to shoot back. This could not help but bring on further incidents and he had better understand the full implications of this matter."[85] "I want," he stressed, "to lay out the current alarming situation the way the President sees it. He wants Khrushchev to know this. This is the thrust of the situation now. . . . A real war will begin, in which millions of Americans and Russians will die. We want to avoid that any way we can, and I'm sure that the government of the USSR has the same wish. However, taking time to find a way out is very risky."[86] Within the White House and in the Pentagon were influential parties "itching for a fight."[87] "The president is in a grave situation," Robert Kennedy said, "and does not know how to get out of it. We are under very severe stress. In fact we are under pressure from our military to use force against Cuba. . . . Even though the President himself is very much against starting a war over Cuba, an irreversible chain of events could occur against his will. That is why the President is appealing directly to Chairman Khrushchev for his help in liquidating this conflict."[88]

"The situation," Kennedy said, "might get out of control, with irreversible consequences."[89] "Those missiles," he said, "had to go and they had to go right away. We had to have a commitment by at least tomorrow that those bases would be removed. This was not an ultimatum, but just a statement of fact. He should understand that if they did not remove those bases then we would remove them."[90]

Dobrynin asked what offer they were making. "In this regard," the attorney general replied, "the President considers that a suitable basis for regulating the entire Cuban conflict might be the letter Khrushchev sent on October 26 and the letter in response from the President, which was sent off today to Khrushchev through the U.S. Embassy in Moscow. The most important thing for us," he stressed, "is to get as soon as possible the agreement of the Soviet government to halt further work on the construction of the missile bases in Cuba and take measures under international control that would make it impossible to use these weapons. In exchange the government of the USA is ready, in addition to repealing all measures on the quarantine, to give assurances that there will be no invasion of Cuba."[91] Dobrynin then asked about the missiles in Turkey. "The President doesn't see any insurmountable obstacles in resolving this issue,"[92] Kennedy replied, but any arrangement must never be made public. There could be no quid pro quo, but, he added, if four or five months elapsed, "I am sure these matters could be resolved satisfactorily."[93] He repeated there could be no explicit deal of any kind on Turkey, but he also made it clear to Dobrynin that an understanding was possible, and that provided

Khrushchev removed the missiles in Cuba, and the arrangement was kept secret, the Turkish missiles would disappear after an interlude of several months. If Khrushchev spoke a word of the arrangement to anybody, the arrangement would be null and void. Besides him and his brother, the attorney general said, only two or three people in Washington knew anything about it. The offer came with a veiled threat. There was little time to resolve the situation. Events were developing too quickly, and the president needed a clear answer the next day. The pleas by the president's brother that time was running out was interpreted by the Soviet leadership as meaning that the president was worried he might lose control of the American military, and if Khrushchev did not defuse the crisis quickly, the generals would seize power and act against Cuba on their own. Robert Kennedy's last words, Dobrynin reported, were, "Time will not wait, we must not let it slip away."[94]

After Dobrynin left, the attorney general returned to the White House. The president ordered twenty-four troop transport squadrons of the Air Force Reserve to active duty to prepare to lift invasion forces to Cuba. Bundy compared the evening of the 27th to a tight chess match. The United States had made its move, and it was now up to Khrushchev to make his. Until then, the United States could only hope and wait. "We all agreed in the end," Robert Kennedy later wrote, "that if the Russians were ready to go to nuclear war over Cuba, they were ready to go to nuclear war, and that was that. So we might as well have the showdown then as six months later."[95]

In case his brother's overture to Dobrynin failed, President Kennedy quietly prepared another way out. He asked Rusk to call Andrew Cordier, dean of Columbia University's School of International Affairs and a former deputy secretary general of the United Nations. If it became necessary, Kennedy wanted Cordier to suggest to U Thant that the United Nations publicly call on the Soviet Union to withdraw its missiles from Cuba in exchange for an American withdrawal of the missiles in Turkey.

It would be difficult, Kennedy believed, for the Soviets to refuse such an offer if it were publicly accepted by the United States. Kennedy was ultimately willing to pay the price of a public withdrawal of the Jupiters, but only if it was necessary, and he would need to use U Thant as cover. Kennedy swore those involved in the Cordier backup plan to secrecy to avoid revealing that it originated with the United States.

On Saturday morning, Khrushchev received information from multiple sources that the invasion would be carried out in the next two or three days. "Our intelligence," he wrote, "reported that preparations had been made for an amphibious landing and that invasion was inevitable if we didn't come to an agreement with President Kennedy."[96] He gathered his senior advisers at the Kremlin early Sunday morning Moscow time. They had before them President Kennedy's letter of October 27, containing Kennedy's gambit ignoring the Turkish missile demand. As the nervous Soviet leaders looked at each other, Khrushchev spoke. "There was a time," he told them, "when we advanced, like in October 1917; but in March 1918 we had to retreat, having signed the Brest-Litovsk agreement with the Germans. Our interests dictated this decision—we had to save Soviet power. Now we find ourselves face to face with the danger of war and of nuclear catastrophe, with the possible result of destroying the human race. In order to save the world, we must retreat. I called you together to consult and debate whether you are in agreement with this kind of decision."[97] The meeting was interrupted as Dobrynin's report of his meeting with Robert Kennedy arrived and was read out. They asked the Soviet official who had brought the notes in to read them out loud again. "It goes without saying," Khrushchev recalled, "that the contents of the dispatch increased the nervousness in the hall by some degrees."[98]

"We knew," Khrushchev wrote, "that Kennedy was a young President and that the security of the United States was indeed threatened. For some time we had felt there was a danger that the President would lose control of his military, and now he was admitting this to us himself. Kennedy's message urgently repeated the Americans' demand that we remove the missiles and bombers from Cuba. We could sense from the tone of the message that tension in the United States was indeed rapidly reaching a critical point."[99]

"Comrades," the Soviet premier said, "we have to look for a dignified way out of this conflict. At the same time, of course, we must make sure that we do not compromise Cuba."[100] Khrushchev explained to Andrei Gromyko, his foreign minister, "Comrade Gromyko, we don't have the right to take risks. Once the President announces there will be an invasion, he won't be able to reverse himself."[101] Khrushchev immediately issued orders to the commander of Soviet forces in Cuba: "Allow no one near the missiles. Obey no orders to launch and under no circumstances install the warheads."[102]

Khrushchev later recalled the exchange that made up his mind:

> When I asked the military advisers if they could assure me that holding fast would not result in the death of five hundred million human beings, they looked at me as though I was out of my mind or, what was worse, a traitor. The biggest tragedy, as they saw it, was not that our country might be devastated and everything lost, but that the Chinese or Albanians would accuse us of appeasement or weakness. So I said to myself: To hell with these maniacs. If I can get the United States to assure me that it will not attempt to overthrow the Cuban government, I will remove the missiles.[103]

At 4 p.m. Moscow time (8 a.m. EST), one hour before Radio Moscow broadcast Khrushchev's acceptance of Kennedy's offer to the world, Soviet Defense Minister Rodion Malinovsky ordered the missile sites dismantled. "Remove them," he directed, "as soon as possible. Before something terrible happens."[104]

Khrushchev's acceptance reached Washington at 9 a.m. local time: "Esteemed Mr. President: I have received your message of

October 27, 1962. . . . In order to complete with greater speed the liquidation of the conflict dangerous to the cause of peace . . . the Soviet Government . . . in addition to previously issued instructions on the cessation of further work at building sites for the weapons, has issued a new order on the dismantling of the weapons which you describe as 'offensive,' and their crating and return to the Soviet Union."[105]

Kennedy's response, broadcast over Voice of America, marked the end of the crisis: "I welcome Chairman Khrushchev's statesmanlike decision to stop building bases in Cuba, dismantling offensive weapons and returning them to the Soviet Union. . . . I think that you and I, with our heavy responsibilities for the maintenance of peace, were aware that developments were approaching a point where events could have become unmanageable. So I welcome this message and consider it an important contribution to peace."[106]

President Kennedy carefully avoided turning the outcome into a public humiliation for the Soviet Union. "He instructed all members of the ExComm and government," his brother wrote, "that no interview should be given, no statement made, which would claim any kind of victory. He respected Khrushchev for properly determining what was in his own country's interest and what was in the interest of mankind. If it was a triumph, it was a triumph for the next generation and not for any particular government or people."[107]

The missiles and bombers in Cuba were quietly dismantled and shipped back to the Soviet Union. Castro, who learned of the outcome on the radio, was so enraged by the Soviet capitulation he broke a mirror. Humiliated by being shunted to the sidelines during the crisis, and resentful at being used as a pawn and then having the missiles suddenly and publicly withdrawn, he refused to comply with the implementation of Kennedy and Khrushchev's agreed protocol for the removal of the missiles and would not let UN inspectors on the island to verify their disarmament. As a result, President Kennedy never issued a formal commitment not to invade, although he respected the understanding, and subsequent administrations abided by it. The Turkish Jupiter missiles were quietly removed the following year and replaced with more modern and accurate Polaris submarine-borne ballistic missiles stationed in the Mediterranean. The Jupiter-missile trade remained one of the most closely kept secrets of the U.S. government until the posthumous publication of Robert Kennedy's memoirs seven years later.

The crisis led to a realization on both sides that the world must not come this close again to catastrophe. During the crisis, President Kennedy told Lord Ormsby-Gore, the British ambassador to the United States, "You know, it really is an *intolerable* state of affairs when nations can threaten each other with nuclear weapons. This is just so totally irrational. A world in which there are large quantities of nuclear weapons is an impossible world to handle. We really must try to get on with disarmament if we get through this crisis . . . because this is just too much."[108] The crisis prompted Kennedy and Khrushchev to take steps to pull back from the brink. The leaders installed a "hot line" between the White House and the Kremlin to provide direct and instantaneous communication in the event of future standoffs. The United States and the Soviet Union took the first steps toward disarmament shortly after, signing the Limited Nuclear Test Ban Treaty in the summer of 1963.

The crisis also brought home to the Soviets their strategic inferiority in nuclear weapons. At the time of the crisis, the United States had a seventeen-to-one advantage over the Soviet Union in nuclear weapons. Within a decade the Soviets had reached parity with the United States.

Neither of the leaders remained in power for long after the crisis. President Kennedy was assassinated a little more than a year later, on November 22, 1963, while campaigning in Dallas. Khrushchev was overthrown in a bloodless coup two years after the crisis, in October 1964. The Presidium faulted him for "hare-brained scheming, hasty conclusions, rash decisions and actions based on wishful thinking."[109] Khrushchev's name was stricken from all official references, and he lived the rest of his life in Moscow as a pensioner under close KGB surveillance, dying of natural causes on September 11, 1971.

"The final lesson of the Cuban Missile Crisis," Robert Kennedy wrote, "is the importance of placing ourselves in the other country's shoes. During the crisis, President Kennedy spent more time trying to determine the effect of a particular course of action on Khrushchev or the Russians than on any other phase of what he was doing. What guided all his deliberations was an effort not to disgrace Khrushchev, not to humiliate the Soviet Union, not to have them feel they would have to escalate their response because their national security or national interests so committed them."[110]

Unknown to the Americans at the time, in the event of invasion, Soviet commanders in Cuba were authorized to use nuclear weapons at their discretion. Had President Kennedy chosen the military option, Theodore Sorensen wrote, "we now know that it would have produced a nuclear war. Such an air strike and invasion, we have learned, would have brought in response an immediate nuclear assault upon our forces by Soviet troops in Cuba, equipped with tactical nuclear weapons and authorized to use them on their own initiative, thereby precipitating the world's first nuclear exchange, initially limited perhaps to the tactical weapons level, but inevitably and rapidly escalating to an all-out strategic exchange."[111]

McGeorge Bundy wrote, "In that final sense the teaching of these great events, as the participants learned it and also as it has been learned by others, was not how to 'manage' a grave crisis, but how important it is not to have one. We must make it our business not to pass this way again."[112]

A UGM-27 Polaris ballistic missile launched from a submarine on August 1, 1986. (*Department of Defense*)

Chapter 8

The Reykjavik Summit

1986

I N the twenty-four years that followed the Cuban Missile Crisis, Soviet and American strategic nuclear arsenals grew twentyfold, and with both forces prepared to launch on several minutes' notice, the world lived under constant threat of nuclear annihilation. The superpowers made little progress despite years of arms-control talks, and a series of accords such as the Nuclear Test Ban, Anti-Ballistic Missile, and Strategic Arms Limitation Treaties imposed limits on testing, antimissile systems, and certain types of delivery vehicles, but failed to curb the growth of missiles and warheads. By 1985, midlevel talks in Geneva on strategic reductions stalled, and Soviet Foreign Minister Eduard Shevardnadze called the traditional arms-control process "a well-travelled road that led nowhere."[1] "The world's nations," Soviet Premier Mikhail Gorbachev explained, "were at an impasse. It seemed that the confrontation between East and West would go on forever."[2] "There seemed to be no way out," Shevardnadze wrote, "except to slash the Gordian knot—and destroy the world in the process."[3]

Both countries struggled under the weight of massive defense spending. In the United States, President Ronald Reagan embarked on a three-trillion-dollar military buildup that caused record deficits. In the Soviet Union, the military consumed over 30 percent of the nation's gross national product, and it became evident to the country's leadership that the arms race was bankrupting the Soviet system. "When I became head of state," Gorbachev wrote, "it was already obvious that there was something wrong in this country. . . . Doomed to serve ideology and bear the heavy burden of the arms race, it was strained to the utmost."[4] A steep fall in the price of oil, which provided most of Russia's hard currency, temporarily forced it to stop hard currency payments. The Soviet Union had fallen to fiftieth in the world in infant mortality rates, three times higher than the United States, and life expectancy was on par with Mexico, Brazil, and Costa Rica. "We can't go on living like this,"[5] Gorbachev said to his wife the night before the Politburo appointed him general secretary of the USSR in March 1985. "The rush toward the abyss," he wrote, "had to end."[6]

Reagan and Gorbachev met briefly in November 1985 in Geneva. The meeting produced only a joint statement that "nuclear war cannot be won and must never be fought"[7] and an agreement to meet again, but Soviet leaders left impressed by Reagan's sincerity and sensed an opportunity for meaningful dialogue. "We saw," Shevardnadze wrote, "that Reagan was a person you could deal with, although it was very hard to win him over, to persuade him of the other point of view. But we had the impression that this is a man who keeps his word and that he's someone you can deal with and negotiate with and reach accord."[8]

On September 15, 1986, Gorbachev wrote a four-page letter to President Reagan. Delivered by Shevardnadze during a visit to Washington, it complained of the deterioration in relations and stressed the need for the two leaders to exert a stabilizing influence to prevent the situation from disintegrating further. Gorbachev spoke of "the spirit of candor which is coming to characterize our dialogue," and wondered whether "the US lead-

ership is at all prepared and
ready to seek agreements which
would lead to the termination of
the arms race and to genuine
disarmament?" He pointed out
that despite the ongoing Geneva
talks, "we still have not moved
an inch closer to an agreement
on arms reduction." "I have
come to the conclusion," the
Soviet premier wrote, "that the
negotiations need a major impe-
tus; otherwise they will continue to mark time. . . . They will
lead nowhere unless you and I

U.S. Secretary of State George
Shultz conferring with President
Ronald Reagan. (*National
Archives*)

intervene personally. . . . An idea has come to my mind to suggest to you, Mr. President, that, in the very near future . . . we
have a quick one-on-one meeting, let us say in Iceland or in
London, maybe just for one day, to engage in a strictly confidential, private, and frank discussion (possibly with only our
foreign ministers present). The discussion—which would not be
a detailed one, for its purpose and significance would be to
demonstrate political will—would result in instructions to our
respective agencies to draft agreements on two or three very
specific questions, which you and I could sign during my visit
to the United States."[9]

Reagan embraced the offer. "If such a meeting was to be
held," Reagan's Secretary of State George Shultz explained, "I
told the president privately, we should prefer Reykjavik, an isolated city where the host government would not interfere in
what would surely be tense marathon negotiations and where
ceremony would be at a minimum."[10] Reagan accepted on condition that Gorbachev release a half dozen imprisoned political
dissidents and allow the return of Nicholas Daniloff, Moscow

bureau chief of *U.S. News & World Report*, whom the KGB had seized on trumped-up espionage charges. The day after Daniloff's release on September 29 President Reagan announced that he would meet Gorbachev in Iceland, on October 11 and 12. In his press conference announcing his acceptance, Reagan framed it as a preliminary meeting "in the context of preparations for the General Secretary's visit to the United States."[11]

On October 4, Gorbachev laid out his goals to the Soviet team preparing for Reykjavik. If a new arms race began, he told them, "the pressure on our economy will be inconceivable."[12] He emphasized that to achieve lasting progress, there had to be advantages for the Americans as well. "Nothing will come out of it," he said, "if our proposals lead to a weakening of US security."[13] Gorbachev addressed the Politburo a couple of days before his departure for Reykjavik and told them "intermediate" solutions would not be enough. "If they impose a second round of arms race upon us," Gorbachev warned, "we will lose."[14]

Reagan looked forward to the meeting. "Years before," he observed, recalling his experience as head of the actors' union, "when I'd sat across the bargaining table from the executives who ran the Hollywood studios, I'd learned a few lessons about negotiating: You're unlikely to ever get *all* you want; you'll probably get more of what you want if you don't issue ultimatums and leave your adversary room to maneuver; you shouldn't back your adversary into a corner, embarrass him, or humiliate him; and sometimes the easiest way to get some things done is for the top people to do them alone and in private."[15]

President Reagan arrived in Iceland on Air Force One on Thursday evening, October 9. Gorbachev and the Soviet team arrived by air the following day and settled into their accommodations on a 360-foot-long Soviet cruise ship anchored offshore. On Saturday morning, the Soviet and American motorcades made their way through driving rain to Hofti House, a two-story, white wood clapboard building about a mile outside downtown Reykjavik, perched on a windswept outcrop of land overlooking the ocean. The building, widely rumored to be haunted, had served previously as a French Consulate and the British ambassador's residence, but the British sold it after mysterious noises, paintings inexplicably falling off their hooks, and doors opening by themselves led them to look elsewhere for embassy housing. The Icelandic government, which had taken over Hofti House, maintained it for conferences and entertaining visiting dignitaries, and despite its unusual history, Soviet and American advance teams had chosen it because of its remote location and commanding view of the harbor.

Reagan and Gorbachev arrived promptly at 10:30. After a brief greeting and photo opportunity for more than thirty-five hundred journalists gathered on the front lawn, the two leaders went indoors to a small room on the building's first floor, where Shultz and Shevardnadze joined them. Gorbachev began by handing Reagan a proposal for the United States and Soviet Union to cut their strategic nuclear forces in half. As Gorbachev later wrote:

> Our proposals to cut strategic nuclear arsenals boiled down to the following: negotiations were stuck in endless discussions, the argument was going round in circles and getting nowhere. What was needed was a new approach. We therefore suggested cutting each of the three groups (ground-based intercontinental ballistic missiles, submarine-launched ballistic missiles and strategic bombers) by 50 per cent. It was the first time that the Soviet Union had agreed to such a big reduction in its ground-based ICBM force. This was our most powerful strategic weapon and was considered a major threat by the Americans. It was not meant as a one-sided offer, since the United States were supposed to cut by 50 per cent their major striking force—their nuclear submarines and their strategic bombers, in which they were superior to us. The logic was simple: to reduce the arsenals which guaranteed nuclear deterrence to a much lower level.[16]

Gorbachev also proposed eliminating Soviet and American intermediate-range nuclear forces (INF) in Europe, while allowing France and Britain, whose combined 194 warheads lay technically outside of NATO's command structure, to retain theirs. He suggested freezing existing levels of nuclear missiles in Europe with a range of less than one thousand kilometers (known as short-range INF missiles), an offer less generous than it appeared, as the Soviets had 120 deployed in Europe and NATO had none. In return Gorbachev asked for a commitment from the United States not to withdraw from the Anti-Ballistic Missile (ABM) Treaty for at least ten years. Finally, Gorbachev suggested a comprehensive ban on nuclear testing. "Gorbachev," Shultz remembered, "was brisk, impatient, and confident, with the air of a man who is setting the agenda and taking charge of the meeting. Ronald Reagan was relaxed, disarming in a pensive way, and with an easy manner. He could well afford to be, since Gorbachev's proposals all moved toward U.S. positions in significant ways."[17]

A prime Soviet concern was the presence of NATO intermediate-range missiles in Europe, which Gorbachev called "a pistol held to our head."[18] Deployed in response to Soviet SS-20 INF missiles in Eastern Europe, the U.S. Pershing II ballistic missiles targeted the most densely populated part of the Soviet Union. The Soviets feared the modern Pershing IIs, with their high accuracy and short flight times to the USSR, would be used as first-strike weapons. "Since the American missiles would take a maximum of five minutes to reach their targets," Gorbachev observed, "we were practically unprotected against a possible strike."[19]

Restraining American efforts to establish an anti-missile defense was another Soviet priority. To counter the Soviet threat, Reagan in March 1983 had launched an initiative to develop a space-based system to track and destroy incoming missiles during an attack, called the Strategic Defense Initiative

Soviet Premier Mikhail Gorbachev and U.S. President Ronald Reagan meet at Hofti House. (*National Archives*)

(SDI). Many, including the head of Soviet space research, questioned whether it could be made to work, but Soviet policymakers were consumed by the fear that SDI would militarize space and allow the United States to launch a first strike without fear of retaliation.

Reagan, while encouraged by the Soviet proposal, understood that important differences remained. The Soviet Union's more than five hundred intermediate-range missiles in Asia threatened American allies in the Pacific, and as mobile systems, the Soviets could easily return the weapons to Europe. "Zero INF in Europe is fine," the president told the Soviet leader, "but there must be reduction of these missiles in Asia."[20] Reagan resisted the demand for a ten-year ABM Treaty commitment. Even if all nuclear missiles were eliminated, both sides would still have the capacity to produce them and would need to guarantee against a future madman like Adolf Hitler reintroducing them. Reagan reminded Gorbachev that after World War I, both sides kept their gas masks even though poison gas had been outlawed.

At half past noon they broke for lunch, and Reagan returned to the American Embassy with his senior advisers. "Gorbachev had introduced new and highly significant material," Shultz explained. "Our response, I knew, must be prepared with care, capturing the extensive Soviet concessions and pointing up deficiencies and difficulties from our standpoint. I was glad we had on hand a knowledgeable team with all the expertise we needed. They could rework the president's talking points during the break. Excitement was in the air. I felt it, too. Perhaps we were at a moment of breakthrough after a period, following the Geneva summit, of stalemate in our negotiations."[21] In the embassy's cramped, bug-proof, secure room, Paul Nitze, the State Department senior arms-control adviser, remarked, "This is the best Soviet proposal we have received in twenty-five years."[22]

When the leaders reconvened that afternoon, Reagan outlined his reservations. He welcomed their proposals but pressed for a 50 percent reduction in heavy intercontinental ballistic missiles, and insisted that intermediate-range forces be dealt with on a global basis. The president replied that if they got rid of them globally that would be fine, and he was all for it. He suggested that a joint working group discuss the proposals that evening. "We are getting somewhere," Reagan observed. "The basis for an agreement is within reach."[23]

An understanding also began to form between the two leaders on a more personal level. "Looking back," Reagan later recalled, "it's clear that there was a chemistry between Gorbachev and me that produced something very close to a friendship. He was a tough, hard bargainer. He was a Russian patriot who loved his country. We could—and did—debate from opposite sides of the ideological spectrum. But there was a chemistry that kept our conversations on a man-to-man basis, without hate or hostility. I liked Gorbachev even though he was a dedicated Communist and I was a confirmed capitalist."[24]

With one day remaining, the leaders designated teams to work overnight to narrow the differences. "Let us turn our experts loose," Gorbachev said. "The two of us have said a lot. Let them go to work now."[25] "And so," Shultz wrote, "the first day ended. We had not made any concessions but had received more movement from the Soviets than anyone thought possible. The whole nature of the meeting we had planned at Reykjavik had changed. The working groups meant that a U.S.-Soviet negotiation had been launched."[26]

Reagan returned to the American Embassy, and Gorbachev left for his quarters aboard the *Georg Otts*, the Soviet cruise ship tied up in the harbor. While the two leaders slept, their experts worked to bridge the gap in a marathon all-night session. Headed by Paul Nitze, the seventy-nine-year-old *eminence grise* of the U.S. arms-control community who had negotiated the SALT I strategic arms limitation treaty and the ABM treaty with the Soviets, the U.S. team met for ten and a half hours with their Soviet counterparts, led by Marshal Sergei Akhromeyev, chief of staff of the Soviet armed forces.

Nitze and Akhromeyev focused on finding a formula to reduce strategic weapons. Since the Soviets had both more nuclear weapons overall and superiority in most categories of delivery systems, a straight 50 percent cut across the board would leave the Soviets with lasting nuclear dominance, something no American president could consent to. Nitze pushed instead for equal outcomes by category. He explained:

> We spent a large part of the first six hours of the meeting trying to pin down what "fifty percent reduction" would entail. Akhromeyev explained that the Soviets proposed halving the strategic arsenals of each side "category by category." I was quick to object to that formula. That would mean unequal end points in those categories where one side or the other had the current advantage. For example, the Soviet Union's large relative advantage in ICBM warheads would remain. I thought the sides must strive for equal end results; this would require unequal reductions where the current levels favored one side.[27]

After hours of haggling, when they finished at six thirty Sunday morning Nitze and Akhromeyev had agreed on a ceiling for each side of six thousand warheads and one thousand six hundred delivery vehicles, including ICBMs, submarine-launched missiles, and heavy bombers, which meant greater cuts by the Soviets but reduced each side's strategic arms by half while accommodating the American concern for an equal numerical outcome. Kenneth Adelman, head of the U.S. Arms Control and Disarmament Agency and Reagan's senior arms-control adviser, called it "more progress than we achieved in thousands of hours in hundreds of meetings over the previous five years."[28]

On Sunday morning, after breakfast with their delegations, Reagan, Shultz, Gorbachev, and Shevardnadze arrived at Hofti House for the final session, scheduled to run until twelve thirty in the afternoon, after which the leaders and their teams would fly home. Gorbachev and Reagan reviewed the results from the previous night, and despite the working groups' progress, both leaders thought they could do better. "I thought," Shultz wrote, "here are *stunning breakthroughs* in Soviet-U.S. arms control negotiations—they both know that—and they are both disappointed! But I also agreed with the president that now was the time to press Gorbachev in order to get as much out of this meeting as possible before the negotiators returned to the traditional framework of Geneva."[29]

With a 50 percent reduction in strategic weapons in hand, they returned to the question of intermediate-range missiles. Reagan pressed to abolish them globally, but at a minimum insisted that removal of those weapons from Europe be accompanied by a reduction in Asian systems as well. "I cannot permit," Reagan maintained, "the creation of a situation where we would reduce these missiles to zero in Europe and not make proportional reductions of similar Soviet missiles in Asia. SS-20 missiles are mobile and can be moved easily. Their presence exerts an influence on our Asian allies, not to mention our allies

Premier Gorbachev and President Reagan at a break during the conference.
(*National Archives*)

in Europe."[30] If Gorbachev could not agree to eliminate the weapons globally, Reagan suggested that they reduce their forces to one hundred missiles each in Europe as an intermediate measure. Gorbachev, rejecting an interim solution, focused on removing the weapons from Europe. "If we find a solution on Asian missiles," he asked Reagan, "do you accept zero in Europe?" "Yes," replied Reagan.[31]

As a compromise, Gorbachev suggested eliminating INF missiles in Europe and setting a ceiling of one hundred INF missiles each in Asia. Reagan hesitated. He shot a questioning look to Shultz, who whispered to him, "We should keep after complete elimination, but this is a good deal, better than we were willing to accept before we came here."[32] Reagan accepted the proposal, telling Gorbachev he saw it as an interim step toward a goal of total elimination. Both sides agreed to work toward a ban on nuclear testing in concert with their reductions in nuclear stockpiles, and in what the Americans viewed as a major breakthrough, the Soviets consented to make human rights a regular subject of the two sides' agenda in future discussions. "George and I," Reagan recalled, "couldn't believe what was happening.

We were getting amazing agreements. As the day went on I felt something momentous was occurring. Our noon deadline came and went. We ignored the clock and kept on working, the four of us and our interpreters in that room above the sea."[33]

"The present chance," Gorbachev warned, "might be the only one. I was not in a position a year ago, to say nothing of two or three years ago, to make the kind of proposals I am now making. I might not be able to make the same proposals in a year or so. Time passes. Things change."[34] Gorbachev pointed out that he had been the one making most of the concessions and asked for one in return. "If we are going to reduce nuclear weapons," he said, "we have to be confident that the United States is not going to do anything behind the back of the USSR, and the USSR is not going to do anything behind the back of the United States that would threaten the interests of the other side, degrade the agreement, or create difficulties. So," he asserted, "it is necessary to strengthen the ABM regime."[35] It was essential to include a ten-year period in which both sides committed not to withdraw from the ABM Treaty. Gorbachev understood that the president did not like to make compromises. "But," he told Reagan, "it takes two to tango. With respect to the major questions of arms control and nuclear disarmament, the two leaders were the only partners in sight. Was the President prepared to dance?"[36] "If the parties are undertaking deep reductions in nuclear weapons," Gorbachev said, "there must be an atmosphere of confidence, and to achieve that the conditions of the ABM Treaty must be toughened." He cautioned that "if the fate of the ABM Treaty is not clear then the whole concept collapses and we are back where we were before Reykjavik."[37]

They agreed to a two-hour break, and while President Reagan returned to the American Embassy for lunch, the U.S. team, which had already gotten into the motorcade, was called back to Hofti House. The Soviets, Shevardnadze had told Shultz, had made all the concessions. Now it was the Americans' turn.

"We're at a very serious impasse"[38] on strategic weapons and defense, Shultz explained to the group, and they needed fresh ideas to bridge the gap. "Unless the United States could suggest something dramatic," Reagan's national security adviser, Admiral John Poindexter, felt, "it could be placed in the very difficult position of having been offered large-scale Soviet concessions and having no response other than to reject them due to the SDI conditions."[39] Robert Linhard, an air force colonel and senior National Security Council arms-control expert sitting in the back of the room, scribbled an idea on a legal pad and passed it around to the other members of the American team, who nodded in agreement as they read it. When it reached Shultz, he read it intently before turning to the Soviets seated across the table. "I would like to explore with you," Schultz said, "an idea that I have not discussed with the president, but please hear me out. This is an effort by some of us here to break the impasse. I don't know how the president will react to it. If after the break, you hear some pounding in our area, you'll know that the president is knocking my head against the wall."[40]

Linhard's proposal gave way to the Soviet demand and committed each side to confine itself to research, development, and testing permitted by the ABM Treaty for ten years, and significantly increased the stakes. During the first five years both sides would reduce their strategic offensive arsenals by 50 percent. In the second five-year period they would eliminate all remaining strategic missiles. The United States would destroy its entire force of 1,650 strategic missiles along with 7,800 nuclear warheads, while the Soviets would eliminate their 2,300 long-range missiles with 9,200 warheads. Both countries would retain their nuclear bombers, cruise missiles, and battlefield weapons, but it would remove the most dangerous and destabilizing weapons from their arsenals. After ten years, with all offensive ballistic missiles eliminated, each side would be free to deploy defenses. Shevardnadze agreed the proposal was worth considering.

When President Reagan arrived at half past two and met with the U.S. team to discuss the afternoon session, they told him of the new proposal. The prospect of banning all ballistic missiles raised the discussion to a new level, and the Americans felt comfortable with the offer because American superiority in bomber technology (including the then-secret stealth bomber program) would leave it with an advantage. Reagan liked the proposal, which he found imaginative. "He gets his precious ABM Treaty, and we get all his ballistic missiles. And after that we can deploy SDI in space. Then it's a whole new ball game."[41]

"Before Reagan and Gorbachev resumed their meeting," recalled Jack Matlock, a senior White House arms-control adviser, "the American delegation reviewed the state of play. It seemed almost certain that an agreement could be reached, either by somehow bridging the gap on the remaining differences or by deciding to conclude a treaty to achieve the reductions that had been agreed while continuing negotiations on the disputed points."[42] Emotions ran high on the Soviet side as well. "Everyone was elated, on the one hand, but on the other hand a little bit frightened with what was going on," wrote one member of the Soviet team. "We were in a big game with high stakes, and the stakes were being raised every five minutes."[43] Gorbachev observed, "Both the negotiating teams realized that this was a unique opportunity to break out of the vicious circle of the nuclear arms race."[44]

The leaders reconvened at three thirty, and when Reagan presented Gorbachev with the formula Linhard and Shultz had come up with during the break and pointed out that the Americans had now satisfied the Soviet need for ten years on the ABM Treaty, the Soviets raised an additional demand. During the ten-year nonwithdrawal period, testing of antimissile systems must also be confined to the laboratory. The language of the ABM Treaty left room for ambiguity, as the technology used in the American program did not exist in 1972 when the treaty was written, but Gorbachev insisted on both sides adhering to a strict interpretation confining all strategic defense-related research to laboratories as part of their agreement. Gorbachev contended:

> Your formula fails to meet our position halfway. Our point of view is that we will eliminate strategic nuclear forces in these 10 years. In the meantime, while the USSR and the U.S. are carrying out deep reductions in nuclear weapons we ought to reinforce instead of undermining the ABM Treaty. That's why we are proposing to strengthen the ABM regime in that very crucial period. Why complicate things with other problems which we are uncertain about, the consequences of which are unclear? Why burden an agreement by these weights? You have to agree that it would be more difficult for us to go along with this if you tie us down with aggravating weights. That is why we are proposing that we come to an agreement regarding the 10-year period of non-withdrawal from the ABM Treaty; to carry out research only in laboratories during that period, and then after the period is over and strategic weapons have been eliminated, discuss what to do next.[45]

Gorbachev asked Reagan to consider his request, and both recognized that an agreement was within sight. "This is a rather strange situation," Reagan observed. "We have both put forth specific demands. You are in favor of a 10-year period. I have said that I will not give up SDI. But both of us, obviously, can say that the most important thing is to eliminate nuclear arsenals."[46] Ten years from now, President Reagan told the Soviet leader, he would be a very old man. He and Gorbachev would return to Iceland and each would bring his country's last nuclear missile. Reagan would be so old by then Gorbachev would not recognize him. The president would say, "Hello, Mikhail." Gorbachev would say, "Ron, is that you?" and together they would destroy the last two missiles and throw a tremendous party for the whole world.[47]

Reagan suggested deferring the laboratory testing question until Gorbachev's Washington visit: "What's wrong with saying 'research, development, and testing as permitted by the ABM Treaty? Then, when we meet in Washington in the summer, we can discuss whether testing is allowed under ABM provisions."[48] Gorbachev replied firmly, "Without that there's no package. All of the elements are interrelated. If we come to an agreement on deep reductions of nuclear weapons, we must have assurance that the ABM Treaty will not only be complied with but also strengthened in this crucial period. I repeat, this period is too crucial, it is dangerous to improvise."[49]

Shultz suggested a recess, and the leaders gathered upstairs with their advisers. Gorbachev paced excitedly back and forth. "Everything," he told the Soviet team, "could be decided right now."[50] On the other side of the room, Reagan met with the Americans. Matlock described "a feeling of tension and antici-pation" among both groups. "Euphoria lurked, barely concealed, under the surface of emotions. The U.S. and USSR seemed to be on the verge of the most sweeping commitments in history to reduce mankind's most destructive weaponry."[51] Reagan's chief of staff, Donald Regan, recalled that the discussion "was ani-mated, urgent, informal, and very tense. The noise level was high in both languages; all faces were deadly serious. No one sat down. The President beckoned me to him. 'Don, this is taking too long,' he murmured. He wanted to get back to Washington— he had planned on having Sunday dinner at home. Reagan was annoyed and disappointed. 'I don't see how it can last much longer, Mr. President,' I said. 'But we've got to hang in there—if we can get this package, it'll be worth it.' . . . Reagan sighed and nodded. Now, with both leaders on the edge of exhaustion, our final proposal was ready."[52] The president decided not to make any substantive changes but simply to rework the text of the proposal, putting it into the Soviet format. Reagan was prepared to accept Gorbachev's position on the ten-year nonwithdrawal period for the ABM Treaty, along with every other Soviet point including elimination of all nuclear weapons at the end of the ten years. For Reagan, the only remaining make-or-break obstacle was Gorbachev's demand to confine SDI research to the laboratory. The American team smelled blood. The Soviets "were desperate for an agreement on SDI," Regan observed. "They were in trouble, we could see that."[53]

When the leaders returned, President Reagan read Gorbachev the American revision. It was, Reagan said, "the final option we can offer."[54] Gorbachev pointed out that the American offer proposed cutting "strategic offensive arms" in the first five-year period, but eliminating only ballistic missiles in the second. Why not, Gorbachev suggested, do away with all nuclear weapons, not just ballistic missiles, but cruise missiles, air-launched systems, and tactical weapons as well? "Let me ask this," Reagan said. "Do we have in mind—and I think it would be very good—that by the end of the two five-year periods all nuclear explosive devices would be eliminated, including bombs, battlefield systems, cruise missiles, submarine weapons, intermediate-range systems, and so on?" "It would be fine with me," Reagan ventured, "if we eliminated all nuclear weapons." Gorbachev replied, "We can do that. Let's include all those weapons as well. Let's eliminate them."[55] Shultz said, "Let's do it."[56] Reagan told Gorbachev, "We can turn it all over to the Geneva people and they can draft the agreement and you could come to the United States and sign it."[57]

Gorbachev returned to missile defense and insisted he still needed SDI confined to the laboratory. Shultz suspected correctly that Gorbachev was under orders from the Politburo to extract concessions on SDI. "Everything," Shultz realized, "depended on agreement on how to handle SDI: a ten-year period of nonwithdrawal and strict adherence to the terms of the ABM Treaty during that period. That was their bottom line."[58] Reagan, though, had no intention of backing down on SDI.

"Understand me," he responded, "I cannot retreat from my positions, renounce what I promised our people."59

"I fail to see the magic of the ABM regime," Reagan asserted, "whose only assurance of safety is the doctrine of Mutual Assured Destruction. We are talking about elimination of missiles, about how we should no longer be threatened with the danger that some gloomy day someone will push the button and everything will be destroyed. But even when we destroy these missiles we must have a defense against others. The genie is already out of the bottle."60

He pointed out that down the road someone might build nuclear weapons again. "Who knows," Reagan argued, "what kind of madman might come along after we're gone? We live in a world where governments change; in your own country, there have already been four leaders during my term. I believe you mean it when you say you want peace, but there could be a change. It's the same thing on the other side: I think you know I want peace, but you also know I will not be in a position to personally keep the promises I've made to you. That's why we need insurance that our agreements eliminating nuclear weapons will be kept in the future."61

"We knew from intelligence information," Reagan later acknowledged, "that the Soviets were secretly researching a missile defense system similar to SDI; their technology was inferior to ours, but if we stopped work on SDI and they continued to work on their system, it meant we might wake up one morning to learn that they alone had a defense against missiles. We couldn't afford that. SDI was an insurance policy to guarantee that the Soviets kept the commitments Gorbachev and I were making at Reykjavik. We had had enough experience with Soviet treaty violations to know that kind of insurance was necessary."62

Gorbachev reminded Reagan that laboratory research could continue, but both knew the language would mean the end of

SDI. Restricting research to the laboratory would have halted half to three-quarters of America's scheduled SDI research, and there was little chance Congress would fund the program unless the technology proved effective in open-air tests. Shultz felt that "Gorbachev obviously knew, but did not say directly, that the restrictions he wanted would make the successful development of a strategic defense extremely remote. No doubt he worried that if SDI research proved successful in the near term, the United States would simply not wait for the ten years to expire before deploying. I sensed, too, that SDI was, in a powerful way, propelling the Soviet concessions, in part because they feared that we were farther along technically than we actually were."[63] "We were calling the Soviets' bluff," Donald Regan acknowledged. "If they accepted, nuclear weapons would vanish from the earth. The key to agreement was SDI; without the insurance policy that it provided, the President could never ask Congress and the American people to trust the Soviets, and no treaty could win ratification."[64]

Shevardnadze told the two leaders, "I would like to say just one thing. The two sides are so close to accomplishing a historic task, to decisions of such historic significance, that when future generations read the record of our talks, and saw how close we had come, they will not forgive us if we let this opportunity pass."[65] "The weather," Shultz wrote, "was alternating every half hour or so between dark, driving rain and brilliant sunshine, and the course of our work mirrored the weather. Round and round we went."[66]

"As evening approached," Reagan recalled, "I thought to myself: Look what we have accomplished—we have negotiated the most massive weapons reductions in history. I thought we were in complete agreement and were going to achieve something remarkable. Then, after everything had been decided, or so I thought, Gorbachev threw us a curve. With a smile on his face, he said: 'This all depends, of course, on you giving up SDI.' I couldn't believe it and blew my top. 'I've said again and again the SDI wasn't a bargaining chip. Now, with all we have accomplished here, you do this and throw in this roadblock and everything is out the window.'"[67]

The president told Gorbachev he felt both sides had results they could be proud of: a 50 percent reduction in the first stage and total elimination in the second. Gorbachev would be able to return with the ten-year period he came for, and while Reagan had agreed to defer development, he would have honored his pledge to keep SDI intact. Why, Reagan questioned, should there be any restrictions beyond the ten-year period, when both sides will have gotten what they claimed to want—the elimination of offensive missiles? "You told your people ten years and you got it," Reagan argued. "I told my people I wouldn't give up SDI; so I have to go home saying I haven't."[68] Gorbachev countered, "But you wouldn't have to give it up, because you will still be able to test it in the laboratory. Your opponents won't be able to open their mouth, especially when we are making deep cuts in our nuclear arsenals. Anyway," he added, "our meeting cannot produce a situation that results in a winner and a loser: we must both either win or lose. Otherwise, after the treaty is signed the loser will work to undermine the agreement."[69]

Reagan pointed to his political pressures at home. "I have promised the American people I will not give up SDI," he reminded Gorbachev, and asked for "just this one thing."[70] Gorbachev responded:

> It's not a trivial thing—it is everything. You must understand me. To us the laboratory issue is not a matter of stubbornness or hard-headedness. We are agreeing to deep reductions and, ultimately, the destruction of nuclear weapons. And at the same time, the American side is pushing us to agree to give them the right to create space weapons. Let me be clear. I cannot do without the word "laboratory." I cannot carry back to Moscow an agreement that gives up this limitation of research and testing

to the laboratory. If you agree to this, we could write it all down and I will sign it right now. If this is not possible, then we can say good-bye and forget everything we have discussed.[71]

The president held his ground. "You're asking me to give up SDI," he said. "I have promised the American people I will not give up SDI. I cannot confine work to the laboratory." Gorbachev asked if this was his final position. "If so, we can end our meeting at this point." Reagan replied tersely, "Yes it is."[72]

"All right, then," Gorbachev said, "if you can't do that, let's end it here. We may as well go home and forget about Reykjavik. We cannot accept what you propose. I've said all I can. There is no other possibility. In any case, I know that for me there is no other way."[73]

Reagan argued, "The text now has everything you asked for: not to exercise the right to withdraw from the ABM Treaty for 10 years, strict compliance with its provisions, and the conduct only of the kind of research, development, and testing which are permitted by the treaty, everything except the term 'laboratories.' It is," he said, "a question of one word."[74] Reagan asked in disbelief, "Are you really going to turn down a historic opportunity for the sake of a single word in the text?"[75]

"You say it is the question of one word," Gorbachev replied, "but for us it's not the matter of a word, it's a matter of principle. We cannot agree to a situation in which you are expanding your SDI and going into space with it while reductions of nuclear weapons are going on. If you will agree to banning tests in space, we will sign the document in two minutes. Otherwise, we cannot go along with what you propose. Even though our meeting is ending this way, I have a clear conscience. I did everything I could."[76]

Reagan told the Soviet leader, "I don't know when we'll ever have another chance like this and whether we'll meet soon." Gorbachev said "I don't either."[77]

Reagan scribbled "Am I wrong?" on a note and pushed it over to Shultz. The secretary of state looked at him and whispered back, "No, you are right." Shultz felt it was important to hold firm: "The Soviets, I thought, had agreed to our long-standing proposals. They had done so, I believed, because of SDI. If President Reagan had agreed—by this compromise—to let SDI die, we would have no leverage to propel the Soviets to continue moving our way. I admired the president for hanging in there. If he had given in on SDI, all the other progress we had achieved with the Soviets would have been problematic. Gorbachev came to Reykjavik prepared to make concessions because of the pressure of SDI, but he also came to kill SDI, and he went to the well once too often."[78]

Reagan, a look of resigned disappointment on his face, gathered his papers and stood up. "Let's go, George, we're leaving,"[79] he said, closing his briefing book as he stood up. "I was very disappointed—and *very* angry,"[80] he later admitted. Gorbachev also rose to his feet. The summit was over.

"I remember," Donald Regan recalled, "their haggard features and the hoarse tone of their voices." As they emerged into the narrow corridor, Gorbachev said, "There is still time, Mr. President. We could go back inside to the bargaining table." Reagan replied curtly, "I think not."[81] The klieg lights set up outside caught the drizzling rain in the arctic twilight. Reagan walked toward his limousine. "Our faces," Shultz conceded, "looked stricken and drained."[82]

"Mr. President," Gorbachev called out to him, "you have missed the unique chance of going down in history as a great president who paved the way for nuclear disarmament." "That applies to both of us,"[83] Reagan replied.

"I still feel we can find a deal," Reagan told Gorbachev as they stood on the gravel at the bottom of the steps outside Hofti House. "I don't think you want a deal," Gorbachev answered. "I don't know what more I could have done." "I do," Reagan replied. "You could have said yes."[84]

President Reagan and Premier Gorbachev at the end of the Reykjavik Summit. (*National Archives*)

The president, Donald Regan, and Shultz rode together in Reagan's limousine on the short trip back to the American ambassador's residence. "In the limousine," Regan recalled, "Reagan was somber, and for the first time since I had known him I felt that I was in the presence of a truly disappointed man. . . . Reagan sat in silence for another moment. Then he said, Don, we came so close. It's just such a shame. He placed his thumb and forefinger less than a half inch apart and added. We were *that* close to an agreement."[85]

"The sweep of what had been achieved at Reykjavik was nevertheless breathtaking," Shultz wrote:

Far-reaching concessions to the American positions had been put forward, orchestrated by Gorbachev, over the two days: it was an elaborate chesslike performance. At the end, Gorbachev pulled the rug out. . . . Gorbachev's approach had been brilliant, but he neglected two points: President Reagan's deeply felt commitment to a new, defense-based concept of deterrence; and the fragility of the Soviet arms control concessions. Without SDI as an ongoing propellant, these concessions could wither away over the next ten years. I knew that the genie was out of the bottle: the concessions Gorbachev made at Reykjavik could never, in reality, be taken back. We had seen the Soviets' bottom line. . . . At Reykjavik we had reached virtual agreement on INF and had set out the parameters of START [the Strategic Arms Reduction Treaty]. And we had gotten human rights formally on the negotiating table. . . . [T]he reality was that Reykjavik was a stupendous success.[86]

At his press conference Gorbachev also maintained it had not been a failure. "I suddenly found myself," Gorbachev recalled, "in the enormous press-conference room, with about a thousand waiting journalists. When I came into the room, the merciless, often cynical and cheeky journalists stood up in silence. I sensed the anxiety in the air. I suddenly felt emotional, even shaken. These people standing in front of me seemed to represent mankind waiting for its fate to be decided. At this moment I realized the true meaning of Reykjavik and knew what further course we had to follow." "In spite of all its drama," the Soviet leader announced, "Reykjavik is not a failure—it is a breakthrough, which allowed us for the first time to look over the horizon." Gorbachev believed "Reykjavik showed that an agreement was possible. . . . Reykjavik strengthened our conviction that we had chosen the right course."[87] "I think," he declared, "that the U.S. President and I should reflect on the entire situation that ultimately evolved here at the meeting, and make another attempt to step over the things that divide us."[88] The Soviet Union "will be waiting, without withdrawing the proposals that we have made public."[89]

That evening before midnight, Gorbachev, sheltered under an umbrella on the airport tarmac with the Icelandic prime minister before boarding his plane to Moscow, confided to him, "Mr. Prime Minister, I can understand your disappointment. But there will be more coming out of this meeting than anyone realizes.

For the first time in forty years, both great powers tried to eliminate all nuclear weapons. This is the beginning of the end of
the Cold War."[90]

The United States also realized that for all its frustrations,
Reykjavik had been a great success. "No, it's not a bust. We got
very far. It's like going 99 yards and not scoring on the last
yard,"[91] Donald Regan said to the gathered crowd of media as
he joined the president aboard Air Force One to return to the
United States. All that remained was the final yard.

Back in Washington on Tuesday morning, Shultz shared his
thoughts with the president: "I thought of Christopher
Columbus, who at the time was said to have failed because he
only landed on a couple of islands and didn't bring back any
gold to Spain. But after a while people realized that he had come
upon a New World. 'In a way, you found a new world this week-
end,' I told the president. 'Some of the critics used to say that
your positions were too tough. Others used to say that they were
unrealistic. But at Reykjavik you smoked the Soviets out and
they are stuck with their concessions. So we have to move fast
to lock them in.'"[92]

The Soviets confirmed that their proposals still stood, and
Reagan also kept his offers on the table. "The door is open," he
announced in a nationally televised address from the Oval
Office, "and the opportunity to begin eliminating the nuclear
threat is within reach. . . . We're ready to pick up where we left
off, and we're prepared to go forward whenever and wherever
the Soviets are ready."[93] The essential elements of an INF treaty
and a strategic arms reduction treaty were in place, and within
three weeks, Shultz and Shevardnadze began working to consolidate the gains made at Reykjavik and turn them into something
Reagan and Gorbachev could sign.

Gorbachev realized he could make no progress with Reagan
while insisting on killing SDI, that the technical hurdles to SDI
were greater than he had thought and the Americans might not

be able to implement it after all; and that improving relations would make it less likely Congress would fund SDI research. In February 1987, Gorbachev dropped his demand subjecting an INF agreement to American concessions restricting SDI research to the laboratory. He untied the package of proposals he had presented, removed linkage between SDI and INF, and publicly proposed that "a separate agreement be concluded on it, and without delay."[94] On April 14, Gorbachev told Shultz that the USSR would agree to eliminate its short-range intermediate missiles as well. Within a couple of months, Gorbachev also dropped his insistence on keeping INF missiles in Asia. The White House officially accepted the Soviet proposal on July 29.

Later that year, President Reagan and General Secretary Gorbachev signed the Intermediate-Range Nuclear Forces Treaty, the first to abolish an entire class of nuclear weapons, during a solemn ceremony in the East Room of the White House. The Soviet Union withdrew and destroyed more than fifteen hundred deployed nuclear warheads, and the United States withdrew and destroyed approximately four hundred, for a total reduction of almost two thousand nuclear warheads. The Soviets, who had more deployed, agreed to destroy four times as many warheads as the Americans. The weapons eliminated included the SS-4 missiles that had brought the world so close to destruction in the Cuban Missile Crisis, as well as their modern equivalents. Verification terms were far more extensive than in any previous treaty and included complete inventories of all weapons, on-site inspections, short-notice inspections, and continued monitoring of missile-production sites. After the signing, Gorbachev declared, "What we have achieved is the revival of hope."[95]

A treaty reducing strategic arms followed four years later. On July 31, 1991, President George H. W. Bush and Gorbachev signed the Strategic Arms Reduction Treaty. Following the framework laid down at Reykjavik, START cut American and

Soviet strategic nuclear arsenals by half, to a maximum of six thousand warheads each, deployed on no more than sixteen hundred missiles or heavy bombers. On Christmas Day, five months after the signing of the START agreement, the Soviet Union collapsed, breaking peacefully apart into twelve independent states, and the iron curtain dividing East and West fell.

NOTES

CHAPTER ONE: FRANKLIN AT THE FRENCH COURT

1 Franklin to Joseph Priestley, Jan. 27, 1777, in Benjamin Franklin, *The Writings of Benjamin Franklin*, vol. 7, ed. Albert Smyth (New York: MacMillan, 1907), 18-19.

2 Lord Chatham address to Parliament Nov. 18, 1777, in William Jennings Bryan and Francis Whiting Halsey, eds., *The World's Famous Orations*, vol. 3 (New York: Funk and Wagnalls, 1906), 219.

3 Stacy Schiff, *A Great Improvisation: Franklin, France, and the Birth of America* (New York: Holt, 2005), 14-15.

4 H. W. Brands, *The First American: The Life and Times of Benjamin Franklin* (New York: Random House, 2000), 527.

5 Alfred Owen Aldridge, *Franklin and His French Contemporaries* (New York: New York University Press, 1957), 268.

6 Franklin to Hancock, December 8, 1776, in Francis Wharton, ed., *The Revolutionary Diplomatic Correspondence of the United States*, vol. 2 (Washington, DC: Government Printing Office, 1889), 222. Tadashi Aruga, "Revolutionary Diplomacy and the Franco-American Treaties of 1778," *The Japanese Journal of American Studies*, no. 2 (1985), 81. Schiff, *A Great Improvisation*, 59.

7 David Schoenbrun, *Triumph in Paris: The Exploits of Benjamin Franklin* (New York: Harper & Row, 1976), 82-83. Gerald Stourzh, *Benjamin Franklin and American Foreign Policy* (Chicago: University of Chicago Press, 1969), 136-137. Benjamin Franklin, *Letters from France: The Private Diplomatic Correspondence of Benjamin Franklin 1776-1785*, ed. Brett Woods (New York: Algora Publishing, 2006), 10.

8 Commissioners to Vergennes, January 5, 1777, in Wharton, *Revolutionary Diplomatic Correspondence*, vol. 2, 246.

9 Ibid.

10 Ibid.

11 James Breck Perkins, *France in the American Revolution* (Boston: Houghton Mifflin, 1911), 228.

12 Laura Charlotte Sheldon, *France and the American Revolution: 1763-1788* (Ithaca, NY: Andrus & Church, 1900), 48.

13 Morris to commissioners, December 21, 1777, in Wharton, *Revolutionary Diplomatic Correspondence*, vol. 2, 236. Committee of Secret Correspondence

to commissioners, December 21, 1776, in Wharton, *Revolutionary Diplomatic Correspondence,* vol. 2, 230. Personal pledge of commissioners, February 2, 1777, in Wharton, *Revolutionary Diplomatic Correspondence,* vol. 2, 260.

14 Benjamin Harrison et al., Committee of Secret Correspondence to the Commissioners at Paris, December 30, 1776, in Wharton, *Revolutionary Diplomatic Correspondence,* vol. 2, 240.

15 Commissioners to Vergennes, March 18, 1777, in *New York Historical Society Collections, 1887* (New York: New York Historical Society, 1887), 27.

16 Frank W. Brecher, *Securing American Independence: John Jay and the French Alliance* (Westport, CT: Praeger Publishers, 2003), 67.

17 Deane in Open letter to Joseph Reed, 1784, in Silas Deane and Charles Isham, *The Deane Papers, 1774-1799,* vol. 5 (New York: New York Historical Society, 1888), 438.

18 Perkins, *France in the American Revolution,* 229.

19 Schiff, *A Great Improvisation,* 99.

20 American Commissioners: Memorial for Comte de Vergennes and Conde d'Aranda, September 25, 1777, in Mary A. Giunta, ed., *Documents of the Emerging Nation: U.S. Foreign Relations, 1775-1789* (Wilmington, DE: Scholarly Resources, in cooperation with the National Historical Publications and Records Commission, 1998), 47.

21 Richard Henry Lee, *Life of Arthur Lee: Joint Commissioner of the U.S. to the Court of France, and Sole Commissioner to the Courts of Spain and Prussia, During the Revolutionary War* (Boston: Wells and Lilly, 1829), 335.

22 Ibid.

23 Aruga, "Revolutionary Diplomacy," 87.

24 Lee, *Life of Arthur Lee,* 357.

25 Franklin, Deane, and Lee to Vergennes, December 8, 1777, in Wharton, *Revolutionary Diplomatic Correspondence,* vol. 2, 444-445.

26 Lee, *Life of Arthur Lee,* 362.

27 Edward S. Corwin, *French Policy and the American Alliance of 1788* (Princeton, NJ: Princeton University Press, 1916), 156.

28 Ibid., 156-157.

29 Sheldon, *France and the American Revolution,* 61.

30 Ibid., 66.

31 Perkins, *France in the American Revolution,* 232.

32 Weldon A. Brown, *Empire or Independence: A Study in the Failure of Reconciliation, 1774-1783* (Port Washington, NY: Kennikat Press, 1966), 186.

33 Corwin, *French Policy and the American Alliance,* 150.

34 Perkins, *France in the American Revolution,* 125.

35 Ibid., 58.

36 Ron Avery, "The Story of Valley Forge," http://www.ushistory.org/valley-forge/history/vstory.html.

37 Ibid.

38 Washington to Governor George Clinton, Valley Forge, February 16, 1778, in George Washington and Jared Sparks, ed., *The Writings of George Washington: Being His Correspondence, Addresses, Messages, and Other Papers, Official and Private, Selected and Published from the Original Manuscripts* (Boston: G. W. Boynton, 1834), 239.

39 Ibid.

40 Brown, *Empire or Independence*, 186.

41 Schiff, *A Great Improvisation*, 132.

42 Lee, *Life of Arthur Lee*, 375-378; also Schiff, *A Great Improvisation*, 127.

43 Corwin, *French Policy and the American Alliance*, 154.

44 Brown, *Empire or Independence*, 194.

45 Treaty of Amity and Commerce, in Samuel Flagg Bemis, *The Diplomacy of the American Revolution* (Bloomington: Indiana University Press, 1965), 61-65.

46 Walter Isaacson, *Benjamin Franklin: An American Life* (New York: Simon & Schuster, 2003), 347.

CHAPTER TWO: THE LOUISIANA PURCHASE

1 Peter Kastor, ed. *The Louisiana Purchase: Emergence of an American Nation* (Washington, DC: Congressional Quarterly Press, 2002), 168.

2 Francois Barbé-Marbois, *The History of Louisiana, Particularly of the Cessation of That Colony to the United States of America* (Philadelphia: Carey & Lea, 1830), 240-241.

3 Jefferson to de Nemours, April 25, 1802, in Thomas Jefferson and Pierre Samuel Du Pont de Nemours, *The Correspondence of Jefferson and Du Pont de Nemours,* ed. Gilbert Chinard (New York: Burt Franklin, 1972), 47.

4 Barbé-Marbois, *History of Louisiana*, 30.

5 Kastor, *Louisiana Purchase*, 168.

6 Barbé-Marbois, *History of Louisiana*, 230.

7 John Keats, *Eminent Domain: The Louisiana Purchase and the Making of America* (New York: Charterhouse, 1973), 288; also Emil Ludwig, *Napoleon* (New York: Boni & Liveright, 1926), 106.

8 Livingston to Jefferson, March 12, 1803, in *State Papers and Correspondence Bearing Upon the Purchase of the Territory of Louisiana* (Washington, DC: U.S. Department of State, 1903), 144.

9 Jefferson to Monroe, January 13, 1803, in *State Papers and Correspondence*, 69.

10 George Dangerfield, *Chancellor Robert R. Livingston of New York, 1746-1813* (New York: Harcourt, Brace, 1960), 361.

11 Barbé-Marbois, *History of Louisiana*, 275.

12 George Morgan, *Life of James Monroe* (New York: AMS Press, 1969), 245.

13 Barbé-Marbois, *History of Louisiana*, 276.

14 Ibid., 275.

15 Jon Kukla, *A Wilderness So Immense: The Louisiana Purchase* (New York: Knopf, 2003), 213.

16 Lewis Stewarton, *The Revolutionary Plutarch: Exhibiting the Most Distinguished Characters, Literary, Military, and Political, in the Recent Annals of the French Republic* (London: J. Murray, 1806), 344.

17 Morgan, *Life of James Monroe*, 232.

18 Ibid.

19 Joan Dayan, *Haiti, History, and the Gods* (Berkeley, CA: University of California Press, 1998), 162.

20 Barbé-Marbois, *History of Louisiana*, 242.

21 Ibid., 276.

22 Ibid., 278.

23 Livingston to Madison, April 11, 1803, in *State Papers and Correspondence*, 158.

24 Ibid.

25 Barbé-Marbois, *History of Louisiana*, 278.

26 Livingston to Madison, April 13, 1803, in *State Papers and Correspondence*, 159-163.

27 Barbé-Marbois, *History of Louisiana*, 302.

28 Livingston to Madison, April 13, 1803, in *State Papers and Correspondence*, 159-163.

29 Ibid.

30 Ibid.

31 Ibid.

32 Ibid.

33 Livingston to Madison, April 17, 1803, in *State Papers and Correspondence*, 172-175.

34 Ibid.

35 Ibid.

36 Ibid.

37 Barbé-Marbois to Talleyrand, April 21, 1803, Documents of the French Government Archives, Library of Congress Manuscript Division.

38 Ibid.

39 Livingston to Madison, April 17, 1803, in *State Papers and Correspondence*, 172-175.

40 Barbé-Marbois, *History of Louisiana*, 283.

41 Ibid., 285.

42 Ibid., 286.

43 Ibid.

44 Ibid., 282.

45 Ibid., 292.

46 Ibid., 238.

47 Charles Cerami, *Jefferson's Great Gamble: The Remarkable Story of Jefferson, Napoleon and the Men Behind the Louisiana Purchase* (Naperville, IL: Sourcebooks, 2003), 195.

48 Henry Adams, *History of the United States During the Administration of Thomas Jefferson* (New York: Library of America, 1986), 220.

49 Monroe's Journal, in *State Papers and Correspondence*, 165-172.

50 Ibid.

51 Barbé-Marbois, *History of Louisiana*, 300.

52 Ibid., 298.

53 Monroe's Journal, in *State Papers and Correspondence*, 165-172.

54 Barbé-Marbois, *History of Louisiana*, 310-311.

55 Jefferson to Williamson, April 30, 1803, in *State Papers and Correspondence*, 182.

56 Barbé-Marbois, *History of Louisiana*, 312.

57 Christopher Herold, *The Age of Napoleon* (New York: Harper & Row, 1963), 310.

58 Livingston to Madison, May 20, 1803, in *State Papers and Correspondence*, 200.

59 Curtis Manning Geer, *The Louisiana Purchase and the Westward Movement* (Philadelphia: G. Barrie, 1904), 211.

CHAPTER THREE: THE CONGRESS OF VIENNA

1 Treaty of Paris, May 30, 1814, Article 32.

2 Talleyrand to King Louis XVIII, October 9, 1814, in Charles Maurice Talleyrand, *The Correspondence of Prince Talleyrand and King Louis XVIII During the Congress of Vienna* (New York: Harper & Brothers, 1881), 15.

3 Circular to Ambassadors by M. Talleyrand, October 3, 1814, in Talleyrand, *Correspondence of Prince Talleyrand*, 15n.

4 Harold Nicolson, *The Congress of Vienna: A Study in Allied Unity, 1812–22* (New York: Viking Compass, 1946), 142.

5 Ibid.

6 Ibid., 170.

7 Charles Webster, *The Congress of Vienna* (London: Foreign Office, 1918), 120.

8 Talleyrand to King Louis XVIII, October 25, 1814, in Talleyrand, *Correspondence of Prince Talleyrand*, 45-46.

9 Ibid.

10 Susan Mark Alsop, *The Congress Dances* (New York: Harper & Row, 1984), 152.

11 Adam Zamoyski, *Rites of Peace: The Fall of Napoleon and the Congress of Vienna* (New York: HarperCollins, 2007), 299.

12 Ibid., 389.

13 Talleyrand to King Louis XVIII, November 12, 1814, in Talleyrand, *Correspondence of Prince Talleyrand*, 67.

14 Ibid., 66.

15 Zamoyski, *Rites of Peace*, 295.

16 Talleyrand to King Louis XVIII, October 31, 1814, in Talleyrand, *Correspondence of Prince Talleyrand*, 56.

17 Talleyrand to King Louis XVIII, November 25, 1814, in Talleyrand, *Correspondence of Prince Talleyrand*, 87.

18 Guglielmo Ferrero, *The Reconstruction of Europe: Talleyrand and the Congress of Vienna 1814-1815* (New York: G. P. Putnam's Sons, 1941), 187.

19 Duff Cooper, *Talleyrand* (Stanford, CA: Stanford University Press, 1932), 240.

20 Talleyrand to King Louis XVIII, September 17, 1814, in Talleyrand, *Correspondence of Prince Talleyrand*, 77.

21 Golo Mann, *Secretary of Europe: The Life of Friedrich Gentz, Enemy of Napoleon*, tr. William H. Woglom (New Haven: Yale University Press, 1946), 213.

22 Zamoyski, *Rites of Peace*, 333-334.

23 Ibid., 369.

24 Alsop, *Congress Dances*, 167.

25 Ferrero, *Reconstruction of Europe*, 263.

26 Zamoyski, *Rites of Peace*, 361.

27 Ibid., 363-4.

28 Ibid.

29 Talleyrand to King Louis XVIII, December 15, 1814, in Talleyrand, *Correspondence of Prince Talleyrand*, 111.

30 Ferrero, *Reconstruction of Europe*, 268.

31 Paul Johnson, *The Birth of the Modern: World Society 1815-1830* (New York: HarperCollins, 1991), 94.

32 Ferrero, *Reconstruction of Europe*, 268-272.

33 Talleyrand to King Louis XVIII, December 20, 1814, in Talleyrand, *Correspondence of Prince Talleyrand*, 115-116.

34 Zamoyski, *Rites of Peace*, 377.

35 Ibid., 373.

36 Ibid., 380.

37 Talleyrand to King Louis XVIII, December 28, 1814, in Talleyrand, *Correspondence of Prince Talleyrand*, 120.

38 Ibid., 123.

39 Henry Kissinger, *A World Restored: Metternich, Castlereagh and the Problems of Peace 1812-22* (London: Weidenfeld and Nicolson, 1957), 167-8.

40 Zamoyski, *Rites of Peace*, 390.

41 Ibid., 391.

42 Ibid.

43 Ibid.

44 Cooper, *Talleyrand*, 255.

45 Alsop, *Congress Dances*, 172.

46 Declaration of the Powers, on the Abolition of the Slave Trade, February 8, 1815.

47 Zamoyski, *Rites of Peace*, 448.

48 Nicolson, *Congress of Vienna*, 226.

49 Johnson, *Birth of the Modern*, 79.

CHAPTER FOUR: THE PORTSMOUTH TREATY

1 William Roscoe Thayer, *John Hay* (Boston: Houghton, Mifflin, 1908), 401.

2 Eugene Trani, *The Treaty of Portsmouth: An Adventure in American Diplomacy* (Lexington: University of Kentucky Press, 1969), 41.

3 Theodore Roosevelt, *Theodore Roosevelt: An Autobiography* (New York: Charles Scribner's Sons, 1913), 555.

4 Ibid.

5 Ibid.

6 Joseph Bishop, *Theodore Roosevelt and His Time Shown in His Own Letters* (New York: Charles Scribner's Sons, 1920), 382.

7 Roosevelt to Lodge, May 15, 1905, in Theodore Roosevelt, *The Letters of Theodore Roosevelt*, vol. 4, *The Square Deal, 1903-1905*, ed. Elting Morison (Cambridge, MA: Harvard University Press, 1951), 1179.

8 U.S. Department of State, *Papers Relating to the Foreign Relations of the United States, 1905* (Washington, DC: U.S. Government Printing Office, 1906), 807.

9 Ibid.

10 Bishop, *Theodore Roosevelt and His Time*, 392.

11 Roosevelt to Meyer, December 26, 1904, in Bishop, *Theodore Roosevelt and His Time*, 356.

12 Edmund Morris, *Theodore Rex* (New York: Random House, 2001), 390; also Morinosuke Kajima, *The Diplomacy of Japan, 1844-1922: Anglo-Japanese Alliance and Russo-Japanese War* (Tokyo: Kajima Institute of International Peace, 1976), 222.

13 Kajima, *Diplomacy of Japan*, 222-223.

14 M. A. De Wolf Howe, *George Von Lengerke Meyer: His Life and Public Services* (New York: Dodd, Mead, 1920), 159.

15 Frederick W. Marks, *Velvet on Iron: The Diplomacy of Theodore Roosevelt* (Lincoln: University of Nebraska Press, 1981), 51.

16 Morris, *Theodore Rex*, 402.

17 Sergei Witte, *The Memoirs of Count Witte.*, ed. and trans. Sidney Harcave (Armonk, NY: M. E. Sharpe, 1990), xiv.

18 Raymond Esthus, *Double Eagle and Rising Sun: The Russians and Japanese at Portsmouth in 1905* (Durham, NC: Duke University Press, 1988), 3.

19 Sterling Fishman, *Sergius Witte and His Part in the Portsmouth Peace Conference* (Madison: University of Wisconsin Press, 1953), 19.

20 Alfred Emanuel Smith, *New Outlook* (Outlook Publishing, 1915), 675.

21 Raymond Esthus, "Nicholas II and the Russo-Japanese War." *Russian Review*, vol. 40, no. 4 (Oct., 1981), 5.

22 *The Outlook*, July 22, 1905, 718.

23 Lancelot Lawton, *Empires of the Far East* (London: G. Richards, 1912), 247.

24 Roosevelt to Meyer, July 7, 1905, in Roosevelt, *Letters of Theodore Roosevelt*, vol. 4, 1262. The chief legal counsel to the Japanese delegation was an American, Henry Willard Denison, who although a foreigner had been a senior advisor to the Japanese Ministry of Foreign Affairs for many years, and served as a rusted expert on international law.

25 Tokyo *Asahi Shimbun*, July 9, 1905.

26 Esthus, *Double Eagle and Rising Sun*, 59.

27 Witte (Harcave), *Memoirs of Count Witte*, 431.

28 V. N. Kokovtsov, *Out of My Past* (Stanford, CA: Stanford University Press, 1935), 55; also Trani, *Treaty of Portsmouth*, 112; also Esthus, *Double Eagle and Rising Sun*, 61.

29 George Smalley, *Anglo-American Memories* (New York: G. P. Putnam's Sons, 1911), 362.

30 Chris Wallace, *Character: Profiles in Presidential Courage* (New York: Rugged Land, 2004), 183.

31 J. J. Korostovetz, *Diary of Korostovetz: Pre-War Diplomacy, the Russo-Japanese Problem* (London: British Periodicals, 1920), 44.

32 Witte (Harcave), *Memoirs of Count Witte*, 439.

33 Korostovetz, *Pre-War Diplomacy*, 51.

34 Kajima, *Diplomacy of Japan*, 242.

35 Ibid., 245.

36 Ibid.

37 Korostovetz, *Pre-War Diplomacy*, 67.

38 *New York Times*, August 12, 1905.

39 Kajima, *Diplomacy of Japan*, 276.

40 Ibid.

41 Harold William Vazeille Temperley and George Peabody Gooch, *British Documents on the Origins of the War, 1898-1914: The Anglo-Russian Rapprochement, 1903-07* (London: Foreign Office, 1938), 97; also Esthus, *Double Eagle and Rising Sun*, 108.

42 Howard Beale, *Theodore Roosevelt and the Rise of America to World Power* (Baltimore: Johns Hopkins University Press, 1956), 296.

43 Roosevelt to John St. Loe Strachey, July 17, 1905, in Bishop, *Theodore Roosevelt and His Time*, 401.

44 Kajima, *Diplomacy of Japan*, 325-326.

45 Roosevelt to Kaneko, August 22, 1905, in Roosevelt, *Letters of Theodore Roosevelt*, vol. 4, 1308.

46 Bishop, *Theodore Roosevelt*, 407; also Sergei Witte, *Memoirs of Count Witte*, ed. and trans. Abraham Yarmolinsky (Garden City, NY: Doubleday, Page, 1921), 157; also Tyler Dennett, *Roosevelt and the Russo-Japanese War* (Garden City, NY: Doubleday, Page, 1925), 269.

47 Henry Pringle, *Theodore Roosevelt: A Biography* (New York: Harcourt, Brace, 1931), 271; also Jules Jusserand, *What Me Befell* (Boston: Houghton Mifflin, 1933), 304; also, Beale, *Theodore Roosevelt*, 304.

48 Temperley, *British Documents*, 106; also Roosevelt, *Letters of Theodore Roosevelt*, vol. 4, 4; also Dennett, *Roosevelt and the Russo-Japanese War*, 275; also Morris, *Theodore Rex*, 413.

49 Bishop, *Theodore Roosevelt*, 407.

50 Roosevelt to Nicholas II, August 21, 1905, in Roosevelt, *Letters of Theodore Roosevelt*, vol. 4, 1307.

51 Morris, *Theodore Rex*, 413; also Dennett, *Roosevelt and the Russo-Japanese War*, 270.

52 Morris, *Theodore Rex*, 413.

53 Korostovetz, *Pre-War Diplomacy*, 98.

54 Esthus, *Double Eagle and Rising Sun*, 100.

55 Ibid., 110.

56 Roosevelt to Meyer, August 25, 1905, in Roosevelt, *Letters of Theodore Roosevelt*, vol. 4, 1314.

57 Korostovetz, *Pre-War Diplomacy*, 99.

58 Esthus, *Double Eagle and Rising Sun*, 148.

59 Komura to Katsura, August 28, 1905, in Kajima, *Diplomacy of Japan*, 344.

60 Esthus, *Double Eagle and Rising Sun*, 158.

61 Foreign Ministry to Komura, August 28, 1905, in Kajima, *Diplomacy of Japan*, 349.

62 Ibid.

63 Witte (Harcave), *Memoirs of Count Witte*, 440.

64 Esthus, *Double Eagle and Rising Sun*, 164.

65 Trani, *Treaty of Portsmouth*, 156.

66 William Harbaugh, *Power and Responsibility: The Life and Times of Theodore Roosevelt* (New York: Farrar, Straus and Cudahy, 1961), 271.

67 Osaka *Mainichi Shimbun*, November 1905.

68 Arthur Brown, *The Mastery of the Far East: The Story of Korea's Transformation and Japan's Rise to Supremacy in the Orient* (New York: Charles Scribner's Sons, 1919), 191.

69 Pringle, *Theodore Roosevelt*, 387.

70 Edward Jewitt Wheeler, ed., *Index of Current Literature, 1906* (New York: Current Literature Publishing, 1906), 357.

71 Bishop, *Theodore Roosevelt*, 422.

72 *Advocate of Peace*, May 1909, 111.

73 Theodore Roosevelt to Kermit Roosevelt, December 5, 1906, in Theodore Roosevelt, *Letters to Kermit from Theodore Roosevelt 1902-1908*, ed. Will Irwin (New York: Charles Scribner's Sons, 1946), 174.

74 Edward Wagenknecht, *The Seven Worlds of Theodore Roosevelt* (New York: Longman's Green, 1958), 308.

CHAPTER FIVE: THE PARIS PEACE CONFERENCE

1 Henry Kissinger, *Diplomacy* (New York: Simon & Schuster, 1994), 218.

2 Robert Lansing, *The Peace Negotiations: A Personal Narrative* (Boston: Houghton Mifflin, 1921), 22.

3 Ibid., 23.

4 Charles Seymour, *Letters from the Paris Peace Conference* (New Haven, CT: Yale University Press, 1965), xxxii.

5 Ibid., xxi.

6 Ibid., 78.

7 Alfred F. Havighurst, *Britain in Transition: The Twentieth Century* (Chicago: University of Chicago Press, 1985), 149.

8 J. W. Schulte Nordholt, *Woodrow Wilson: A Life for World Peace* (Berkeley: University of California Press, 1991), 287.

9 Robert Lansing, *The Big Four and Others of the Peace Conference* (New York: Houghton Mifflin, 1921), 10.

10 Ibid., 85.

11 Seymour, *Letters from the Paris Peace Conference*, 55.

12 Billy Hughes to Governor General Ronald Munro Ferguson, January 17, 1919, in Papers of Ronald Craufurd Munro Ferguson, 1912-1935, National Library of Australia Collections.

13 Harold Nicolson, *Peacemaking 1919* (London: Constable, 1933), 77.

14 John Maynard Keynes, *The End of Laissez-Faire: The Economic Consequences of the Peace* (Amherst, NY: Prometheus Books, 2004), 38.

15 David Lloyd George, *Memoirs of the Peace Conference* (New Haven, CT: Yale University Press, 1939), 139.

16 Ibid., 140.

17 Margaret MacMillan, *Paris 1919* (New York: Random House, 2001), 97.

18 Ray Stannard Baker and Woodrow Wilson, *Woodrow Wilson and World Settlement* (New York: Doubleday, 1922), 235.

19 Edward House, *The Intimate Papers of Colonel House*, ed. Charles Seymour (Boston: Houghton Mifflin, 1928), 280.

20 MacMillan, *Paris 1919*, 86.

21 Lansing, *Peace Negotiations*, 43.

22 House, *Intimate Papers of Colonel House*, 479-480.

23 MacMillan, *Paris 1919*, 91.

24 Lloyd George, *Memoirs of the Peace Conference*, 181.

25 House, *Intimate Papers of Colonel House*, 300.

26 Ibid., 303.

27 MacMillan, *Paris 1919*, 94.

28 Ibid., 92.

29 Ibid., 93.

30 House, *Intimate Papers of Colonel House*, 314.

31 MacMillan, *Paris 1919*, 95.

32 *New York Herald*, February 23, 1919 (Paris ed.).

33 Lansing, *Peace Negotiations*, 81.

34 Ibid., 172.

35 Elmer Bendiner, *A Time for Angels: The Tragicomic History of the League of Nations* (New York: Knopf, 1975), 106.

36 Lloyd George, *Memoirs of the Peace Conference*, 200.

37 Nicolson, *Peacemaking 1919*, 270. (Old newspapers fact from Seymour, *Letters from the Paris Peace Conference*, 164.)

38 MacMillan, *Paris 1919*, 169.

39 Ibid., 180.

40 Woodrow Wilson, *The Papers of Woodrow Wilson,* vol. 61, ed. Arthur S. Link (Princeton, NJ: Princeton University Press, 1994), 191.

41 MacMillan, *Paris 1919*, 187.

42 Lloyd George, *Memoirs of the Peace Conference*, 331.

43 MacMillan, *Paris 1919*, 184.

44 Nicolson, *Peacemaking 1919*, 203.

45 MacMillan, *Paris 1919*, 189.

46 Ibid., 189.

47 Ibid., 185.

48 Lloyd George, *Memoirs of the Peace Conference*, 294.

49 Seymour, *Letters from the Paris Peace Conference*, 45.

50 Lansing, *Peace Negotiations*, 235.

51 Seymour, *Letters from the Paris Peace Conference*, 135.

52 Ibid., 155.

53 Ibid.

54 Ibid., 137.

55 House, *Intimate Papers of Colonel House*, 337.

56 Ibid., 271, 274.

57 Lloyd George, *Memoirs of the Peace Conference*, 260.

58 House, *Intimate Papers of Colonel House*, 345.

59 Lloyd George, *Memoirs of the Peace Conference*, 203.

60 Ibid., 201.

61 MacMillan, *Paris 1919*, 212.

62 Philip Bobbitt, *The Shield of Achilles* (New York: Knopf, 2002), 408.

63 Nicolson, *Peacemaking 1919*, 288.

64 Winston Churchill, *The Great War* (London: George Newnes, 1933), 1415.

65 Ibid., 1413.

66 House, *Intimate Papers of Colonel House*, 384.

67 Ibid., 389.

68 Ibid., 377.

69 Nicolson, *Peacemaking 1919*, 291.

70 Ibid.

71 House, *Intimate Papers of Colonel House*, 395.

72 Ibid.

73 Ibid., 396.

74 Ibid., 399-400.

75 Ibid., 402-3.

76 Ibid., 400-402.

77 Ibid., 405.

78 Ibid., 406-7.

79 Nicolson, *Peacemaking 1919*, 198.

80 Ibid., 92.

81 Ibid., 68.

82 Lloyd George, *Memoirs of the Peace Conference*, 538.

83 House, *Intimate Papers of Colonel House*, 446.

84 MacMillan, *Paris 1919*, 465.

85 Lansing, *Peace Negotiations*, 97.

86 Lloyd George, *Memoirs of the Peace Conference*, 200.

87 Nicolson, *Peacemaking 1919*, 115.

88 Ibid., 329.

89 Lloyd George, *Memoirs of the Peace Conference*, 647.

90 MacMillan, *Paris 1919*, 466.

91 Ibid., 470.

92 Ibid.

93 Ibid., 471.

94 Ibid., 474.

95 Lansing, *Peace Negotiations*, 272-273.

96 Ibid., 273.

97 Winston Churchill, *The Gathering Storm* (New York: Mariner Books, 1948), 6.

98 House, *Intimate Papers of Colonel House*, 488-9.

99 Lloyd George, *Memoirs of the Peace Conference*, 491.

100 Kissinger, *Diplomacy*, 229.

101 Lloyd George, *Memoirs of the Peace Conference*, 284.

102 Ibid., 266.

CHAPTER SIX: THE EGYPTIAN-ISRAELI ARMISTICE AGREEMENT

1 J. C. Hurewitz, "The United Nations Conciliation Commission for Palestine: Establishment and Definition of Functions." *International Organization* 7, no. 4 (Nov. 1953), 485.

2 Ibid., 486.

3 Jon and David Kimche, *A Clash of Destinies: The Arab-Jewish War and the Founding of the State of Israel* (New York: Praeger Publishers, 1960), 265.

4 Nobel Peace Prize Presentation Speech by Gunnar Jahn, chairman of the Nobel Committee, 1950, http://nobelprize.org/nobel_prizes/peace/laureates/1950/press.html; also Ralph J. Bunche, *Selected Speeches and Writings*, ed. Charles P. Henry (Ann Arbor: University of Michigan Press, 1995), 269.

5 Nobel Peace Prize Presentation Speech by Gunnar Jahn, chairman of the Nobel Committee, 1950.

6 Walter Eytan, *The First Ten Years: A Diplomatic History of Israel* (New York: Simon and Schuster, 1958), 29-30.

7 Statement by Acting Mediator at Opening Meeting of Egyptian-Israeli Negotiations, Rhodes, January 13, 1949, UN Archives.

8 Draft Declaration on Assurances as Regards Action by Armed Forces and Security, January 14, 1949, in *Documents on the Foreign Policy of Israel, vol. 3: Armistice Negotiations with the Arab States December 1948-July 1949* (Jerusalem: Israel State Archives, 1983), 21-22; and Tentative Draft Agenda (Revised Version), UN Archives.

9 Eytan to Sharett, January 13, 1949, in *Documents on the Foreign Policy of Israel, vol. 3*, 18.

10 Eytan, *First Ten Years*, 30; also Dan Kurzman, *Genesis 1948: The First Arab-Israeli War* (New York: World Publishing, 1970), 681.

11 Peggy Mann, *Ralph Bunche, UN Peacemaker* (New York: Coward, McCann & Geoghegan, 1975), 248.

12 Neil Caplan, "A Tale of Two Cities: The Rhodes and Lausanne Conferences, 1949." *Journal of Palestine Studies* 21, no. 3 (Spring 1992), 8; also Mann, *Ralph Bunche*, 246.

13 Eytan to Sharett, January 16, 1949, in *Documents on the Foreign Policy of Israel, vol. 3*, 28.

14 Ibid.

15 Eytan, *First Ten Years*, 39.

16 Bunche's notes, 6, UCLA Archives.

17 Bunche to Secretary General, January 20, 1949, UN Archives.

18 Bunche's notes, 7, UCLA Archives.

19 Ibid., 9.

20 Ibid.

21 Eytan to Sharett, January 24, 1949, in *Documents on the Foreign Policy of Israel, vol. 3*, 67.

22 Bunche to Secretary General, January 23, 1949, UN Archives.

23 Bunche's notes, 9-10, UCLA Archives.

24 Ibid., 12.

25 Mann, *Ralph Bunche*, 252.

26 Benjamin Rivlin, ed., *Ralph Bunche: The Man and His Times* (New York: Holmes & Meier, 1990), 177-178.

27 Ibid., 178.

28 Caplan, *A Tale of Two Cities*, 8.

29 Sharett to Eytan, January 24, 1949, in *Documents on the Foreign Policy of Israel, vol. 3: Armistice Negotiations with the Arab States December 1948-July 1949 Companion Volume* (Jerusalem: Israel State Archives, 1983), 15.

30 Brian Urquhart, *Ralph Bunche: An American Life* (New York: Norton, 1993), 206.

31 Mann, *Ralph Bunche*, 253.

32 Bunche to Secretary General, January 27, 1949, UN Archives.

33 Lie to Bunche, January 30, 1949, UN Archives.

34 Urquhart, *Ralph Bunche*, 204.

35 Rivlin, *Ralph Bunche*, 185.

36 Bunche's notes, 15, UCLA Archives.

37 Ibid.

38 Ibid.

39 Bunche to Eytan, January 31, 1949, in *Documents on the Foreign Policy of Israel, vol. 3*, 96-97.

40 Caplan, *A Tale of Two Cities*, 9.

41 Bunche's notes, 18, UCLA Archives.

42 Ibid.

43 Bunche to Secretary General, February 4, 1949, UN Archives.

44 Bunche's notes, 20, UCLA Archives.

45 Eytan, *First Ten Years*, 31.

46 Mann, *Ralph Bunche*, 248.

47 Ibid., 250.

48 Ibid., 247.

49 Bunche's notes, 27, UCLA Archives.

50 Urquhart, *Ralph Bunche*, 224.

51 Mann, *Ralph Bunche*, 253.

52 Ibid., 253-254.

53 Eytan, *First Ten Years*, 32.

54 Urquhart, *Ralph Bunche*, 224.

55 Bunche to Secretary General, February 5, 1949, UN Archives.

56 Bunche to Secretary General, February 6, 1949, UN Archives.

57 Eytan to Sharett, February 7, 1949, in *Documents on the Foreign Policy of Israel, vol. 3*, 216.

58 *Documents on the Foreign Policy of Israel, vol. 3: Armistice Negotiations with the Arab States December 1948-July 1949 Companion Volume*, 136.

59 Urquhart, *Ralph Bunche*, 207.

60 Bunche's notes, 21-22, UCLA Archives.

61 Eytan, *First Ten Years*, 35.

62 Bunche to Secretary General, February 10, 1949, UN Archives.

63 Eytan to Sharett, February 10, 1949, in *Documents on the Foreign Policy of Israel, vol. 3*, 234.

64 Eytan, *First Ten Years*, 33.

65 Bunche to Secretary General, February 13, 1949, UN Archives.

66 Caplan, *A Tale of Two Cities*, 10.

67 Eytan to Sharett, February 16, 1949, in *Documents on the Foreign Policy of Israel, vol. 3*, 252.

68 Eytan to Sharett, February 17, 1949, in *Documents on the Foreign Policy of Israel, vol. 3*, 254.

69 Bunche to Secretary General, February 19, 1949, UN Archives.

70 Bunche to Secretary General, February 20, 1949, UN Archives.

71 Ibid.

72 Ibid.

73 Bunche's notes, 34, UCLA Archives.

74 Mann, *Ralph Bunche*, 255.

75 Eytan, *First Ten Years*, 31.

76 *Documents on the Foreign Policy of Israel, vol. 3, Armistice Negotiations with the Arab States December 1948-July 1949. Companion Volume*, 133.

77 Caplan, *A Tale of Two Cities*, 11.

78 Nuchhi R. Currier, "'Nation shall not rise up against nation . . .,'" *UN Chronicle* 40, no. 3 (2003), http://www.un.org/Pubs/chronicle/2003/issue3/0303p37.asp; Harry Kreisler, "A Life in Peace and War: Conversation With Sir Brian Urquhart," Conversations with History series, Institute of International Studies, University of California, Berkeley (March 19, 1996), http://globetrotter.berkeley.edu/UN/Urquhart/urquhart5.html.

79 Mann, *Ralph Bunche*, 257.

80 Nobel Peace Prize Presentation Speech by Gunnar Jahn, chairman of the Nobel Committee, 1950.

CHAPTER SEVEN: THE CUBAN MISSILE CRISIS

1 John Lewis Gaddis, *The Cold War: A New History* (New York: Penguin, 2005), 75.

2 Nikita Khrushchev, *Khrushchev Remembers*, trans. and ed. Strobe Talbott (Boston: Little, Brown, 1970), 494.

3 Arthur M. Schlesinger Jr., *A Thousand Days: John F. Kennedy in the White House* (New York: Mariner Books, 2002), 802-803.

4 McGeorge Bundy, *Danger and Survival: Choices About the Bomb in the First Fifty Years* (New York: Vintage Books, 1990), 398.

5 This and the following quotations from President John F. Kennedy "Radio-TV Address of the President to the Nation from the White House," October 22, 1962, National Security Archive.

6 Theodore C. Sorensen, *Counselor: A Life at the Edge of History* (New York: HarperCollins, 2008), 298.

7 Aleksandr Fursenko and Timothy Naftali, *Khrushchev's Cold War: The Inside Story of an American Adversary* (New York: Norton, 2006), 470.

8 Khrushchev to Kennedy, October 23, 1962, National Security Archive.

9 Khrushchev, *Khrushchev Remembers*, 497.

10 Kennedy to Khrushchev, October 23, 1962, National Security Archive.

11 David L. Larson, ed., *The "Cuban Crisis" of 1962: Selected Documents and Chronology* (Boston: Houghton Mifflin, 1963), 108-109; also Elie Abel, *The Missile Crisis* (Philadelphia: J.B. Lippincott, 1966), 125.

12 Sheldon M. Stern, *Averting "The Final Failure": John F. Kennedy and the Secret Cuban Missile Crisis Meetings* (Stanford, CA: Stanford University Press, 2003), 176.

13 Mark J. White, *Missiles in Cuba: Kennedy, Khrushchev, Castro and the 1962 Crisis* (Chicago: Ivan R. Dee, 1997), 115; also Robert F. Kennedy, *Thirteen Days: A Memoir of the Cuban Missile Crisis* (New York: Norton, 1999), 49.

14 Aleksandr Fursenko and Timothy Naftali, *One Hell of a Gamble: Khrushchev, Castro, and Kennedy 1958-1964* (New York: Norton, 1997), 251.

15 White, *Missiles in Cuba*, 118.

16 Fursenko, *One Hell of a Gamble*, 253.

17 Khrushchev to Kennedy, October 24, 1962, National Security Archive.

18 Nikita Khrushchev, *Memoirs of Nikita Khrushchev*, vol. 3, *Statesman (1953-1964)*, ed. Sergei Khrushchev (University Park: Pennsylvania State University Press, 2007), 350.

19 Arthur M. Schlesinger Jr., *Robert Kennedy and His Times* (New York: Houghton Mifflin, 1978), 514.

20 White, *Missiles in Cuba*, 120.

21 Kennedy, *Thirteen Days*, 55.

22 Internal State Department Correspondence. Roger Hilsman to Secretary Rusk, October 26, 1962, National Security Archive.

23 Fursenko, *One Hell of a Gamble*, 256.

24 George W. Ball, *The Past Has Another Pattern: Memoirs* (New York: Norton, 1982), 300.

25 Fursenko, *One Hell of a Gamble*, 279; also Stern, *Averting the Final Failure*, 303.

26 Theodore C. Sorensen, *Kennedy* (New York: Konecky & Konecky, 1965), 710.

27 "Kennedy talked Khrushchev triumphed," *New York Times*, May 22, 2008.

28 Stern, *Averting the Final Failure*, 225.

29 Ibid, 241.

30 Kennedy, *Thirteen Days*, 59.

31 Theodore C. Sorensen, *Decision-Making in the White House: The Olive Branch or the Arrows* (New York: Columbia University Press, 2005), 31.

32 Kennedy to Khrushchev, October 25, 1962, National Security Archive.

33 U.S. Ambassador Adlai Stevenson United Nations Security Council Address Exchange with Soviet Ambassador Valerian Zorin delivered October 25, 1962, United Nations Archives.

34 Fursenko, *One Hell of a Gamble*, 259.

35 Stern, *Averting the Final Failure*, 236.

36 Fursenko, *One Hell of a Gamble*, 259.

37 Ibid, 260.

38 Khrushchev, *Khrushchev Remembers*, 497.

39 Ibid.

40 Ball, *Past Has Another Pattern*, 302.

41 Schlesinger, *Thousand Days*, 826.

42 Michael Tatu, *Power in the Kremlin: From Khrushchev to Kosygin* (New York: Viking Press, 1970), 266-267.

43 Kennedy, *Thirteen Days*, 69.

44 Fursenko, *One Hell of a Gamble*, 270.

45 Ibid.

46 Ball, *Past Has Another Pattern*, 302.

47 Ibid.

48 Ibid.

49 Sorensen, *Counselor*, 288.

50 Ball, *Past Has Another Pattern*, 306.

51 Stern, *Averting the Final Failure*, 84.

52 Khrushchev, *Memoirs of Nikita Khrushchev*, vol. 3, 341.

53 Khrushchev to Kennedy, October 26, 1962, National Security Archive.

54 Dean Rusk, *As I Saw It* (New York: Penguin Books, 1991), 239.

55 Ball, *Past Has Another Pattern*, 304.

56 Sorensen, *Kennedy*, 712.

57 Stern, *Averting the Final Failure*, 266.

58 Khrushchev to Kennedy, October 27, 1962, National Security Archive.

59 Bundy, *Danger and Survival*, 445.

60 Stern, *Averting the Final Failure*, 319.

61 Ball, *Past Has Another Pattern*, 306.

62 Stern, *Averting the Final Failure*, 300.

63 Ibid.

64 Ibid, 303.

65 Ibid, 304.

66 Ibid.

67 Ibid.

68 Ibid, 305.

69 Ibid, 306.

70 Kennedy, *Thirteen Days*, 73.

71 Bundy, *Danger and Survival*, 405.

72 Stern, *Averting the Final Failure*, 371.

73 Schlesinger, *Robert Kennedy and His Times*, 520.

74 This and the following quotations from the Scali-Fomin meeting are from Bundy, *Danger and Survival*, 438-439.

75 Kurt Wiersma and Ben Larson. *Fourteen Days in October: The Cuban Missile Crisis* (http://library.thinkquest.org/11046/media/fourteen_days_in_october.pdf), 16.

76 Sorensen, *Kennedy*, 714.

77 Ibid.

78 Kennedy, *Thirteen Days*, 81.

79 Ibid, 97.

80 Kennedy to Khrushchev, October 27, 1962, National Security Archive.

81 Kennedy, *Thirteen Days*, 83.

82 White, *Missiles in Cuba*, 140.

83 Stern, *Averting the Final Failure*, 369.

84 Khrushchev, *Khrushchev Remembers*, 551-552.

85 Memorandum for the Secretary of State from the Attorney General October 30, 1962, National Security Archive.

86 Dobrynin Cable to the USSR Foreign Ministry, 27 October 1962, National Security Archive.

87 Ibid.

88 Khrushchev, *Khrushchev Remembers*, 497.

89 Dobrynin Cable to the USSR Foreign Ministry, 27 October 1962, National Security Archive.

90 Memorandum for the Secretary of State from the Attorney General. October 30, 1962, National Security Archive.

91 Dobrynin Cable to the USSR Foreign Ministry, 27 October 1962, National Security Archive.

92 Ibid.

93 Memorandum for the Secretary of State from the Attorney General. October 30, 1962, National Security Archive.

94 Schlesinger, *Robert Kennedy and His Times*, 522.

95 Kennedy, *Thousand Days*, 829.

96 Khrushchev, *Memoirs of Nikita Khrushchev*, vol. 3, 340.

97 Fursenko, *One Hell of a Gamble*, 284.

98 Ibid, 285.

99 Khrushchev, *Khrushchev Remembers*, 498.

100 Ibid.

101 Stern, *Averting the Final Failure*, 384.

102 Ibid.

103 Bundy, *Danger and Survival*, 444; also Schlesinger, *Robert Kennedy and His Times*, n529 (originally from Norman Cousins, "The Cuban Missile Crisis: An Anniversary," *Saturday Review*, October 15, 1977).

104 Stern, *Averting the Final Failure*, 384.

105 Khrushchev communiqué to Kennedy, October 28, 1962, National Security Archive.

106 Statement by President Kennedy, October 28, 1962, National Security Archive.

107 Kennedy, *Thirteen Days*, 98.

108 Schlesinger, *Robert Kennedy and His Times*, 530.

109 Ibid, 530.

110 Kennedy, *Thirteen Days*, 95.

111 Sorensen, *Counselor*, 296.

112 Bundy, *Danger and Survival*, 462.

Chapter Eight: The Reykjavik Summit

1 Eduard Shevardnadze, *The Future Belongs to Freedom* (London: Sinclair-Stevenson, 1991), 81.

2 Mikhail Gorbachev, *On My Country and the World* (New York: Columbia University Press, 2000), 171.

3 Shevardnadze, *Future Belongs to Freedom*, 81.

4 Jack Matlock Jr., *Reagan and Gorbachev: How the Cold War Ended* (New York: Random House, 2005), 106.

5 Mikhail Gorbachev, *Memoirs* (New York: Doubleday, 1995), 165.

6 Gorbachev, *On My Country and the World*, 172.

7 Gorbachev, *Memoirs*, 411.

8 Don Oberdorfer, *From the Cold War to a New Era: The United States and the Soviet Union, 1983-1991* (Baltimore: Johns Hopkins University Press, 1998), 154.

9 Gorbachev to Reagan, September 15, 1986, National Security Archive.

10 George Shultz, *Turmoil and Triumph: Diplomacy, Power and the Victory of the American Ideal* (New York: MacMillan, 1993), 743.

11 Edmund Morris, *Dutch: A Memoir of Ronald Reagan* (New York: Random House, 1999), 591.

12 Anatoly Chernyaev Meeting Notes, October 4, 1986, National Security Archive.

13 Ibid.

14 Chernyaev Notes from the Politburo Session, October 8, 1986, National Security Archive.

15 Ronald Reagan, *An American Life* (New York: Simon & Schuster, 1990), 637.

16 Gorbachev, *Memoirs*, 417.

17 Shultz, *Turmoil and Triumph*, 758.

18 Gorbachev, *Memoirs*, 444.

19 Ibid.

20 U.S. Meeting Notes, October 11, 1986 (White House Memorandum of Conversation: Reagan-Gorbachev Meetings in Reykjavik.), National Security Archive.

21 Shultz, *Turmoil and Triumph*, 760.

22 Ibid., 761.

23 U.S. and Soviet Meeting Notes, October 11, 1986, National Security Archive.

24 Reagan, *An American Life*, 707.

25 U.S. and Soviet Meeting Notes, October 11, 1986, National Security Archive.

26 Shultz, *Turmoil and Triumph*, 762.

27 Paul Nitze, *From Hiroshima to Glasnost: At the Center of Decision* (New York: Grove Weidenfeld, 1989), 430.

28 Kenneth L. Adelman, *The Great Universal Embrace: Arms Summitry–A Skeptic's Account* (New York: Simon and Schuster, 1989), 53.

29 Shultz, *Turmoil and Triumph*, 765.

30 U.S. and Soviet Meeting Notes, October 12, 1986, National Security Archive.

31 Ibid.

32 Shultz, *Turmoil and Triumph*, 766.

33 Reagan, *An American Life*, 677.

34 U.S. and Soviet Meeting Notes, October 12, 1986, National Security Archive.

35 Soviet Meeting Notes, October 12, 1986, National Security Archive.

36 Ibid.

37 Matlock, *Reagan and Gorbachev*, 224.

38 Oberdorfer, *From the Cold War to a New Era*, 196.

39 Ibid., 197.

40 Shultz, *Turmoil and Triumph*, 768.

41 Oberdorfer, *From the Cold War to a New Era*, 199.

42 Matlock, *Reagan and Gorbachev*, 228.

43 William C. Wohlforth, *Witnesses to the End of the Cold War* (Baltimore: Johns Hopkins University Press, 1996), 179.

44 Gorbachev, *Memoirs*, 418.

45 Soviet Meeting Notes, October 12, 1986, National Security Archive.

46 U.S. and Soviet Meeting Notes, October 12, 1986, National Security Archive.

47 Ibid.

48 Shultz, *Turmoil and Triumph*, 772.

49 U.S. and Soviet Meeting Notes, October 12, 1986, National Security Archive.

50 Oberdorfer, *From the Cold War to a New Era*, 201.

51 Matlock, *Reagan and Gorbachev*, 232.

52 Donald T. Regan, *For the Record: From Wall Street to Washington* (New York: Harcourt Brace Jovanovich, 1988), 349-350.

53 Peter Schweizer, *Victory: The Reagan Administration's Secret Strategy That Hastened the Collapse of the Soviet Union* (New York: Atlantic Monthly Press, 1994), 276.

54 Soviet Meeting Notes, October 12, 1986, National Security Archive.

55 U.S. and Soviet Meeting Notes, October 12, 1986, National Security Archive.

56 Ibid.

57 Oberdorfer, *From the Cold War to a New Era*, 203.

58 Shultz, *Turmoil and Triumph*, 768.

59 Soviet Meeting Notes, October 12, 1986, National Security Archive.

60 Ibid.

61 Reagan, *An American Life*, 678.

62 Ibid., 677.

63 Shultz, *Turmoil and Triumph*, 770.

64 Regan, *For the Record*, 348.

65 U.S. and Soviet Meeting Notes, October 12, 1986, National Security Archive.

66 Shultz, *Turmoil and Triumph*, 765.

67 Reagan, *An American Life*, 677.

68 Shultz, *Turmoil and Triumph*, 771.

69 U.S. and Soviet Meeting Notes, October 12, 1986, National Security Archive.

70 Oberdorfer, *From the Cold War to a New Era,* 203.

71 Oberdorfer, *From the Cold War to a New Era,* 203-204; also U.S. and Soviet Meeting Notes, October 12, 1986, National Security Archive.

72 U.S. and Soviet Meeting Notes, October 12, 1986, National Security Archive.

73 Matlock, *Reagan and Gorbachev,* 234.

74 Shultz, *Turmoil and Triumph*, 772.

75 Matlock, *Reagan and Gorbachev,* 235.

76 U.S. and Soviet Meeting Notes, October 12, 1986, National Security Archive.

77 Ibid.

78 Shultz, *Turmoil and Triumph*, 773.

79 Morris, *Dutch*, 599.

80 Reagan, *An American Life*, 679.

81 Morris, *Dutch*, 599.

82 Shultz, *Turmoil and Triumph*, 773.

83 Morris, *Dutch*, 599.

84 Reagan, *An American Life*, 679.

85 Regan, *For the Record*, 351.

86 Shultz, *Turmoil and Triumph*, 775.

87 Gorbachev, *Memoirs*, 419-420,

88 Oberdorfer, *From the Cold War to a New Era,* 206.

89 Ibid.

90 Morris, *Dutch*, 599.

91 Oberdorfer, *From the Cold War to a New Era*, 207.

92 Shultz, *Turmoil and Triumph*, 775.

93 Michael Mandelbaum and Strobe Talbott, *Reagan and Gorbachev* (New York: Random House, 1987), 180-181.

94 Oberdorfer, *From the Cold War to a New Era*, 217.

95 Gorbachev, *Memoirs*, 449.

BIBLIOGRAPHY

CHAPTER ONE: FRANKLIN AT THE FRENCH COURT, 1778

Franklin Manuscript Sources

The Bancroft Collection. Manuscripts and Archives Division, New York Public Library, New York.

The Diplomatic Correspondence of the American Revolution, vols. 1-12. Edited by Jared Sparks. Boston: Hale and Gray & Bowen, 1830.

The Franklin Papers Archive. Yale University. www.FranklinPapers.org.

The Revolutionary Diplomatic Correspondence of the United States, vols. 1-6. Edited by Francis Wharton. Washington, DC: Government Printing Office, 1889.

Stevens, Benjamin Franklin, comp. *Facsimiles of Manuscripts in European Archives Relating to America, 1773-1783*. London: 1898.

Franklin Book Sources

Aldridge, Alfred Owen. *Benjamin Franklin: Philosopher and Man*. Philadelphia: J.B. Lippincott, 1965.

———. *Franklin and His French Contemporaries*. New York: New York University Press, 1957.

Alsop, Susan Mary. *Yankees at the Court: The First Americans in Paris*. Garden City, NY: Doubleday, 1982.

Bailyn, Bernard. *To Begin the World Anew: The Genius and Ambiguities of the American Founders*. New York: Vintage Books, 2004.

Bemis, Samuel Flagg. *The Diplomacy of the American Revolution*. Bloomington: Indiana University Press, 1965.

Brands, H. W. *The First American: The Life and Times of Benjamin Franklin*. New York: Random House, 2000.

Brecher, Frank W. *Securing American Independence: John Jay and the French Alliance*. Westport, CT: Praeger Publishers, 2003.

Brown, Weldon A. *Empire or Independence: A Study in the Failure of Reconciliation, 1774-1783*. Port Washington, NY: Kennikat Press, 1966.

Bryan, William Jennings, and Francis Whiting Halsey, eds. *The World's Famous Orations*, vol. 3. New York: Funk and Wagnalls, 1906.

Burlingame, Roger. *Benjamin Franklin, Envoy Extraordinary: The Secret Missions and Open Pleasures of Benjamin Franklin in London and Paris*. New York: Coward-McCann, 1967.

Chinard, Gilbert, and James Brown Scott. *The Treaties of 1778 and Allied Documents*. Baltimore: Johns Hopkins University Press, 1928.

Corwin, Edward S. *French Policy and the American Alliance of 1778*. Princeton, NJ: Princeton University Press, 1916.

Cuneo, John. *Benjamin Franklin: Ingenious Diplomat*. New York: McGraw Hill, 1969.

Deane, Silas, and Charles Isham. *The Deane Papers, 1774-1799*. Vols. 1-3. New York: New York Historical Society, 1888.

Doren, Carl Van. *Benjamin Franklin*. New York: Penguin, 1991.

Dull, Jonathan R. *A Diplomatic History of the American Revolution*. New Haven, CT: Yale University Press, 1985.

———. *Franklin the Diplomat: the French Mission*. Philadelphia: American Philosophical Society, 1982.

Fleming, Thomas. *The Man Who Dared the Lightning: A New Look at Benjamin Franklin*. New York: William Morrow, 1971.

Franklin, Benjamin. *Letters from France: The Private Diplomatic Correspondence of Benjamin Franklin 1776-1785*. Edited by Brett Woods. New York: Algora Publishing, 2006.

———. *The Writings of Benjamin Franklin*. Vol. 7. Edited by Albert Smyth. New York: MacMillan, 1907.

Giunta, Mary A., ed. *Documents of the Emerging Nation: U.S. Foreign Relations, 1775-1789*. Wilmington, DE: Scholarly Resources, in cooperation with the National Historical Publications and Records Commission, 1998.

Griffin, Appleton Prentiss Clark, ed. *List of Works Relating to the French Alliance in the American Revolution*. Washington, DC: Government Printing Office, 1907.

Hale, Edward Everett, and Edward E. Hale Jr. *Franklin in France: From Original Documents Most of Which Are Now Published for the First Time*, vols. 1 and 2. Boston: Roberts Brothers, 1887.

Hardman, John, and Munro Price, eds. *Louis XVI and the Comte de Vergennes: Correspondence, 1774-1787*. Oxford: Voltaire Foundation, 1998.

Hoffman, Ronald, and Peter J. Albert, eds. *Diplomacy and Revolution: The Franco-American Alliance of 1778.* Charlottesville, VA: University Press of Virginia, 1981.

Hutson, James H. *John Adams and the Diplomacy of the American Revolution.* Lexington, KY: University Press of Kentucky, 1980.

Isaacson, Walter. *Benjamin Franklin: An American Life.* New York: Simon & Schuster, 2003.

Lee, Richard Henry. *Life of Arthur Lee: Joint Commissioner of the U.S. to the Court of France, and Sole Commissioner to the Courts of Spain and Prussia, During the Revolutionary War.* Boston: Wells and Lilly, 1829.

Middlekauff, Robert. *The Glorious Cause: The American Revolution, 1763-1789.* Oxford: Oxford University Press, 1982.

Morris, Richard. *The Peacemakers: The Great Powers and American Independence.* New York: Harper & Row, 1965.

New York Historical Society Collections, 1887. New York: New York Historical Society, 1888.

Perkins, James Breck. *France in the American Revolution.* Boston: Houghton Mifflin, 1911.

Price, Munro. *Preserving the Monarchy: The Comte De Vergennes, 1774-1787.* Cambridge, England: Cambridge University Press, 1995.

Schiff, Stacy. *A Great Improvisation: Franklin, France, and the Birth of America.* New York: Holt, 2005.

Schoenbrun, David. *Triumph in Paris: The Exploits of Benjamin Franklin.* New York: Harper & Row, 1976.

Sheldon, Laura Charlotte. *France and the American Revolution: 1763-1788.* Ithaca, NY: Andrus & Church, 1900.

Stinchcombe, William. *The American Revolution and the French Alliance.* Syracuse, NY: Syracuse University Press, 1969.

Steell, Willis. *Benjamin Franklin of Paris.* New York: Minton, Balch, 1928.

Stourzh, Gerald. *Benjamin Franklin and American Foreign Policy.* Chicago: University of Chicago Press, 1969.

Washington, George. *The Writings of George Washington: Being His Correspondence, Addresses, Messages, and Other Papers, Official and Private, Selected and Published from the Original Manuscripts.* Edited by Jared Sparks. Boston: G. W. Boynton, 1834.

Franklin Periodical Sources

Aruga, Tadashi. "Revolutionary Diplomacy and the Franco-American Treaties of 1778." *The Japanese Journal of American Studies*, no. 2. (1985): 59-100.

CHAPTER TWO: THE LOUISIANA PURCHASE, 1803

Louisiana Purchase Manuscript Sources

Documents of the French Government Archives. Manuscript Division, Library of Congress, Washington, DC.

Robert Livingston Papers. Manuscripts and Archives Division, New York Public Library, New York.

Robert Livingston Papers. New York Historical Society Library, New York.

Monroe's Memoranda. Monroe MSS. State Department Archives. U.S. Department of State, Washington, DC.

State Papers and Correspondence Bearing Upon the Purchase of the Territory of Louisiana. Washington, DC: U.S. Department of State, 1903.

U.S. Government House Document 431, 57th Cong., 2d sess., 1903. Washington, DC.

Louisiana Purchase Book Sources

Adams, Henry. *History of the United States of America.* Vols. 1-2. New York: Charles Scribner's Sons, 1889-91.

–––. *History of the United States During the Administration of Thomas Jefferson.* New York: Library of America, 1986.

Ammon, Henry. *James Monroe: The Quest for National Identity.* New York: McGraw-Hill, 1971.

Barbé-Marbois, Francois. *The History of Louisiana, Particularly of the Cessation of That Colony to the United States of America.* Philadelphia: Carey & Lea, 1830.

Barry, James. *The Louisiana Purchase.* New York: Franklin Watts, 1973.

Bernard, Jack. *Talleyrand: A Biography.* New York: G. P. Putnam's Sons, 1973.

Blanchard, Rufus, ed. *Documentary History of the Cession of Louisiana to the United States.* Chicago: R. Blanchard, 1903.

Brant, Irving. *James Madison.* Vol. 4. Indianapolis: Bobbs-Merrill, 1959.

Brecher, Frank W. *Negotiating the Louisiana Purchase: Robert Livingston's Mission to France 1801-1804*. Jefferson, NC: McFarland, 2006.

Brodie, Fawn. *Thomas Jefferson: An Intimate History*. New York: Norton, 1974.

Brown, Charles. *An Interesting Account of the Project of France Respecting Louisiana*. Martinsburg, WV: John Alburtis, 1803.

———. *Monroe's Embassy*. Philadelphia: John Conrad, 1803.

Bryan, George. *The Spy in America*. Philadelphia: J.B. Lippincott, 1943.

Castelot, Andre. *Napoleon*. New York: Harper & Row, 1971.

Cerami, Charles. *Jefferson's Great Gamble: The Remarkable Story of Jefferson, Napoleon and the Men Behind the Louisiana Purchase*. Naperville, IL: Sourcebooks, 2003.

Chidsey, Donald Barr. *The Louisiana Purchase*. New York: Crown Publishers, 1972.

Cresson, W. P. *James Monroe*. Chapel Hill: University of North Carolina Press, 1946.

Dangerfield, George. *Chancellor Robert R. Livingston of New York, 1746-1813*. New York: Harcourt, Brace, 1960.

Daniels, Jonathan. *Ordeal of Ambition: Jefferson, Hamilton, Burr*. Garden City, NY: Doubleday, 1970.

Dayan, Joan. *Haiti, History, and the Gods*. Berkeley: University of California Press, 1998.

DeConde, Alexander. *This Affair of Louisiana*. New York: Charles Scribner's Sons, 1976.

DeVoto, Bernard. *The Louisiana Purchase*. Springfield, OH: Crowell-Collier, 1953.

Ellis, Joseph. *American Creation: Triumphs and Tragedies at the Founding of the Republic*. New York: Random House, 2007.

Fleming, Thomas. *The Louisiana Purchase*. Hoboken, NJ: John Wiley & Sons, 2003.

Geer, Curtis Manning. *The Louisiana Purchase and the Westward Movement*. Philadelphia: G. Barrie, 1904.

Gilman, Daniel C. *James Monroe*. Boston: Houghton, Mifflin, 1898.

Haswell, Jock. *Spies and Spymasters: A Concise History of Intelligence*. London: Thames & Hudson, 1977.

Herold, J. Christopher. *The Age of Napoleon*. New York: Harper & Row, 1963.

Hitchcock, Ripley. *The Louisiana Purchase and the Exploration, Early History and Building of the West.* Boston: Ginn, 1903.

Hosmer, James. *The History of the Louisiana Purchase.* New York: D. Appleton, 1902.

Howard, James Q. *History of the Louisiana Purchase.* Chicago: Callaghan, 1902.

Jefferson, Thomas, and Pierre Samuel Du Pont de Nemours. *The Correspondence of Jefferson and Du Pont de Nemours.* Edited by Gilbert Chinard. Reprint, New York: Burt Franklin, 1972.

Johnson, Paul. *Napoleon.* New York: Viking, 2003.

Kaminski, John P., ed. *The Founders on the Founders: Word Portraits from the American Revolutionary Era.* Charlottesville: University of Virginia Press, 2008.

Kastor, Peter, ed. *The Louisiana Purchase: Emergence of an American Nation.* Washington, DC: Congressional Quarterly Press, 2002.

———. *The Nation's Crucible.* New Haven, CT: Yale University Press, 2004.

Keats, John. *Eminent Domain: The Louisiana Purchase and the Making of America.* New York: Charterhouse, 1973.

Ketcham, Ralph. *James Madison.* New York: Macmillan, 1971.

Kukla, Jon. *A Wilderness So Immense: The Louisiana Purchase.* New York: Knopf, 2003.

Labbe, Dolores, ed. *The Louisiana Purchase and Its Aftermath 1800-1830.* Lafayette, LA: Center for Louisiana Studies, University of Southwestern Louisiana, 1998.

Lewis, James. *The Louisiana Purchase: Jefferson's Noble Bargain.* Charlottesville, VA: Thomas Jefferson Foundation, 2003.

Livingston, Robert. *Original Letters of Robert R. Livingston, 1801-1803.* New Orleans: Louisiana Historical Society, 1953.

Ludwig, Emil. *Napoleon.* New York: Boni & Liveright, 1926.

Lyon, E. Wilson. *Louisiana in French Diplomacy 1759-1804.* Norman: University of Oklahoma Press, 1934.

———. *The Man Who Sold Louisiana: The Career of Francois Barbé-Marbois.* Norman: University of Oklahoma Press, 1942.

Madelin, Louis. *Talleyrand.* Paris: J. Tallandier, 1979.

Madison, James. *The Papers of James Madison.* Vols. 4 and 5. Edited by Robert J. Brugger. Charlottesville: University of Virginia Press, 1986.

Malone, Dumas. *Jefferson and His Time.* Vol. 4, *Jefferson the President.* Boston: Little, Brown, 1948.

Monroe, James. *The Writings of James Monroe*, vol. 4. Edited by
    Stanislaus Murray Hamilton. New York: G. P. Putnam's Sons,
    1900.

———. *The Autobiography of James Monroe*. Edited by Stuart Brown
    and Donald Baker. Syracuse, NY: Syracuse University Press, 1959.

———. *The Memoir of James Monroe Relating to United States
    Claims...* Charlottesville, VA: Gilmer, Davis, 1828.

Morgan, George. *Life of James Monroe*. New York: AMS Press, 1969.

Orieux, Jean *Talleyrand*. New York: Knopf, 1974.

Peterson, Merrill. *James Madison: A Biography in His Own Words*.
    New York: Newsweek, 1974.

Preston, Daniel, ed. *A Comprehensive Catalogue of the
    Correspondence and Papers of James Monroe*. Westport, CT:
    Greenwood Press, 2001.

Richard, Carl. *The Louisiana Purchase*. Lafayette, LA: Center for
    Louisiana Studies, University of Southwestern Louisiana, 1995.

Rodriguez, Junius, ed. *The Louisiana Purchase: A Historical and
    Geographical Encyclopedia*. Santa Barbara, CA: ABC-CLIO, 2002.

Rutland, Robert. *James Madison: The Founding Father*. New York:
    Macmillan, 1987.

Schom, Alan. *Napoleon Bonaparte*. New York: HarperCollins, 1997.

Skolnick, Richard. *1803: Jefferson's Decision: The United States
    Purchases Louisiana*. New York: Chelsea House, 1969.

Sprague, Marshall. *So Vast, So Beautiful a Land*. Athens, OH:
    Swallow/Ohio University Press, 1991.

Stewarton, Lewis. *The Revolutionary Plutarch: Exhibiting the Most
    Distinguished Characters, Literary, Military, and Political, in the
    Recent Annals of the French Republic*. London: J. Murray, 1806.

*Treaty and Conventions Entered Into and Ratified by the United
    States of America and the French Republic Relative to the Cession
    of Louisiana*. Washington, DC: Government Printing Office, 1803.

Whitaker, Arthur. *The Mississippi Question, 1795-1803: A Study in
    Trade, Politics, and Diplomacy*. New York: Appleton-Century,
    1934.

Winship, Albert E., and Robert W. Wallace. *The Louisiana Purchase:
    As It Was, and as It Is*. Chicago: A. Flanagan, 1903.

Louisiana Purchase Periodical Sources

Aiton, Arthur. "The Diplomacy of the Louisiana Cession." *American
    Historical Review* 36 (July 1931): 701-720.

Bowman, Albert. "Pichon, the United States and Louisiana." *Diplomatic History: The Journal of the Society for Historians of American Foreign Relations* 1 (1977): 257-270.

Hill, F. T. "Adventures in American Diplomacy: The Inside History of the Louisiana Purchase." *Atlantic Monthly* (1857) Vol. 113 (May 1914): 649-659.

McLemore, R. A. "Jeffersonian Diplomacy in the Purchase of Louisiana, 1803." *Louisiana Historical Quarterly* 18 (1935): 346-353.

Parsons, Edward. "The Letters of Robert R. Livingston: The Diplomatic Story of the Louisiana Purchase." *Proceedings of the American Antiquarian Society*, New Series, 52: 363-407.

Sparks, Jared. "The History of the Louisiana Purchase." *North American Review* 28 (April 1829): 389.

Turner, Fredrik Jackson. "The Diplomatic Contest for the Mississippi Valley." *Atlantic Monthly* 93 (1904): 676-691 and 807-817.

CHAPTER THREE: THE CONGRESS OF VIENNA, 1815

Congress of Vienna Book Sources

Alsop, Susan Mark. *The Congress Dances.* New York: Harper & Row, 1984.

Bartlett, C. J. *Castlereagh.* Toronto: Macmillan, 1966.

Bobbitt, Philip. *The Shield of Achilles.* New York: Knopf, 2002.

Breunig, Charles. *The Age of Revolution and Reaction: 1789-1850.* New York: Norton, 1970.

Castlereagh, Robert Stewart. *Correspondence, Despatches and Other Papers of Viscount Castlereagh, Second Marquess of Londonderry.* Edited by Charles William Vane. London: William Shoberl, 1852.

Chapman, Tim. *The Congress of Vienna: Origins, Processes and Results.* New York: Routledge, 1998.

Cooper, Duff. *Talleyrand.* Stanford, CA: Stanford University Press, 1932.

Dallas, Gregor. *The Final Act: The Roads to Waterloo.* New York: Holt, 1996.

Ferrero, Guglielmo. *The Reconstruction of Europe: Talleyrand and the Congress of Vienna 1814-1815.* New York: G. P. Putnam's Sons, 1941.

Freksa, Frederick, comp. *A Peace Congress of Intrigue: Vienna, 1815.* Translated by Harry Hansen. New York: Century, 1919.

Johnson, Paul. *The Birth of the Modern: World Society 1815-1830*. New York: HarperCollins, 1991.

King, David. *Vienna 1814: How the Conquerors of Napoleon Made Love, War, and Peace at the Congress of Vienna*. New York: Harmony Books, 2008.

Kissinger, Henry. *Diplomacy*. New York: Simon & Schuster, 1994.

———. *A World Restored: Metternich, Castlereagh and the Problems of Peace 1812-22*. London: Weidenfeld and Nicolson, 1957.

Mann, Golo. *Secretary of Europe: The Life of Friedrich Gentz, Enemy of Napoleon*. Translated by William H. Woglom. New Haven, CT: Yale University Press, 1946.

McGuigan, Dorothy Gies. *Metternich and the Duchess*. Garden City, NY: Doubleday, 1975.

Metternich, Klemens. *Metternich: The Autobiography, 1773-1815*. London: Ravenhall Books, 2004.

Nicolson, Harold. *The Congress of Vienna: A Study in Allied Unity, 1812-22*. New York: Viking Compass, 1946.

Orieux, Jean. *Talleyrand: The Art of Survival*. New York: Knopf, 1974.

Spiel, Hilde. *The Congress of Vienna: An Eyewitness Account*. Philadelphia: Chilton Book Co., 1968.

Talleyrand, Charles Maurice. *The Correspondence of Prince Talleyrand and King Louis XVIII During the Congress of Vienna*. New York: Harper & Brothers, 1881.

———. *Memoirs of the Prince De Talleyrand*. Vols. 1-3. Edited by the Duc De Broglie. New York: G. P. Putnam's Sons, 1891.

Troyat, Henri. *Alexander of Russia: Napoleon's Conqueror*. New York, Dutton, 1982.

Webster, Charles. *The Congress of Vienna*. London: Foreign Office, 1918.

———. *The Foreign Policy of Castlereagh: 1812-1815*. London: G. Bell and Sons, 1931.

Zamoyski, Adam. *Rites of Peace: The Fall of Napoleon and the Congress of Vienna*. New York: HarperCollins, 2007.

Congress of Vienna Periodical Sources

Kissinger, Henry A. "The Congress of Vienna: A Reappraisal." *World Politics* 8, no. 2. (Jan. 1956): 264-280.

Chapter Four: The Portsmouth Treaty, 1905

Portsmouth Treaty Manuscript Sources

Collection of Documents Concerning Negotiations between Russia and Japan about the Conclusion of the Peace Treaty May 24-October 3. Moscow: Russian Ministry of Foreign Affairs, 1906.

Japanese Foreign Office, Diplomatic Correspondence. A History of the Russo-Japanese Negotiations, vols. 1 and 2. Tokyo: Foreign Office Circulation.

Japanese Foreign Office, Diplomatic Correspondence. Record of the Russo-Japanese Peace; Including the Informal Discussions of the Plenipotentiaries of the Two Nations. Tokyo: Foreign Office.

Japanese Ministry of Foreign Affairs Archives (Microfilm Collection), including Telegram Series Reel 55, pp. 17, 808-817, 811, Monoto Ichiro to Komura Jutaro, August 2, 1904. Library of Congress, Washington, DC.

Meyer Diary. George von Lengerke Meyer Papers. Library of Congress, Washington, DC.

Protocols of the Portsmouth Peace Conference and Text of the Treaty between Russia and Japan. Moscow: Russian Ministry of Foreign Affairs, 1906.

Records of the Department of State, National Archives Numerical Series, 1906-1910: 3919—Treaty Negotiations between Russia and Japan. Also Dispatches from Foreign Legations Japan 1858-1906 (1953), and Dispatches from United States Ministers to Russia 1808-1906 (1953). National Archives, Washington, DC.

Cecil Spring Rice Correspondence with Theodore Roosevelt. Library of Congress, Washington, DC.

Theodore Roosevelt Papers and Diaries. Library of Congress, Washington, DC.

U.S. Department of State. Papers Relating to the Foreign Relations of the United States, 1905. Washington, DC: Government Printing Office: 1906.

Portsmouth Treaty Book Sources

Albrecht-Carrie, Renee. *A Diplomatic History of Europe Since the Congress of Vienna.* New York: Harper, 1958.

Asakawa, Kanichi. *The Russo-Japanese Conflict: Its Causes and Issues.* Boston: Houghton Mifflin, 1904.

Auchincloss, Louis. *Theodore Roosevelt.* New York: Times Books,

2001.

Bailey, Thomas. *A Diplomatic History of the American People.* Englewood Cliffs, NJ: Pretence-Hall, 1974.

Beale, Howard. *Theodore Roosevelt and the Rise of America to World Power.* Baltimore: Johns Hopkins University Press, 1956.

Bemis, Samuel Flagg. *A Diplomatic History of the United States.* New York: Holt, 1942.

Bernstein, Herman, ed. *The Willy-Nicky Correspondence.* New York: Knopf, 1918.

Bing, E. J., ed. *The Secret Letters of the Last Tsar: Being the Confidential Correspondence Between Nicholas II and His Mother, Dowager Empress Maria Fedorovna.* New York: Longmans, Green, 1938.

Bishop, Joseph. *Theodore Roosevelt and His Time Shown in His Own Letters.* New York: Charles Scribner's Sons, 1920.

Blum, John. *The Republican Roosevelt.* Cambridge, MA: Harvard University Press, 1961.

Borton, Hugh et al. *A Selected List of Books and Articles on Japan in English, France, and German.* Washington, DC: Committee on Japanese Studies, American Council of Learned Societies, 1954.

Brown, Arthur. *The Mastery of the Far East: The Story of Korea's Transformation and Japan's Rise to Supremacy in the Orient.* New York: Charles Scribner's Sons, 1919.

Burleigh, Bennet. *Empire of the East, or, Japan and Russia at War, 1904-1905.* London: George Bell & Sons, 1905.

Butt, Archie. *The Letters of Archie Butt, Personal Aide to President Roosevelt.* Edited by Lawrence Abbott. Garden City, NY: Doubleday, Page, 1924.

Cassell, John. *Cassell's History of the Russo-Japanese War.* London: Cassell and Co., 1905.

Chessman, G. Wallace. *Theodore Roosevelt and the Politics of Power.* New York: Little, Brown, 1969.

Collin, Richard. *Theodore Roosevelt: Culture, Diplomacy and Expansion.* Baton Rouge: Louisiana State University Press, 1985.

Dalton, Kathleen. *Theodore Roosevelt: A Strenuous Life.* New York: Knopf, 2002.

De Wolf Howe, M. A. *George Von Lengerke Meyer: His Life and Public Services.* New York: Dodd, Mead, 1920.

Dennett, Tyler. *John Hay.* New York: Dodd, Mead, 1933.

–––. *Roosevelt and the Russo-Japanese War*. Garden City, NY: Doubleday, Page, 1925.

Dennis, Alfred L. P. *Adventures in American Diplomacy, 1896-1906*. New York: Dutton, 1928.

Dillon, Emily Joseph. *The Eclipse of Russia*. London: J. M. Dent & Sons, 1918.

Donald, Aida D. *Lion in the White House: A Life of Theodore Roosevelt*. New York: Basic Books, 2007.

Esthus, Raymond. *Double Eagle and Rising Sun: The Russians and Japanese at Portsmouth in 1905*. Durham, NC: Duke University Press, 1988.

–––. *Theodore Roosevelt and the International Rivalries*. Waltham, MA: Ginn-Blaisdell, 1970.

–––. *Theodore Roosevelt and Japan*. Seattle: University of Washington Press, 1967.

Fishman, Sterling. *Sergius Witte and His Part in the Portsmouth Peace Conference*. Madison: University of Wisconsin Press, 1953.

Gaimusho (Foreign Ministry). *Komura Gaikoshi*. Tokyo: Japanese Foreign Office, 1953.

Gatewood, Willard B., Jr. *Theodore Roosevelt and the Art of Controversy*. Baton Rouge: Louisiana State University Press, 1970.

Gordon, John Steele. *An Empire of Wealth: The Epic History of American Economic Power*. New York: HarperCollins, 2004.

Gould, Lewis. *The Presidency of Theodore Roosevelt*. Lawrence: University Press of Kansas, 1991.

Graber, Doris Appel. *Crisis Diplomacy: A History of United States Intervention Policy*. Washington, DC: Public Affairs Press, 1959.

Grew, E. Sharpe. *War in the Far East: A History of the Russo-Japanese Struggle*. London: Virtue, 1905.

Griswold, A. W. *The Far Eastern Policy of the United States*. New York: Harcourt, Brace, 1938.

Handlin, Oscar, et al. eds. *Harvard Guide to American History*. Cambridge, MA: Belknap Press, 1955.

Harbaugh, William. *Power and Responsibility: The Life and Times of Theodore Roosevelt*. New York: Farrar, Straus and Cudahy, 1961.

Hayashi, Tadasu. *The Secret Memoirs of Count Tadasu Hayashi*. Edited by A. M. Pooley. New York: G. P. Putnam's Sons, 1915.

Hershey, Amos. *The International Law and Diplomacy of the Russo-Japanese War*. New York: Macmillan, 1906.

Horecky, Paul, ed. *Russia and the Soviet Union*. Chicago: University of Chicago Press, 1965.

Ishii, Viscount. *Diplomatic Commentaries*. Edited by William R. Langdon. Baltimore: Johns Hopkins University Press, 1936.

Jukes, Geoffrey. *The Russo-Japanese War: 1904-1905*. Oxford: Osprey Publishing, 2002.

Jusserand, Jules. *What Me Befell*. Boston: Houghton Mifflin, 1933.

Kajima, Morinosuke. *The Diplomacy of Japan, 1844-1922: Anglo-Japanese Alliance and Russo-Japanese War*. Tokyo: Kajima Institute of International Peace, 1976.

Kaneko, Kentaro. *Japan: Continuing the History to the Close of 1905, with the Provisions of the Treaty of Portsmouth Between Russia and Japan, and Supplementary Chapters*. Edited by David Murray. New York: G. P. Putnam's Sons, 1906.

Kawakami, Kiyoshi. *American-Japanese Relations*. New York: Revell, 1912.

Kissinger, Henry. *Diplomacy*. New York: Simon & Schuster, 1994.

Kokovtsov, V. N. *Out of My Past*. Stanford, CA: Stanford University Press, 1935.

Korostovetz, J. J. *Diary of Korostovetz: Pre-War Diplomacy, the Russo- Japanese Problem*. London: British Periodicals, 1920.

Kuropatkin, A. N. *The Russian Army and the Japanese War*. Edited by E. D. Swinton. Translated by A. B. Lindsay. New York: Dutton, 1909.

Lawton, Lancelot. *Empires of the Far East*. London: G. Richards, 1912.

Levine, Isaac, ed. *Letters from the Kaiser to the Czar*. New York: Frederick A. Stokes, 1920.

Lorant, Stefan. *The Life and Times of Theodore Roosevelt*. Garden City, NY: Doubleday, 1959.

Marks, Fredrik W. *Velvet on Iron: The Diplomacy of Theodore Roosevelt*. Lincoln: University of Nebraska Press, 1981.

Merli, Frank, and Theodore Wilson, eds. *Makers of American Diplomacy: From Benjamin Franklin to Henry Kissinger*. New York: Charles Scribner's Sons, 1974.

Michelson, Alexander M., Paul N. Apostol, and Michael W. Bernatzky. *Russian Public Finance During the War: Revenue and Expenditure*. New Haven, CT: Yale University Press, 1928.

Miller, Nathan. *Theodore Roosevelt: A Life*. New York: Morrow, 1992.

Milyovkov, Paul. *Russia and Its Crisis*. Chicago: University of
    Chicago Press, 1906.

Morley, Charles. *A Guide to Research in Russian History*. Syracuse,
    NY: Syracuse University Press, 1951.

Morris, Edmund. *Theodore Rex*. New York: Random House, 2001.

Morse, Hosea Ballou, and Harley MacNair. *Far Eastern International
    Relations*. Boston: Houghton, Mifflin, 1931.

Mowry, George. *The Era of Theodore Roosevelt*. New York: Harper,
    1958.

Nish, Ian. *Japanese Foreign Policy 1869-1942*. London: Routledge &
    K. Paul, 1977.

Ogawa, Gotaro. *Expenditures of the Russo-Japanese War*. New York:
    Oxford University Press, 1923.

Okamoto, Shumpei. *The Japanese Oligarchy and the Russo-Japanese
    War*. New York: Columbia University Press, 1970.

Ono, Giichi. *War and Armament Expenditures of Japan*. New York:
    Oxford University Press, 1922.

Paleologue, Maurice. *The Turning Point: Three Critical Years (1904,
    05, 06)*. Translated by F. Appleby Holt. New York: Robert Speller
    & Sons, 1957.

Phillips, William. *Ventures in Diplomacy*. Boston: Beacon Press,
    1953.

Plischke, Elmer. *American Foreign Relations: A Bibliography of
    Official Sources*. New York: Johnson Reprint, 1966.

Pringle, Henry. *Theodore Roosevelt: A Biography*. New York:
    Harcourt, Brace, 1931.

Randall, Peter E. *There Are No Victors Here!: A Local Perspective on
    the Treaty of Portsmouth*. Portsmouth, NH: Portsmouth Marine
    Society, 1985.

Repington, Charles. *The War in the Far East, 1904-1905*. New York:
    Dutton, 1905.

Rice, Cecil Spring. *The Letters and Friendships of Sir Cecil Spring
    Rice*. Edited by Stephen Gwynn. Boston: Houghton, Mifflin, 1929.

Roosevelt, Theodore. *The Letters of Theodore Roosevelt*. Vol. 4, *The
    Square Deal, 1903-1905*. Edited by Elting Morison. Cambridge,
    MA: Harvard University Press, 1951.

———. *The Selected Letters of Theodore Roosevelt*. Edited by H. W.
    Brands. New York: Cooper Square Press, 2001.

———. *Letters to Kermit from Theodore Roosevelt, 1902-1908*. Edited
    by Will Irwin. New York: Charles Scribner's Sons, 1946.

———. *Theodore Roosevelt: An Autobiography.* New York: Charles Scribner's Sons, 1913.

Rosen, Roman Romanovich. *Forty Years of Diplomacy.* New York, Knopf, 1922.

Seton-Watson, Hugh. *The Decline of Imperial Russia.* London: Methuen, 1952.

Smalley, George. *Anglo-American Memories.* New York: G. P. Putnam's Sons, 1911.

Smith, Alfred Emanuel. *New Outlook.* Outlook Publishing, 1915.

Stone, Melville. *Fifty Years a Journalist.* Garden City, NY: Doubleday, Page, 1921.

———. *M.E.S.: His Book, a Tribute and a Souvenir of the Twenty-Five Years, 1893-1918, of the Service of Melville E. Stone as General Manager of the Associated Press.* New York: Harper & Brothers, 1918.

Sullivan, Mark. *Our Times.* New York: Charles Scribner's Sons, 1927.

Takahashi, Sakue. *International Law Applied to the Russo-Japanese War.* London: Stevens and Sons, 1908.

Takeuchi, Tatsuji. *War and Diplomacy in the Japanese Empire.* New York: Russell & Russell, 1935.

Temperley, Harold William Vazeille, and George Peabody Gooch. *British Documents on the Origins of the War, 1898-1914: The Anglo-Russian Rapprochement, 1903-07.* London: Foreign Office, 1938.

Thayer, William Roscoe. *John Hay.* Boston: Houghton, Mifflin, 1915.

———. *Theodore Roosevelt: An Intimate Biography.* Boston: Houghton, Mifflin, 1919.

Trani, Eugene. *The Treaty of Portsmouth: An Adventure in American Diplomacy.* Lexington: University of Kentucky Press, 1969.

Treat, Payson J. *Diplomatic Relations Between the United States and Japan, 1895-1905.* Vol. 3. Gloucester, MA: P. Smith, 1963.

Tyler, Sidney. *The Japan-Russia War.* Philadelphia: P.W. Ziegler, 1905.

Uyehara, Cecil H. *Checklist of Archives in the Japanese Ministry of Foreign Affairs, Tokyo, Japan, 1868-1945.* Washington, DC: Photoduplication Service, Library of Congress, 1954.

Wagenknecht, Edward. *The Seven Worlds of Theodore Roosevelt.* New York: Longman's Green, 1958.

Wallace, Chris. *Character: Profiles in Presidential Courage.* New York: Rugged Land, 2004.

Wheeler, Edward Jewitt, ed. *Index of Current Literature, 1906.* New York: Current Literature Publishing, 1906.

White, John Albert. *The Diplomacy of the Russo-Japanese War.* Princeton, NJ: Princeton University Press, 1964.

Witte, Sergei. *Memoirs of Count Witte.* Edited and translated by Abraham Yarmolinsky. Garden City, NY: Doubleday, Page, 1921.

———. *The Memoirs of Count Witte.* Edited and translated by Sidney Harcave. Armonk, NY: M. E. Sharpe, 1990.

Zabriskie, Edward. *American-Russian Rivalry in the Far East, 1895-1914: A Study in Diplomacy and Power Politics.* Philadelphia: University of Pennsylvania Press, 1946.

Portsmouth Treaty Periodical Sources

Aldanov, Mark. "Count Witte." *The Russian Review* 1 (Nov. 1, 1941): 56-64.

Bennett, Col. Drew. "The Russo-Japanese War: Defining Victory." *Marine Corps Gazette* (Nov. 2002).

Collum, C. "Prince Katsura." *The Contemporary Review* 104 (Nov. 1913): 656-662.

Corbet, R. G. "Japan and the Peace." *Imperial and Asiatic Quarterly Review* (January 1906): 36-42.

Dennett, Tyler. "President Roosevelt's Secret Pact with Japan." *Current History* 21 (1924-25): 15-21.

Dillon, E. J. "The Official Narrative of the Peace Conference." *Harper's Weekly* 49 (Sept. 16, 1905): 1334-1337.

———. "The Peace Conference at Portsmouth, N.H." *Harper's Weekly* 49 (Aug. 26, 1905): 1222-1224.

———. "Sergius Witte." *The American Monthly Review of Reviews* 32 (Sept. 3, 1905): 292-295.

———. "Sergius Witte and Jutaro Komura." *Harper's Weekly* 49 (Sept. 2, 1905): 1262-1264 and 1279.

———. "The Story of How Peace Was Brought About." *The Contemporary Review* (Feb. 1907): 270-292.

———. "The Story of the Peace Negotiations." *The Contemporary Review* 88 (Oct. 1905): 457-478.

———. "What the Peace of Portsmouth Means to Russia." *Harper's Weekly* 49 (Sept. 16, 1905): 1337, 1351.

Esthus, Raymond. "Nicholas II and the Russo-Japanese War." *Russian Review* 40, no. 4 (Oct. 1981): 396-411.

Fay, Sidney B. "The Kaiser's Secret Negotiations with the Czar 1904-1905." *American Historical Review* 24 (Oct. 1 1918): 48-72.

Goodwin, Robert K. "Russia and the Portsmouth Peace Conference." *American Slavonic and East European Review* 9, no. 4 (December 1950): 279-291.

Gordon, D. C. "Roosevelt's 'Secret Yankee Trick.'" *Pacific Historical Review* 30 (1961): 351-358.

Griffis, Rev. William Elliot. "The Elder Statesmen of Japan: The Power behind the Portsmouth Treaty." *North American Review* 182 (1906): 215-227.

Hall, Luella. "A Partnership in Peacemaking: Theodore Roosevelt and Wilhelm II." *Pacific Historical Review* 13 (1944): 390-411.

Howells, W. D. "The Peacemakers at Portsmouth." *Harper's Weekly* 49 (Aug. 26, 1905): 1225, 1244.

Kaneko, Ketaro. "American Millions for Japan's War." *World's Work* (May 1905): 6124-6126.

Kinnosuke, Adachi. "Japan's Elder Statesmen and the Peace." *The American Monthly Review of Reviews* 32 (Oct. 4, 1905): 430-432.

Komura, Shoji. "Jutaro Komura, My Father." *Contemporary Japan* (March 4, 1933): 641-649.

Kublin, Hyman. "The Japanese Socialists and the Russo-Japanese War." *Journal of Modern History* 22, no. 4 (Dec. 1950): 322-39.

Long, John Wendell. "The Diplomacy of the Portsmouth Conference, 1905." Unpublished Master's Essay. Columbia University Department of History, 1965.

May, Ernest. "The Far Eastern Policy of the United States in the Period of the Russo-Japanese War: A Russian View." *American Historical Review* 62 (1957): 345-351.

McWilliams, C. F. "What Russia Has to Pay For." *Harper's Weekly* 49 (Sept. 30, 1905): 1406-1409.

Millard, T. F. "The Financial Prospects of Japan." *Scribner's Magazine* 38 (Sept. 1905): 369-379.

———. "The Fruits of Japan's Victory." *Scribner's Magazine* 38, no. 2 (Aug. 1905): 240-251.

Parsons, Edward. "Roosevelt's Containment of the Russo-Japanese War." *Pacific Historical Review* 38 (Feb. 1969): 21-43.

Stead, Alfred. "Peace in the Far East." *The Fortnightly Review*, New Series, 74 (July-Dec. 1905): 593-603.

Stead, William T. "How St. Petersburg Received News of Peace." *The American Monthly Review of Reviews* 32, no. 4 (Oct. 1905): 426-429.

Stone, Melville E. "The Portsmouth Conference." *The Saturday Evening Post* 187 (Jan. 30, 1915): 3-4, 48.

Thorson, Winston B. "American Public Opinion and the Portsmouth Peace Conference." *The American Historical Review* 53, no. 3 (April 1948): 439-464.

Van Norman, Louis. "The Making of a Modern Treaty of Peace." *The American Monthly Review of Reviews* 32, no. 4 (Oct. 1905): 418-425.

White, J. A. "Portsmouth 1905: Peace or Truce?" *Journal of Peace Research* 6, no. 4, Special Issue on Peace Research in History (1969): 359-366.

"Roosevelt as Russia's Helper." *The American Monthly Review of Reviews* 32, no. 4 (Oct. 1905): 475.

"Russia and Japanese Finances." *The American Monthly Review of Reviews* 32, no. 3 (Sept. 1905): 381-382.

"The Peace and After." *The American Monthly Review of Reviews* 32, no. 5 (Nov. 1905): 598-600.

"The Peace of Portsmouth and Its Consequences." *Harper's Weekly* 49, (Sept. 16, 1905): 1332.

"The Portsmouth Peace Conference." *North American Review* 171 (November 1905): 646-647.

"The Progress of the World." *The American Monthly Review of Reviews* 32, no. 3 (Sept. 1905): 259-266.

Also, numerous contemporaneous news reports from *Outlook* magazine and the *New York Observer*.

CHAPTER FIVE: THE PARIS PEACE CONFERENCE, 1919

Paris Peace Conference Manuscript Sources

U.S. Department of State. Papers Relating to the Foreign Relations of the United States, The Paris Peace Conference. 13 vols. Washington, DC: Government Printing Office, 1942-1947

Paris Peace Conference Book Sources

Andelman, David A. *A Shattered Peace: Versailles 1919 and the Price We Pay Today.* Hoboken, NJ: John Wiley & Sons, 2008.

Baker, Ray Stannard, and Woodrow Wilson. *Woodrow Wilson and World Settlement.* New York: Doubleday, 1922.

Bartlett, Vernon. *Behind the Scenes at the Peace Conference.* London: George Allen & Unwin, 1919.

Baruch, Bernard. *The Making of the Reparation and Economic Sections of the Treaty.* New York: Harper & Brothers Publishers, 1920.

Bendiner, Elmer. *A Time for Angels: The Tragicomic History of the League of Nations.* New York: Knopf, 1975.

Bobbitt, Philip. *The Shield of Achilles.* New York: Knopf, 2002.

Callahan, Edith. *Glimpses of the Peace Conference.* Louisville, KY: Catholic Messenger Press, 1920.

Carter, Joseph. *1918: Year of Crisis, Year of Change.* Englewood Cliffs, NJ: Prentice-Hall, 1968.

Churchill, Winston. *The Gathering Storm.* New York: Mariner Books, 1948.

———. *The Great War.* London: George Newnes, 1933.

Czernin, Ferdinand. *Versailles, 1919.* New York: G. P. Putnam's Sons, 1964.

Dillon, Dr. E.J. *The Inside Story of the Peace Conference.* New York: Harper & Brothers Publishers, 1920.

Elcock, Howard. *Portrait of a Decision: The Council of Four and the Treaty of Versailles.* London: Eyre Methuen, 1972.

Floto, Inga. *Colonel House in Paris: A Study of American Policy at the Paris Peace Conference 1919.* Princeton, NJ: Princeton University Press, 1980.

Fromkin, David. *A Peace to End All Peace: The Fall of the Ottoman Empire and the Creation of the Modern Middle East.* New York: Holt, 1989.

Gelfand, Lawrence E. *The Inquiry: American Preparations for Peace, 1917-1919.* New Haven, CT: Yale University Press, 1963.

Greene, Theodore P., ed. *Wilson at Versailles.* Lexington, MA: D. C. Heath, 1957.

Hankey, Lord Maurice. *The Supreme Control at the Paris Peace Conference 1919.* London: George Allen & Unwin, 1963.

Hansen, Harry. *The Adventures of the Fourteen Points.* New York: Century, 1919.

Haskins, Charles, and Robert Lord. *Some Problems of the Peace Conference.* Cambridge, MA: Harvard University Press, 1920.

Havighurst, Alfred F. *Britain in Transition: The Twentieth Century.* Chicago: University of Chicago Press, 1985.

Henig, Ruth. *Versailles and After: 1919-1933.* New York: Routledge, 1995.

House, Edward, and Charles Seymour, eds. *What Really Happened at Paris*. New York: Charles Scribner's Sons, 1921.

House, Edward. *The Intimate Papers of Colonel House*. Edited by Charles Seymour. Boston: Houghton Mifflin, 1928.

Keynes, John Maynard. *The End of Laissez-Faire: The Economic Consequences of the Peace*. Amherst, NY: Prometheus Books, 2004.

Kissinger, Henry. *Diplomacy*. New York: Simon & Schuster, 1994.

Lansing, Robert. *The Big Four and Others of the Peace Conference*. New York: Houghton Mifflin, 1921.

———. *The Peace Negotiations: A Personal Narrative*. Boston: Houghton Mifflin, 1921.

Levin, N. Gordon, Jr., ed. *Woodrow Wilson and the Paris Peace Conference*. Lexington, MA: D. C. Heath, 1972.

Lloyd George, David. *Memoirs of the Peace Conference*. New Haven, CT: Yale University Press, 1939.

MacMillan, Margaret. *Paris 1919*. New York: Random House, 2001.

Mantoux, Paul. *The Deliberations of the Council of Four*. Edited by Arthur Link. Princeton, NJ: Princeton University Press, 1992.

Mayer, Arno J. *Politics and Diplomacy of Peacemaking: Containment and Counterrevolution at Versailles, 1918-1919*. New York: Knopf, 1967.

Merli, Frank, and Theodore Wilson, eds. *Makers of American Diplomacy from Benjamin Franklin to Henry Kissinger*. New York: Charles Scribner's Sons, 1974.

Nicolson, Harold. *Peacemaking 1919*. London: Constable, 1933.

Nordholt, J. W. Schulte. *Woodrow Wilson: A Life for World Peace*. Berkeley: University of California Press, 1991.

Oren, Michael B. *Power, Faith and Fantasy: America in the Middle East, 1776 to the Present*. New York: Norton, 2007.

Parkerson, John Taylor. *Looking Back to Glory*. New York: J. T. Parkerson, 1933.

Seymour, Charles. *Letters from the Paris Peace Conference*. New Haven, CT: Yale University Press, 1965.

Simonds, Frank H. *How Europe Made Peace Without America*. New York: Doubleday, Page, 1927.

Sinclair, David. *Hall of Mirrors*. London: Century, 2001.

Stevenson, Frances. *Lloyd George: A Diary*. London: Hutchinson of London, 1971.

Stokes, Harold Phelps. *Dispatches, 1919-1921*. Greenwich, CT: privately printed, 1922.

Tardieu, Andre. *The Truth about the Treaty*. Indianapolis: Bobbs-Merrill, 1921.

Temperley, Harold, ed. *A History of the Peace Conference of Paris*. Vols. 1-5. London: H. Frowde and Hodder & Stoughton, 1920.

Thompson, Charles T. *The Peace Conference Day by Day*. New York: Brentano's Publishers, 1920.

Trachtenberg, Marc. *Reparation in World Politics*. New York: Columbia University Press, 1980.

Walworth, Arthur. *Wilson and His Peacemakers*. New York: Norton, 1986.

Williams, Wythe. *The Tiger of France: Conversations with Clemenceau*. New York: Duell, Sloane and Pearce, 1949.

Wilson, Woodrow. *The Papers of Woodrow Wilson*. Edited by Arthur S. Link. Princeton, NJ: Princeton University Press, 1994.

Paris Peace Conference Periodical Sources

Finch, Geo. "The Peace Conference of Paris, 1919." *The American Journal of International Law* 13, no. 2. (April 1919): 159-186.

Marks, Sally. "Behind the Scenes at the Paris Peace Conference of 1919." *The Journal of British Studies* 9, no. 2. (May 1970): 154-180.

"Peace Conference Delegates at Paris," *The American Journal of International Law* 13, no. 1 (Jan. 1919): 79-81.

Seidel, Andrew. "The Use of the Physical Environment in Peace Negotiations." In "Politics and Design Symbolism," special issue, *Journal of Architectural Education* 32, no. 2, (Nov. 1978): 19-23.

Trask, David F. "General Tasker Howard Bliss and the 'Sessions of the World,' 1919." *Transactions of the American Philosophical Society*, New Series, 56, no. 8 (1966): 1-80.

CHAPTER SIX: THE EGYPTIAN-ISRAELI ARMISTICE AGREEMENT

Arab-Israeli Accord Interview Sources

Dr. Lawrence Finkelstein, former assistant to Dr. Ralph Bunche, in interview with the author, September 22, 2008.

Professor Benjamin Rivlin, former assistant to Dr. Ralph Bunche, in interview with the author, September 24, 2008.

Arab-Israeli Accord Manuscript Sources

Documents on the Foreign Policy of Israel. Vol. 3, *Armistice Negotiations with the Arab States, December 1948-July 1949.* Jerusalem: Israel State Archives, 1983.

Documents on the Foreign Policy of Israel. Vol. 3, *Armistice Negotiations with the Arab States, December 1948-July 1949. Companion Volume.* Jerusalem: Israel State Archives, 1983.

Ralph Bunche Archives, Ralph Bunche Institute, City University of New York Graduate Center, New York.

Ralph Bunche Collection, UCLA Library Archives Division, Los Angeles.

Ralph Bunche Papers, New York Public Library, New York.

United Nations Archives and Records Management Section, United Nations Headquarters, New York.

Arab-Israeli Accord Book Sources

Acheson, Dean. *Present at the Creation: My Years in the State Department.* New York: Norton, 1969.

Bernadotte, Folke. *To Jerusalem.* London: Hodder & Stoughton, 1951.

Bilby, Kenneth. *New Star in the Near East.* Garden City, NY: Doubleday, 1950.

Bunche, Ralph J. *Selected Speeches and Writings.* Edited by Charles P. Henry. Ann Arbor: University of Michigan Press, 1995.

Caplan, Neil. *Futile Diplomacy.* Vol. 3, *The United Nations, The Great Powers, and Middle East Peacemaking 1948-1954.* Totowa, NJ: F. Cass, 1983.

Cleveland, William L. *A History of the Modern Middle East*, 3rd ed. Boulder, CO: Westview Press, 2004.

Cordier, Andrew W., and Wilder Foote, eds. *Public Papers of the Secretaries-General of the United Nations.* Vol. 1, *Trygve Lie 1946-1953.* New York: Columbia University Press, 1969.

Eban, Abba. *An Autobiography.* New York: Random House, 1977.

Eytan, Walter. *The First Ten Years: A Diplomatic History of Israel.* New York: Simon & Schuster, 1958.

Frye, Richard N., ed. *The Near East and the Great Powers.* Cambridge, MA: Harvard University Press, 1951.

Gelber, Yoav. *Palestine 1948: War, Escape and the Emergence of the Palestinian Refugee Problem.* Portland, OR: Sussex Academic Press, 2001.

Haskins, Jim. *Ralph Bunche: A Most Reluctant Hero*. New York: Hawthorn Books, 1974.

Henry, Charles P. *Ralph Bunche: Model Negro or American Other?* New York: New York University Press, 1999.

Kimche, Jon and David. *A Clash of Destinies: The Arab-Jewish War and the Founding of the State of Israel*. New York: Praeger Publishers, 1960.

Kurzman, Dan. *Genesis 1948: The First Arab-Israeli War*. New York: World Publishing, 1970.

Lie, Trygve. *In the Cause of Peace: Seven Years with the United Nations*. New York: Macmillan, 1954.

Lindsay, Beverly, ed. *Ralph Johnson Bunche: Public Intellectual and Nobel Peace Laureate*. Chicago: University of Illinois Press, 2007.

Mann, Peggy. *Ralph Bunche, UN Peacemaker*. New York: Coward, McCann & Geoghegan, 1975.

Mansfield, Peter. *A History of the Middle East*. New York: Penguin, 1991.

Pelcovits, Nathan. *The Long Armistice: UN Peacekeeping and the Arab-Israeli Conflict, 1958-1960*. Boulder, CO: Westview Press, 1993.

Rabin, Yitzhak. *The Rabin Memoirs*. Boston: Little, Brown, 1979.

Rivlin, Benjamin, ed. *Ralph Bunche: The Man and His Times*. New York: Holmes & Meier, 1990.

Smith, Richard Harris. *OSS: The Secret History of America's First Central Intelligence Agency*. Guilford, CT: Lyons Press, 2005.

Touval, Saadia. *The Peace Brokers: Mediators in the Arab-Israeli Conflict, 1948-1979*. Princeton, NJ: Princeton University Press, 1982.

Urquhart, Brian. *Ralph Bunche: An American Life*. New York: Norton, 1993.

Arab-Israeli Accord Periodical Sources

Caplan, Neil. "A Tale of Two Cities: The Rhodes and Lausanne Conferences, 1949." *Journal of Palestine Studies* 21, no. 3 (Spring 1992): 5-34.

Currier, Nuchhi. "Nation Shall Not Rise Up Against Nation." *UN Chronicle* 3 (2003).

Gazit, Mordechai. "American and British Diplomacy and the Bernadotte Mission." *The Historical Journal* 29, no. 3 (Sept. 1986): 677-696.

Heller, Joseph. "Failure of a Mission: Bernadotte and Palestine, 1948." *Journal of Contemporary History* 14, no. 3 (July 1979): 515-534.

Hurewitz, J. C. "The United Nations Conciliation Commission for Palestine: Establishment and Definition of Functions." *International Organization* 7, no. 4 (Nov. 1953): 482-497.

Urquhart, Sir Brian. "'May I Speak a Word or Two Against Brotherhood?'" *UN Chronicle* 3 (2003).

Also, contemporaneous periodical reports, including "Israel Sees New Hope for a Negotiated Peace," *New York Times*, October 31, 1948, by Sydney Gruson.

Arab-Israeli Accord Lecture Sources

Naeser, Ingrid. "Ralph Bunche and the Continued Palestine Conflict." Paper presented at the annual meeting of the International Studies Association, Montreal, Quebec, Canada, March 17, 2004. http://www.allacademic.com/meta/p_mla_apa_research_citation/0/7/3/2/5/p73254_index.html (accessed September 2, 2009).

CHAPTER SEVEN: THE CUBAN MISSILE CRISIS, 1962

Cuban Missile Crisis Interview Sources

Professor Sergei Khrushchev (Nikita Khrushchev's son and the editor of his memoirs), in interview with the author, September 23, 2008.

Theodore Sorensen, in interview with the author, June 9, 2008.

Cuban Missile Crisis Manuscript Sources

The Cuban Missile Crisis: Declassified Documents. National Security Archive, George Washington University, Washington, DC.

Cuban Missile Crisis Collection, Cold War International History Project, Woodrow Wilson Center for Scholars, Washington, DC.

U.S. Department of State. Papers Relating to the Foreign Relations of the United States, 1961-1963. Vol. 11, Cuban Missile Crisis and Aftermath. Washington, DC: Government Printing Office, 1997.

Cuban Missile Crisis Book Sources

Abel, Elie. *The Missile Crisis*. Philadelphia: Lippincott, 1966.

Allison, Graham, and Philip Zelikow. *Essence of Decision: Explaining the Cuban Missile Crisis*. New York: Longman, 1999.

Allyn, Bruce J., James G. Blight and David A. Welch, eds. *Back to the Brink: Proceedings of the Moscow Conference on the Cuban Missile Crisis, January 27-28, 1989*. Lanham, MD: University Press of America, 1992.

Ball, George W. *The Past Has Another Pattern: Memoirs*. New York: Norton, 1982.

Beschloss, Michael. *The Crisis Years: Kennedy and Khrushchev 1960-1963*. New York: HarperCollins, 1991.

Blight, James G., and David A. Welch. *On The Brink: Americans and Soviets Reexamine the Cuban Missile Crisis*. New York: Hill and Wang, 1989.

Blight, James G., Bruce J. Allyn, and David A. Welch. *Cuba on the Brink: Castro, the Missile Crisis, and the Soviet Collapse*. New York: Rowman & Littlefield Publishers, 2002.

Brugioni, Dino. *Eyeball to Eyeball*. New York: Random House, 1991.

Bundy, McGeorge. *Danger and Survival: Choices About the Bomb in the First Fifty Years*. New York: Vintage Books, 1990.

Chang, Laurence, and Peter Kornbluh. *The Cuban Missile Crisis, 1962: A National Security Archive Documents Reader, Revised to Include Recently Declassified Documents*. New York: New Press, 1998.

Detzer, David. *The Brink: Cuban Missile Crisis 1962*. New York: Thomas Y. Crowell Publishers, 1979.

Dobbs, Michael. *One Minute to Midnight*. New York: Knopf, 2008.

Dobrynin, Anatoly. *In Confidence: Moscow's Ambassador to America's Six Cold War Presidents*. Seattle: University of Washington Press, 1995.

Feklisov, Alexander. *The Man behind the Rosenbergs*. New York: Enigma Books, 2004.

Frankel, Max. *High Noon in the Cold War: Kennedy, Khrushchev and the Cuban Missile Crisis*. New York: Ballantine Books, 2005.

Fursenko, Aleksandr, and Timothy Naftali. *Khrushchev's Cold War: The Inside Story of an American Adversary*. New York: Norton, 2006.

———. *One Hell of a Gamble: Khrushchev, Castro, and Kennedy 1958-1964*. New York: Norton, 1997.

Gaddis, John Lewis. *The Cold War: A New History*. New York: Penguin, 2005.

———. *Strategies of Containment: A Critical Appraisal of American National Security During the Cold War.* New York: Oxford University Press, 2005.

Garthoff, Raymond. *Reflections on the Cuban Missile Crisis.* Washington, DC: Brookings Institution, 1989.

Gribkov, General Anatoli I., and General William Y. Smith. *Operation Anadyr: U.S. and Soviet Generals Recount the Cuban Missile Crisis.* Chicago: Edition Q, 1994.

Hilsman, Roger. *To Move a Nation: The Politics of Foreign Policy in the Administration of John F. Kennedy.* Garden City, NY: Doubleday, 1967.

Horelick, Arnold L., and Myron Rush. *Strategic Power and Soviet Foreign Policy.* Chicago: University of Chicago Press, 1966.

Ikle, Fred Charles. *How Nations Negotiate.* New York: Harper & Row, 1964.

Katzenbach, Nicholas deB. *Some of It Was Fun: Working with RFK and LBJ.* New York: Norton, 2008.

Kennedy, Robert F. *Thirteen Days: A Memoir of the Cuban Missile Crisis.* New York: Norton, 1999.

Khrushchev, Nikita. *Khrushchev Remembers.* Translated and edited by Strobe Talbott. Boston: Little, Brown, 1970.

———. *Memoirs of Nikita Khrushchev.* Vol. 3, *Statesman (1953-1964).* Edited by Sergei Khrushchev. University Park: Pennsylvania State University Press, 2007.

Khrushchev, Sergei. *Khrushchev on Khrushchev: An Inside Account of the Man and His Era, by His Son, Sergei Khrushchev.* Edited and translated by William Taubman. Boston: Little, Brown, 1990.

———. *Nikita Khrushchev and the Creation of a Superpower.* University Park: Pennsylvania State University Press, 2001.

Larson, David L., ed. *The "Cuban Crisis" of 1962: Selected Documents and Chronology.* Boston: Houghton Mifflin, 1963.

May, Ernest R., and Philip Zelikow, eds. *The Kennedy Tapes: Inside the White House During the Cuban Missile Crisis.* New York: Norton, 2002.

McNamara, Robert S. *The Essence of Security: Reflections in Office.* New York: Harper & Row, 1968.

Merli, Frank, and Theodore Wilson, eds. *Makers of American Diplomacy from Benjamin Franklin to Henry Kissinger.* New York: Charles Scribner's Sons, 1974.

Nathan, James A. *Anatomy of the Cuban Missile Crisis.* Westport, CT: Greenwood Press, 2001.

Nitze, Paul. *From Hiroshima to Glasnost: At the Center of Decision.* New York: Grove Weidenfeld, 1989.

Pachter, Henry. *Collision Course: the Cuban Missile Crisis and Coexistence.* New York: Praeger Publishers, 1963.

Rusk, Dean. *As I Saw It.* New York: Penguin, 1991.

Schlesinger, Arthur M., Jr. *A Thousand Days: John F. Kennedy in the White House.* New York: Mariner Books, 2002.

———. *Robert Kennedy and His Times.* New York: Houghton Mifflin, 1978.

Sorenson, Theodore C. *Decision-Making in the White House: The Olive Branch or the Arrows.* New York: Columbia University Press, 2005.

———. *Kennedy.* New York: Konecky and Konecky, 1965.

———. *Counselor: A Life at the Edge of History.* New York: HarperCollins, 2008.

Stern, Sheldon M. *Averting "The Final Failure": John F. Kennedy and the Secret Cuban Missile Crisis Meetings.* Stanford, CA: Stanford University Press, 2003.

———. *The Week the World Stood Still: Inside the Secret Cuban Missile Crisis.* Stanford, CA: Stanford University Press, 2005.

Tatu, Michael. *Power in the Kremlin: From Khrushchev to Kosygin.* New York: Viking Press, 1970.

Taylor, General Maxwell. *Swords and Plowshares: A Memoir.* New York: Da Capo, 1972.

White, Mark J. *Missiles in Cuba: Kennedy, Khrushchev, Castro and the 1962 Crisis.* Chicago: Ivan R. Dee, 1997.

Weiner, Tim. *Legacy of Ashes: The History of the CIA.* New York: Random House, 2008.

Weintal, Edward, and Charles Bartlett. *Facing the Brink: An Intimate Study of Crisis Diplomacy.* New York: Charles Scribner's Sons, 1967.

Wiersma, Kurt, and Ben Larson. *Fourteen Days in October: The Cuban Missile Crisis.* http://library.thinkquest.org/11046/media/fourteen_days_in_october.pdf.

Zubok, Vladislav, and Constantine Pleshakov. *Inside the Kremlin's Cold War: From Stalin to Khrushchev.* Cambridge, MA: Harvard University Press, 1996.

Cuban Missile Crisis Periodical Sources

Hershberg, Jim. "Anatomy of a Controversy: Anatoly F. Dobrynin's Meeting with Robert F. Kennedy, Saturday, 27 October 1962." *The Cold War International History Project Bulletin* Issue 5 (Spring 1995).

Thrall, Nathan and Jesse James Wilkins. "Kennedy Talked, Khrushchev Triumphed." *New York Times*, May 22, 2008.

Cuban Missile Crisis Film Sources

Morris, Errol, director. *The Fog of War*. DVD. Sony Pictures, 2003.

Chapter Eight: The Reykjavik Summit, 1986

Reykjavik Summit Interview Sources

Ambassador Kenneth Adelman, former director of the U.S. Arms Control and Disarmament Agency, in interviews with the author, September 30, 2008, and October 31, 2008.

Ambassador Thomas Graham, former special representative for the president on arms control, nonproliferation, and disarmament, and acting director and general counsel of the U.S. Arms Control and Disarmament Agency, in interview with the author, October 2, 2008.

Ambassador Max Kampelman, former head of the U.S. delegation to the Geneva Negotiations on Nuclear and Space Arms Reduction, and counselor to the U.S. Department of State, in interview with the author, October 20, 2008.

Ambassador Jack Matlock, former senior director of the U.S. National Security Council and U.S. ambassador to the Soviet Union, in interview with the author, October 2, 2008.

Richard Perle, former assistant secretary of defense for international security policy, in interview with the author, October 7, 2008.

Admiral John Poindexter, former national security adviser (assistant to the president for national security affairs), in interview with the author, November 10, 2008.

George Shultz, former secretary of state, in interview with the author, February 11, 2009.

Reykjavik Summit Manuscript Sources

Original transcripts and notes from the American and Soviet governments, as well as formerly classified material surrounding the

negotiation on both sides compiled by the National Security
Archive, George Washington University, Washington, DC.
The Gorbachev Foundation Collection, the Hoover Institution,
Stanford University, Stanford, CA.
The Kataev Collection, the Hoover Institution, Stanford University,
Stanford, CA.

Reykjavik Summit Book Sources

Adelman, Kenneth L. *The Great Universal Embrace: Arms
Summitry—A Skeptic's Account.* New York: Simon & Schuster,
1989.
Anderson, Martin, and Annelise Anderson. *Reagan's Secret War: The
Untold Story of His Fight to Save the World from Nuclear
Disaster.* New York: Crown Publishers, 2009.
Binnendijk, Hans, ed. *National Negotiating Styles.* Washington, DC:
Foreign Service Institute, U.S. Department of State, 1987.
Blacker, Coit. *Reluctant Warriors: The United States, the Soviet
Union and Arms Control.* New York: Freeman, 1987.
Brady, Linda P. *The Politics of Negotiation: America's Dealings with
Allies, Adversaries, and Friends.* Chapel Hill: University of North
Carolina Press, 1991.
Brown, Archie. *The Gorbachev Factor.* Oxford, England: Oxford
University Press, 1996.
Chernyaev, Anatoly. *My Six Years with Gorbachev.* University Park:
Pennsylvania State University Press, 2000.
Doder, Dusko, and Louise Branson. *Gorbachev: Heretic in the
Kremlin.* New York: Penguin, 1991.
Eberstadt, Nicholas. *The Poverty of Communism.* New Brunswick, NJ:
Transaction Publishers, 1988.
Einhorn, Robert J. *Negotiating from Strength: Leverage in U.S.-Soviet
Arms Control Negotiations.* New York: Praeger Publishers, 1985.
Ekedahl, Carolyn McGiffert, and Melvin A. Goodman. *The Wars of
Eduard Shevardnadze,* 2nd ed., rev. and updated. Washington, DC:
Brassey's, 2001.
Gaddis, John Lewis. *The Cold War: A New History.* New York:
Penguin, 2005.
———. *Strategies of Containment: A Critical Appraisal of American
National Security During the Cold War.* New York: Oxford
University Press, 2005.

———. *The United States and the End of the Cold War: Implications, Reconsiderations, Provocations*. New York: Oxford University Press, 1992.

Genest, Marc. *Negotiating in the Public Eye: The Impact of the Press on the Intermediate-Range Nuclear Force Negotiations*. Stanford, CA: Stanford University Press, 1995.

Glitman, Maynard W. *The Last Battle of the Cold War: An Inside Account of Negotiating the Intermediate Range Nuclear Forces Treaty*. New York: Palgrave MacMillan, 2006.

Gorbachev, Mikhail. *Memoirs*. New York: Doubleday, 1995.

———. *On My Country and the World*. New York: Columbia University Press, 2000.

———. *Perestroika: New Thinking for Our Country and the World*. New York: Harper & Row, 1987.

Gorbachev, Mikhail, and Zdenek Mlynar. *Conversations with Gorbachev: On Perestroika, the Prague Spring and the Crossroads of Socialism*. Translated by George Shriver. New York: Columbia University Press, 2002.

Graham, Thomas, Jr. *Disarmament Sketches: Three Decades of Arms Control and International Law*. Seattle: University of Washington Press, 2002.

Jensen, Lloyd. *Bargaining for National Security: The Postwar Disarmament Negotiations*. Columbia: University of South Carolina, 1988.

Kampelman, Max M., *Entering New Worlds: The Memoirs of a Private Man in Public Life*. New York: HarperCollins, 1991.

Kengor, Paul, and Patricia Clark Doerner. *The Judge: William P. Clark, Ronald Reagan's Top Hand*. San Francisco: Ignatius Press, 2007.

Kissinger, Henry. *Diplomacy*. New York: Simon & Schuster, 1994.

Mandelbaum, Michael, ed. *The Other Side of the Table: The Soviet Approach to Arms Control*. New York: Council on Foreign Relations Press, 1990.

Mandelbaum, Michael, and Strobe Talbott. *Reagan and Gorbachev*. New York: Random House, 1987.

Matlock, Jack, Jr. *Reagan and Gorbachev: How the Cold War Ended*. New York: Random House, 2005.

Medvedev, Zhores A. *Gorbachev*. New York, Norton, 1986.

Mikheyev, Dmitry. *The Rise and Fall of Gorbachev*. Indianapolis: Hudson Institute, 1992.

Morris, Edmund. *Dutch: A Memoir of Ronald Reagan.* New York: Random House, 1999.

Nitze, Paul. *From Hiroshima to Glasnost: At the Center of Decision.* New York: Grove Weidenfeld, 1989.

Oberdorfer, Don. *From the Cold War to a New Era: The United States and the Soviet Union, 1983-1991.* Baltimore: Johns Hopkins University Press, 1998.

Palazchenko, Pavel. *My Years with Gorbachev and Shevardnadze: The Memoir of a Soviet Interpreter.* University Park: Pennsylvania State University Press, 1997.

Reagan, Ronald. *An American Life.* New York: Simon & Shuster, 1990.

Regan, Donald T. *For the Record: From Wall Street to Washington.* New York: Harcourt Brace Jovanovich, 1988.

Reynolds, David. *Summits: Six Meetings That Shaped the Twentieth Century.* New York: Basic Books, 2007.

Rueckert, George L. *Global Double Zero: The INF Treaty from Its Origins to Implementation.* Westport, CT: Greenwood Press, 1993.

Schweizer, Peter. *Victory: The Reagan Administration's Secret Strategy That Hastened the Collapse of the Soviet Union.* New York: Atlantic Monthly Press, 1994.

Scott, Robert Travis, ed. *The Race for Security: Arms and Arms Control in the Reagan Years.* Lexington, MA: Lexington Books, 1987.

Sherr, Alan. *The Other Side of Arms Control: Soviet Objectives in the Gorbachev Era.* Boston: Unwin Hyman, 1988.

Shevardnadze, Eduard. *The Future Belongs to Freedom.* London: Sinclair-Stevenson, 1991.

Shultz, George. *Turmoil and Triumph: Diplomacy, Power and the Victory of the American Ideal.* New York: MacMillan, 1993.

Shultz, George, and Sidney Drell, eds. *Implications of the Reykjavik Summit on Its Twentieth Anniversary: Conference Report,* conference held October 11-12, 2006, at the Hoover Institution, Stanford University. Stanford, CA: Hoover Institution Press, 2007.

Shultz, George, Steven Andreasen, and Sidney Drell, eds. *Reykjavik Revisited: Steps Toward a World Free of Nuclear Weapons.* Stanford, CA: Hoover Institution Press, 2008.

Smith, Raymond. *Negotiating with the Soviets.* Bloomington: Indiana University Press, 1989.

Talbott, Strobe. *Deadly Gambits: The Regan Administration and Stalemate in Nuclear Arms Control.* New York: Knopf, 1984.

———. *The Master of the Game: Paul Nitze and the Nuclear Peace.* New York: Knopf, 1988.

Thompson, Kenneth W. *Negotiating Arms Control: Missed Opportunities and Limited Successes.* Lanham, MD: University Press of America, 1991.

Vigor, P. H. *The Soviet View of Disarmament.* New York: St. Martin's Press, 1986.

Wohlforth, William C. *Cold War Endgame: Oral History, Analysis, Debates.* University Park: Pennsylvania State University Press, 2003.

———, ed. *Witnesses to the End of the Cold War.* Baltimore: Johns Hopkins University Press, 1996.

Reykjavik Summit Periodical Sources

Adomeit, Hannes. "Gorbachev's Policy toward the West: Smiles and Iron Teeth." *Proceedings of the Academy of Political Science* 36, no. 4, Soviet Foreign Policy (1987): 93-105.

Greenstein, Fred I. "The Impact of Personality on the End of the Cold War: A Counterfactual Analysis." *Political Psychology* 19, no.1 (March 1998): 1-16.

Hyland, William G. "Gorbachev III." *Foreign Affairs* 66, no. 1 (Fall 1987): 7-21.

Kapur, Harish. "Reykjavik Summit." *Economic and Political Weekly* 21, no. 47 (Nov. 22, 1986): 2039.

Larrabee, F. Steven, and Allen Lynch. "Gorbachev: The Road to Reykjavik." *Foreign Policy* 65 (Winter 1986-1987): 3-28.

Mandelbaum, Michael, and Strobe Talbott. "Reykjavik and Beyond." *Foreign Affairs* 65, no. 2 (Winter 1986): 215-235.

Perle, Richard. "Reykjavik as a Watershed in U.S.-Soviet Arms Control." *International Security* 12, no. 1 (Summer 1987): 175-178.

Schlesinger, James. "Reykjavik and Revelations: A Turn of the Tide?" in "America and the World 1986," special issue, *Foreign Affairs* 65, no. 3, (1986): 426-446.

"Setback for Reagan?" *Economic and Political Weekly* 21, no. 44/45 (Nov. 1-8, 1986): 1913-1914.

Sharp, Jane M. O. "After Reykjavik: Arms Control and the Allies." *International Affairs* 63, no. 2 (Spring 1987): 239-257.

Wallace, Michael D., Peter Suedfeld, and Kimberly A. Thachuk. "Failed Leader or Successful Peacemaker?: Crisis, Behavior, and the Cognitive Processes of Mikhail Sergeyevitch Gorbachev." *Political Psychology* 17, no. 3 (Sept. 1996): 453-472.

General Diplomacy and Negotiating Theory Sources

Bendahmane, Diane, and John McDonald Jr. *International Negotiation: Art and Science.* Washington, DC: Center for the Study of Foreign Affairs, Foreign Service Institute, U.S. Department of State, 1992.
———., eds. *Perspectives on Negotiation: Four Case Studies and Interpretations.* Washington, DC: Center for the Study of Foreign Affairs, Foreign Service Institute, U.S. Department of State, 1986.
Berton, Peter, Hiroshi Kimura, and William Zartman, eds. *International Negotiation: Actors, Structure/Process, Values.* New York: St. Martin's Press, 1999.
Crocker, Chester A., Fen Osler Hampson, and Pamela Aall, eds. *Grasping the Nettle: Analyzing Cases of Intractable Conflict.* Washington, DC: United States Institute of Peace Press, 2005.
Fisher, Roger, Andrea Kupfer Schneider, Elizabeth Borgwardt, and Brian Ganson. *Coping with International Conflict: A Systematic Approach to Influence in International Negotiation.* Upper Saddle River, NJ: Prentice Hall, 1997.
Fisher, Roger, and William Ury. *Getting to Yes: Negotiating Agreement Without Giving In.* New York: Penguin, 1981.
Harvard Business School. *Harvard Business Essentials: Negotiation.* Boston: Harvard Business School Press, 2003.
Ikle, Fred Charles. *How Nations Negotiate.* New York: Harper & Row, 1964.
Kissinger, Henry. *Diplomacy.* New York: Simon & Schuster, 1994.
Kremenyuk, Victor, ed. *International Negotiation: Analysis, Approaches, Issues.* San Francisco: Jossey-Bass, 2002.
Lewicki, Roy J., David M. Saunders, and Bruce Barry. *Negotiation.* Boston: McGraw Hill, 2006.
McDonald, John. *Strategy in Poker, Business and War.* New York: Norton, 1950.
Raiffa, Howard. *The Art and Science of Negotiation.* Cambridge, MA: Harvard University Press, 1982.

Ury, William. *Getting Past No: Negotiating Your Way from Confrontation to Cooperation*. New York: Bantam Books, 1991.

Watkins, Michael, and Susan Rosegrant. *Breakthrough International Negotiation: How Great Negotiators Transformed the World's Toughest Post-Cold War Conflicts*. San Francisco: Jossey-Bass, 2001.

Zartman, I. William, and Maureen R. Berman. *The Practical Negotiator*. New Haven, CT: Yale University Press, 1982.

INDEX

Page numbers followed by *ph* indicate a photograph. Those followed by *m* indicate a map.

ACKNOWLEDGMENTS

For their help in the many stages of the project, special thanks to
Ambassador Kenneth Adelman, Jason Andris, Secretary General Kofi
Annan, Louis Auchincloss, James Bacon, Jessie Betts, Professor Neil
Caplan, Kevin Carmody, Gregor Dallas, Alexis Dufresne, Professor
Steven Ericson, Dr. Lawrence Finkelstein, Peter Fitzpatrick, Thomas
Fleming, Anthony Fountain, Professor Alison Frank, Laura Frost,
Kevin Galligan, John Steele Gordon, Ambassador Thomas Graham,
Charles Hale, Ariana Hartsock, Professor James Hershberg,
Ambassador Max Kampelman, JC Khoury, Professor Sergei
Khrushchev, Jon Kukla, Peter Laverack, Carol Leadenham, Richard
Leonard, Douglas Loutit, Professor Margaret MacMillan, David
Mandy, Elizabeth Marshall, Ambassador Jack Matlock, Michael
Meyers, Professor Carla Mulford, Don Oberdorfer, Amanda Packard,
Dennis Paul, Richard Perle, Admiral John Poindexter, Natasha
Porfirenko, Jeff Rankin, Professor Benjamin Rivlin, Professor Shabtai
Rosenne, Stacy Schiff, Anthony Schulte, Charles Scribner III,
Elizabeth Sheinkman, George Shultz, Theodore Sorensen, Van Taylor,
Nicholas Thompson, Professor Eugene Trani, Jim Uebbing, Sir Brian
Urquhart, Ike Williams, Alastair Wood, William Zachary, Irina
Zaytseva, and Tanner Zucker.

Thanks also to my publisher, Bruce H. Franklin, for his unwaver-
ing support; to Ron Silverman, for his meticulous editing; Tracy
Dungan for his maps, and to Trudi Gershenov, for her beautiful jack-
et design.